Yan Yan

Other Kaplan Books for College-Bound Students

College Admissions and Financial Aid

Parent's Guide to College Admissions

Straight Talk on Paying for College: Lowering the Cost of Higher Education

The Unofficial, Unbiased Guide to the 328 Most Interesting Colleges

Test Preparation

ACT

AP Biology

AP Calculus AB: An Apex Learning Guide

AP Chemistry: An Apex Learning Guide

AP English Language & Composition: An Apex Learning Guide

AP English Literature & Composition

AP Macroeconomics/Microeconomics: An Apex Learning Guide

AP Physics B: An Apex Learning Guide

AP Psychology

AP Statistics: An Apex Learning Guide

AP U.S. Government & Politics: An Apex Learning Guide

AP History: An Apex learning Guide

SAT & PSAT

SAT 1600

SAT Math Mania

SAT Math Workbook

SAT Vocab Velocity

SAT Verbal Workbook

SAT Vocabulary Flashcards Flip-O-Matic

SAT II: Biology E/M

SAT II: Chemistry

SAT II: Mathematics Levels IC and IIC

SAT II: Physics

SAT II: Spanish

SAT II: U.S. History

SAT II: World History

SAT II: Writing

What Smart Girls Know About the SAT

AP* MACROECONOMICS/ MICROECONOMICS

2004 Edition
An Apex Learning Guide

By Richard G. Brunelle

Simon & Schuster

NEW YORK · LONDON · SYDNEY · TORONTO

Kaplan Books
Published by Simon & Schuster
1230 Avenue of the Americas
New York, New York 10020

For bulk sales to schools, colleges, and universities, please contact: Order Department, 100 Front Street, Riverside, NJ 08075. Phone: 800-223-2336. Fax: 800-943-9831.

Contributing Editor: Seppy Basili and John Zeitlin
Project Editor: Angela Cress
Cover Design: Cheung Tai
Production Editor: Maude Spekes
Production Artist: Jan Gladish
Production Manager: Michael Shevlin
Editorial Coordinator: Déa Alessandro
Executive Editor: Del Franz

Special thanks to Dr. Sangeeta Bishop.

Manufactured in the United States of America
Published simultaneously in Canada

January 2004

10 9 8 7 6 5 4 3 2 1

ISBN 0-7432-4164-9

Table of Contents

About the Author vii

SECTION I: THE BASICS

Chapter 1: Understanding the AP Economics Exams 3

SECTION II: THE ESSENTIALS OF ECONOMICS

Chapter 2: Basic Economic Concepts 13

Chapter 3: Supply and Demand 33

SECTION III: MACROECONOMICS

Chapter 4: Macroeconomic Variables 77

Chapter 5: AD/AS Models 97

Chapter 6: Fiscal Policy 117

Chapter 7: Money and Monetary Policy 135

SECTION IV: MICROECONOMICS

Chapter 8: Costs, Revenues and Profits 163

Chapter 9: Market Structures 187

Chapter 10: Efficiency, Equity, and the Role of Government 215

SECTION V: INTERNATIONAL ECONOMICS

Chapter 11: International Economics 237

SECTION VI: FULL-LENGTH PRACTICE TESTS

Macroeconomics Practice Test 261

Answers and Explanations 273

Microeconomics Practice Test 287

Answers and Explanations 299

Scoring Your Practice Tests 310

SECTION VII: GLOSSARIES

Glosary of Macroeconomic Terms 313

Glosary of Microeconomic Terms 335

Kaptest.com/publishing

The material in this book is up to date at the time of publication. However, the College Entrance Examination Board and Educational Testing Service may have instituted changes in the test after the book was published. Be sure to carefully read the materials you receive when you register for the test.

If there are any important late-breaking developments—or any changes or corrections to the Kaplan test preparation materials in this book—we will post that information online at **kaptest.com/publishing**. Check to see if there is any information posted there regarding this book.

About the Author

Richard G. Brunelle was recently appointed Director of the Economic Education, Secondary Schools Program, for the Boston chapter of Financial Executives International, the professional association that promotes teacher training and support for economics courses. He also serves as adjunct faculty in economics, finance, and accounting for the Department of Continuing Education and M.B.A. programs at Nichols College. Until recently, he taught Advanced Placement economics at Ashland High School in Ashland, Massachusetts.

Mr. Brunelle teaches Advanced Placement Economics workshops regularly and has served as an AP Economics Reader for the College Board. In addition to having received numerous grants and fellowships in the area of economic education, he has developed curricula at secondary, college, and graduate levels, and has provided extensive consulting services and training for teachers. He received his master's of business administration from Babson College with distinction, and his master's of education from Northeastern University.

THE BASICS

UNDERSTANDING THE AP ECONOMICS EXAMS

CHAPTER ONE

This book is designed to help you to prepare for the AP Microeconomics and/or Macroeconomics exam. You may be planning to take one, or like many students, both, of the tests. If you have had a good high-school course in economics, taking the exam could earn you college credit and/or placement into advanced coursework at the college level.

If your intention is to take only one exam, read through this section, The Basics, and then turn to the relevant test section. Note that chapter 11, International Economics, applies to *both* macro and microeconomics. Each chapter includes review questions to help you identify your strength and weaknesses. Also included are two practice tests (one each for micro and macro) with answers and explanations. With Kaplan's proven test-taking strategies and the targeted review, you will go into the test with confidence.

ABOUT THE AP ECONOMICS EXAMS

What are the exams?

There are two exams in economics: one in microeconomics and one in macroeconomics. You do not have to take both but may choose to do so. Both exams have the same structure:

Section I

60 multiple-choice questions	70 minutes

Section II

1 long free-response question and 2 short free-response questions	10 minutes for planning
	50 minutes for writing

Total Time	2 hours and 10 minutes

Microeconomics: What's Covered?

The Microeconomics exam covers four major areas: The numbers in parentheses indicate the approximate proportion of multiple-choice questions in each area. For example, 8-12% for Basic Economic Concepts indicates that there are 5 to 7 questions on this subject.

I. Basic Economic Concepts (8–12%)

A. Scarcity: The Nature of Economic Systems

B. Opportunity Costs and Production Possibilities

C. Specialization and Comparative Advantage; The Basis for International Trade

D. The Functions of Any Economic System

II. The Nature and Functions of Product Markets (60–70%)

A. Supply and Demand

B. Models of Consumer Choice

C. Firm Production, Costs, Revenues

D. Product Pricing and Outputs within Different Market Structures

E. Efficiency and Government Policy toward Imperfect Competition

III. Factor Markets (10–15%)

A. Derived Factor Demand

B. Determination of Wages and Other Factor Prices

IV. Efficiency, Equity, and the Role of Government (8–12%)

A. Externalities

B. Public goods

C. Distribution of Income

Macroeconomics: What's Covered?

The Macroeconomics exam covers five major areas: The numbers in parentheses indicate the approximate proportion of multiple-choice questions en each area. For example, 5–10% for Basic Economic Concepts indicates that there will be 3–6 questions on this subject.

I. Basic Economic Concepts (5–10%)

A. Scarcity: the Nature of Economic Systems

B. Opportunity Costs and Production Possibilities

C. Specialization and Comparative Advantage: The Basis for International Trade

D. The Functions of Any Economic System

E. Demand, Supply, Price Determination

II. Measurement of Economic Performance *(8–12%)*

A. Gross National Product, Gross Domestic Product, and National Income

B. Inflation and Price Indices

C. Unemployment

III. National Income and Price Determination *(70–75%)*

A. Aggregate Supply

B. Aggregate Demand

C. Money and Banking

D. Fiscal–Monetary Mix

E. Trade-Offs between Inflation and Unemployment

IV. Economic Growth *(4–6%)*

V. International Finance, Exchange Rates, and Balance of Payments *(4–6%)*

ANATOMY OF THE EXAM

Section I consists of 60 multiple-choice questions. Most of the questions are not straight recall questions; rather, they require you to apply concepts in an analytical way. Section I accounts for two-thirds of your final grade.

Section II consists of three free-response questions (one long and two short). These brief problem-solving questions often involve several subjects. The longer question is worth twice as much as each short question. This section accounts for one-third of your final grade. You should note that these do not require full paragraph explanations. Rather, a short description and graph, when appropriate, are sufficient.

HOW IS THE EXAM SCORED?

Section I: The raw score for Section I is calculated by taking the number of questions answered correctly, and subtracting 1/4 point for every wrong response. An unanswered question is not considered wrong, so if you leave a question blank, 1/4 point will not be deducted.

If you answered all 60 questions and had 50 correct answers and 10 incorrect answers, your raw score would be calculated as follows:

$$\text{Raw Score} = \text{\# correct} - \left(\frac{1}{4}\right)(\text{\# incorrect})$$

$$= 50 - \frac{1}{4}(10)$$

$$50 - 2.5 = 47.5$$

$$= 47.5$$

All 'negative" raw scores are rounded up to zero. If you did get all the multiple-choice questions wrong, you would get a score of zero.

Section II: Section II counts for one-third of the overall grade. The free-response questions include one long question and two short questions, each with a different point value depending on the rubrics. Typically, the long question is worth 9–12 points, and each short question is worth 4–6 points. Regardless of the number of points each has, the long question counts for half of this section (1/6 of the overall grade), and each short question counts for one quarter of this section (1/12 of the overall grade).

You *can* earn partial credit on your free-response answers. The graders are looking for logical reasoning, so even if some of your data is wrong, you can still earn some credit. Make sure you present the steps to your reasoning—don't just list the final answer itself.

Total Composite Score: The scores from Sections I and II are combined to give a composite score. (Remember, the multiple-choice section is 2/3 of the composite grade and the free-response section is 1/3 of the composite grade.) The composite score is then converted into an AP grade, reported on a 5-point scale:

    5 — Extremely well qualified

    4 — Well qualified

    3 — Qualified

    2 — Possibly qualified

    1 — No recommendation*

HOW DO I GET MY GRADE?

AP Grade Reports are sent in July to your home, high school, and any colleges designated by you. You may designate the colleges you would like to receive your grade on the exam answer sheet, so make sure you bring this information with you on test day.

The reports include all your AP exam history, unless you request a particular grade to be withheld. To withhold a grade, or to forward your grade to other colleges after the exam, contact AP Services.

AP Grades by phone are available for $13 per call beginning in early July. A touch-tone phone is needed. The toll-free number is (888) 308-0013.

REGISTRATION

To register for the exam, contact your school guidance counselor or AP Coordinator. If your school does not administer the exam, contact AP Services for schools in your area that do.

---

* No recommendation to receive college credit or advanced placement

FEES

The fee for each AP Exam is $82, as of this printing. However, you may take both economics exams for a single fee if they are taken in the same year. The College Board offers a $22 reduction to those with acute financial need. Additionally, some school districts subsidize exam fees when appropriate. A portion of the exam fee may be refunded if you do not take the test. (Note: If you take only one economics exam, you will not be refunded any money.)

WHAT YOU NEED TO BRING

- Photo I.D.
- Your secondary school code number (see your guidance counselor or AP coordinator)
- Your social security number
- Several sharpened No. 2 pencils
- A black or dark blue ballpoint pen for the free-response questions
- An eraser
- A watch, in case you can't easily see the clock in your exam room.

WHAT NOT TO BRING

- Do not bring scratch paper. You will make your notes in the test booklet.
- Do not bring a dictionary, notes, correction fluid, or a ruler.
- Do not bring beepers or cell phones, or anything that has a beeper function.
- Do not bring a calculator (calculators are not permitted).
- Do not bring food or drink.
- Do not bring headphones that you'd like to wear while taking the test.

ADDITIONAL RESOURCES

For more information on the exam, contact AP Services at:

AP Services
P.O. Box 6671
Princeton, NJ 08541-6671
Phone: (609) 771-7300 or (888) 225-5427
Fax: (609) 530-0482
TTY: (609) 882-4118
Email: apexams@info.collegeboard.org
Website: www.collegeboard.com/student/testing/ap/about.html

TEST-TAKING STRATEGIES

Now that you've got some idea of the kind of adversary you face in the AP, it's time to start developing your strategy mindset.

While both AP economics exams require prior knowledge of concepts, they also require you to do a fair amount of analysis. Your ability to apply economic concepts is crucial. You must also be able to interpret graphs; in the free-response section as well, you will be expected to include appropriate graphs in your explanations.

You are not expected to recall straight historical data. You would not be asked about the inflation rate in the late 1970s or the U.S. automobile output in 2001. Rather, you would be asked to analyze the possible causes of high inflation or to explain the effects of technological development on the automobile industry.

Try to master all the concepts from your AP course. Practice applying them. And before test day, review the table of contents in your textbook.

If you are tempted to skip some sections from your AP course because you are short of time, understand that this could be a serious mistake. All course topics are covered on the test.

1. For the multiple-choice questions, guess intelligently and with caution.

Random guessing will not help your score and it may very well hurt it. There is a 1/4 point deduction for a wrong answer, but no deduction for an answer left blank. However, if you can eliminate a few answer choices, then your odds of making an intelligent guess will improve. Each multiple-choice question has five possible answers. If you eliminate one answer choice, you have a 1 in 4 chance of being correct. If you eliminate two answer choices you have a 1 in 3 chance of being correct. Since you only lose 1/4 point for an wrong answer, the odds become more advantageous to taking a risk.

2. In the multiple-choice section, answer the easy questions first.

Easy questions are worth just as many points as hard questions. To maximize your score, you need to answer as many questions correctly as possible—but it does not matter if they are easy or hard. And if you run out of time, you will want to be sure to have gotten to all the questions that would earn you points. So on your first pass through the multiple-choice section, answer all the easy questions. Circle the harder questions and come back to them later. Do not waste valuable time on time-consuming questions early in the exam. You're better off spending those extra few minutes answering 3 or 4 easier questions.

As a point of interest, each test question has been refined numerous times. Key criteria used are a) that the question is not ambiguous, b) that there is only one correct answer, and c) that the question asks about an important concept, relationship, or definition. Also note that there is usually an answer that may seem to be correct, but is not 100 percent accurate.

3. In the free-response section, read the question twice before you begin to organize your answer. Prepare an outline and list key terms, graphs, and linkages where appropriate.

Be sure that you are clear on what you are being asked to do: Describe, illustrate, graph, and list mean different things, and if your answers take this into account, your answers will be stronger. Graders are looking for main points, and appropriate and well-labeled graphs (where required). Make sure you make the proper cause-and-effect linkages when needed.

4. Mirror the structure of the free-response question.

If the question is broken down into Roman numerals, for example, stick to the same format. This will ensure that you don't leave out any part of the question. Many free-response questions are divided into parts such as a, b, and c, and you are scored individually for each part. So even if you get part b wrong, for instance, you could still earn full credit for parts a and c.

In economics, the free-response questions are *not* essay questions that require an essay format with paragraphs. They're analytical and visual, and should be answered directly in the question format.

5. Answer the free-response questions directly and explicitly.

Your goal is to have a clear, directed response, not a general, undirected response. Don't jot down everything you know about a topic in hopes of getting something right—that approach won't work. Let the question guide you. Write focused responses to the specific parts of the question.

6. Prioritize the free-response questions according to difficulty.

Again, your goal is to score as many points in this section as possible. During the 10 minutes that you are given to read and make notes, do the easier questions first. Remember that the longer essay question is worth the same as the two shorter ones combined.

7. Draw clear and correctly labeled graphs.

Graphs are an integral part of economics. You should have mastered doing graphs in your preparation for the exam. In addition to those questions that specifically request graphs, you may also include graphs to support your answers on questions where the graph was not specifically requested. Make sure your graphs are large enough so that you can clearly have unambiguous reference points. Labeling your graph correctly with the vertical and horizontal axes is essential.

8. Mark up your test booklet.

When taking the AP exam, it's to your advantage to mark up your test booklet. Draw diagrams such as supply and demand graphs when you need to reason out an answer. Cross out incorrect answer choices. Jot down key notes that will help you answer questions, such as $P\uparrow$ $TR\uparrow$—inelastic. Use the margins to do some simple math if that helps you with the question.

9. Be careful with your answer grid.

Your AP score for the multiple-choice section is based on what appears on your answer grid. So even if you answered every question correctly, you'll get a low score if you put the answers in the wrong place.

Be careful! Keep track of the numbers and the responses that you record. You may skip a question the first time through the exam. Make sure you leave the appropriate space in the answer grid blank. Misaligning your answers even if you catch the error later can cost you valuable time—you'll have to erase and realign your responses. Also, if you do change an answer, make sure that you erase cleanly the original answer choice you had selected.

10. Write neatly.

Penmanship is not graded when the free-response section of the test is graded. However, a reader who must struggle to make out words is bound to have a harder time grading the response. You will not get the benefit of the doubt if the reader cannot read your writing. If your handwriting tends to be hard to read, make an effort to write more legibly than usual. In economics, the free-response questions do not require you to write a large number of words, so you can take the time to be legible.

11. Keep track of time.

It's important to keep track of time as you work through the test. You'll have to pace yourself, or else you'll run out of time. With 70 minutes to answer 60 multiple-choice questions, that means just over one minute per question. Some will take more time than others, of course, so you'll have to keep track of how fast you are proceeding. If you find that you are losing time poring over one tough question, circle it, move on, and go back if you have time.

In the free-response section you will have 10 minutes to make notes on all three questions. Then you will have 50 minutes to write your responses. The first question is the long question and worth 50 percent of the total free-response score. Plan to spend about 25 minutes on it. The other two questions are shorter. Plan to spend about 10 minutes on each. You'll want to leave a couple of minutes for proofreading your answer as well.

12. No cheating.

It is hardly necessary to indicate that such behavior is unacceptable, but you should know that cheating on AP Exams is dealt with quite severely. The effort it takes to cheat is much greater than the effort required to learn the material. Furthermore, the consequences of such behavior are very serious and long-term.

Apart from the illegal component of cheating, you would be shortchanging yourself; if you were placed in an advanced course for which you were not fully prepared, you would find yourself at a serious disadvantage.

KAPLAN

THE ESSENTIALS OF ECONOMICS

BASIC ECONOMIC CONCEPTS

Economics is the study of how resources are used by individuals, by firms, and by society in general. At any given time, resources exist in limited supply. It is this scarcity that creates problems. People have unlimited wants but are faced with limited resources with which to satisfy these wants. The resources available to any economy are categorized as **land** (natural resources), **labor** (human resources), **capital** (capital resources), and **entrepreneurship** (the ability and will of the consumer to efficiently and creatively organize resources for production). The term *capital* in economics refers to the goods used in the production process, such as factories, tools, and equipment. It is not financial capital, which is the money used to acquire the real assets of production.

Students frequently confuse money with economic resources. Economic resources are **factors of production**, or inputs. Money is a **medium of exchange**. It may be true that if an individual had more income he would be able to consume more, but more money does not necessarily allow a country to produce more. If a country created more money without increasing its production of goods and services, it would merely lead to higher prices—and not to a higher standard of living. Money allows an economy to function more efficiently. Without it, people would have to barter one good or service for another good or service. Bartering requires a **coincidence of wants**. That is, without money, individuals would have to find someone who wanted their good, service, or labor, and who had what they wanted in return. This would significantly lower the number of transactions possible. It is much more efficient to sell one's good or service for money and then use that money to buy whatever is wanted.

As a result of the scarcity problem, decisions have to be made. The essential questions facing every economy are: *What to make? How to make it? For whom would it be made?* Economic systems are distinguished by how they answer these questions.

Command economies answer these key questions through a central authority made up of an individual or a number of individuals. **Traditional** economies rely on past customs and practices.

Market economies use a system of supply and demand. Adam Smith was the first to detail the ability of markets to coordinate economic activity. His 18th century book *The Wealth of Nations* describes an "invisible hand" that directs society's resources to their most efficient use. In other words, allowing individuals to pursue their own self-interest usually results in an efficient economy.

Economies do not always fall completely into one system or the other. Many modern economies are mixed in that they have elements of the different systems. That being said, the AP curriculum covers the economics of a *predominantly market economy*. We'll also need to understand the role that government can play when there are less than ideal market conditions or outright market failures.

In a market economy, entities pursue their own self-interest. Consumers buy what they want, and producers must produce what the consumer wants if they intend to stay in business. This power of the consumer to decide the question "What to make?" is called **consumer sovereignty**.

Producers decide "How to make?" by combining resources in the most efficient manner. Competition from other producers provides the incentive for firms to produce quality products in the least costly manner. Firms are organized as:

> **Sole proprietorship**, if one individual is the owner and recognizes all profits as income. The owner and the business are treated as one entity for legal and tax purposes. When the owner dies, the sole proprietorship dies.

> **Partnerships,** if more than one owner is involved and the profits are recognized as income to the individuals in some predetermined prorated portions. The individuals and the company are also treated as combined entities for legal and tax purposes. When one of the partners dies, the partnership dies.

> **Corporations**, if individuals incorporate a business. Then, the business has a separate legal entity for legal and tax purposes. For tax purposes, the income of the business is not recognized as the individual's income: the business exists as a separate legal entity. The owners are stockholders and they can sell their stock without disruption to the continuity of the business. Corporations can continue on long after the original incorporators have passed on.

In a market economy, the factors of production are owned by individuals and not by the state. This is what is meant by **capitalism**. **Property rights** (private ownership) are very important to a market economy, not only to the production side, but also to the consumption side. Think about it—would you buy a car or a house if the legal system did not protect your ownership rights to exclusive use of the purchased items? If ownership rights were not protected, what would happen to the demand for products?

In a market economy, the "For whom?" question is determined by purchasing power. Consumers are part of the demand for goods and services not only because they want them, but also because they have (or haven't) the money to buy them. Individuals earn money by creating income. So the need for purchasing power provides people with the incentive to work, to invest their financial capital, or to provide their natural resources—in return for income. In order to be consumers, we need to be part of the production process. This system of incentives is called the **circular flow model**.

Now we all know that this system works very well, but there are times when we might question the "For whom" results. Poverty and other issues may arise. That is one reason why most advanced countries are mixed economies: If there's a perceived problem with distribution, then governments intercede. To what extent they intercede depends on *value judgments* (otherwise called **normative economic issues**). Governments usually make political decisions that set economic goals addressing perceived problems, while economists usually deal with **positive economic issues**, at least at the principles level. Positive economics looks at what is happening in the economy and why. Let's look at a circular diagram:

There are four sectors to the economy: households, business, government, and foreign. We could draw a circular flow model with all four sectors included but it would wind up looking like some pretty ugly plumbing. So let's keep it simple! Included below are the business and household sectors. Real flows of goods and services go from business to the households. Real flows of resources go from households to business. Money flows go in the opposite directions.

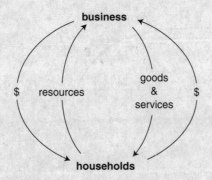

SCARCITY: THE CENTRAL ECONOMIC PROBLEM

Think like an economist! TINSTAAFL! There is no such thing as a free lunch! Because of limited resources and unlimited wants, every decision involves a choice. The cost of every decision is the **opportunity cost**.

Suppose you are going shopping and have $40 to spend. After looking at all your options you narrow down your choices to a new sweatshirt for $40 or a new pair of jeans for $40.

You opt for the new sweatshirt. What is your opportunity cost? It is the *forgone* new pair of jeans. Now we can say that you have given up $40 to buy the new sweatshirt and that is true.

But the real cost is the forgone new jeans. If you think that the real cost is the $40 you could have saved, then you are changing your options. You are saying that your best options are to buy the new jeans for $40 and save $40.

If this is truly what your final options are, then your opportunity cost of buying the new sweatshirt is the forgone savings of $40. Keep in mind that *your* opportunity cost of buying new jeans is not necessarily *another person's* opportunity cost. Charlie, for instance, might forgo the purchase of a new pair of sneakers. It depends on what his next best alternative is.

Every time you decide to spend your money on a good or service, you are helping the economy make a decision on what to produce. This is the "invisible hand" at work. If more people want jeans and have the $40 to buy them, then jeans producers will make more jeans. If people decide they want more sweatshirts, then more sweatshirts would be produced.

Production Possibilities Curve

Let's take a look at a key model, the **production possibilities curve** (PPC), used to illustrate the problem of scarce resources and opportunity cost.

Suppose that the Busy Bee Manufacturing Company produces two products: jeans and sweatshirts. We can construct the following model:

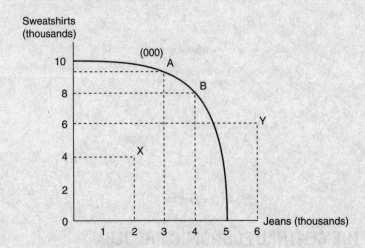

This graph illustrates the company's production possibilities for a given period of time. Busy Bee can use all of the resources available (natural resources, human resources, capital resources, entrepreneurship) to make 10,000 sweatshirts and zero jeans—or it can make 5,000 jeans and zero sweatshirts. It could also produce various other combinations, such as 9,000 sweatshirts and 3,000 jeans.

What if Busy Bee wanted to produce 6,000 sweatshirts and 6,000 jeans? This combination would bring us to point Y. The company could *not* reach that production level with the existing available resources. It would be beyond its production possibilities. A point such as

Y is said to be "unattainable." But what if it wanted to produce 4,000 sweatshirts and 2,000 jeans? This would place us at point X and we would be underutilizing the existing available resources. This would not be efficient. **Economic efficiency** would require firms to operate *on* the production possibilities curve, not at some point inside the curve.

This production possibilities curve illustrates opportunity cost because the company must forgo producing some of the sweatshirts in order to produce more jeans, and it must forgo producing some jeans in order to produce more sweatshirts. The production possibilities curve bows out from the origin (0 sweatshirts, 0 jeans). This is the result of what economists call the **principle of increasing opportunity costs**; that is, as we produce more jeans, we must forgo an increasing number of sweatshirts, and vice versa.

The *bowed-out* production possibilities curve is a key graph in economics because it illustrates the principle of increasing opportunity cost. However you also need to be familiar with a *constant cost* production possibilities curve, which does not deal with the principle of increasing opportunity costs. Constant cost implies that all resources are equally suitable to produce either good; therefore, the opportunity cost remains constant.

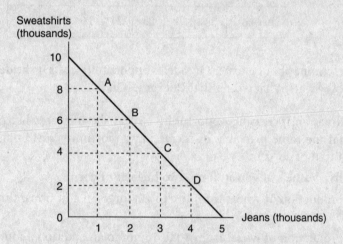

As the firm moves from point D (4,000 jeans/2,000 sweatshirts) to point C (3,000 jeans shirts/4,000 sweatshirts), the opportunity cost is 1,000 jeans for every 2,000 sweatshirts. This trade-off ratio remains constant for each possible level of production. Regardless of the quantity of either good that is produced, the opportunity cost is two sweatshirts for each additional pair of jeans, and 1/2 a pair of jeans for each additional sweatshirt.

In addition to understanding how a PPC graph works, you must also know for the test how to turn a table of information into a production possibilities curve. Consider the following:

Farmer Inadell has a farm where he can grow bushels of wheat or corn on his land. What is the opportunity cost of producing 15 bushels of wheat rather than 10 bushels? What would the PPC graph look like?

Inadell's Bushels							
Wheat	0	5	10	15	20	25	30
Corn	6	5	4	3	2	1	0

The opportunity cost of going from 10 to 15 bushels of wheat is one bushel of corn. In fact, regardless of how much of each good is produced, the opportunity cost of one bushel of corn is five bushels of wheat. This would be a constant cost PPC graph. The curve would be a straight line.

Now let us consider Farmer Outadell. Her farm produces the following possibilities:

Outadell's Bushels							
Wheat	0	5	10	15	20	25	30
Corn	30	28	25	21	16	10	0

What can you determine about Farmer Outadell's opportunity costs if she decides to increase the production of wheat? What would that PPC graph look like?

Farmer Outadell has an increasing opportunity cost as she increases her output of wheat. (Don't forget that the same principle of increasing opportunity cost applies if we look at increasing the output of corn.)

- Produce five bushels of wheat; forgo two bushels of corn.
- Increase production of wheat from five to 10; forgo an additional three bushels of corn.
- Increase production of wheat from 10 to 15; forgo an additional four bushels of corn.
- Increase production of wheat from 15 to 20; forgo an additional five bushels of corn.
- The production possibilities graph would be bowed out from the origin because it would illustrate "increasing costs."

Let's look at some problem types that require a good understanding of the concept of production possibilities.

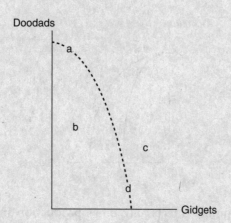

On the graph above, point a is on the production possibility curve (sometimes referred to as the production possibility frontier); therefore, it is economically efficient. Point b is inside the production possibility curve, so it is inefficient. That is, resources are underutilized. Point c is a combination that is unattainable with the present level of resources and technology. Point d, like point a, is economically efficient. Point a denotes more production of doodads than gidgets. Point d denotes more production of gidgets than doodads.

Which point on the PPC should be determined by consumer demand? (What are you going to consume?) Would point c ever be attainable? Only if there were an increase over time of a resource (factor) or technology that would make the resource more productive. This can be illustrated as follows:

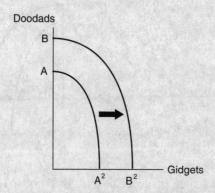

Any increase in resources or technology will increase the production possibilities and the PPC will shift from A, A^2 to B, B^2. Consequently the firm can produce more of both goods. But what if the increase in technology affects only one of the goods being produced?

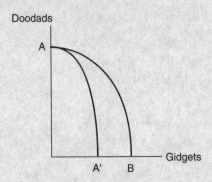

Let's assume that the technology affects only gidget production and not doodad production. In this case, the PPC remains anchored at the same spot on the doodad axis, but the PPC shifts out on the gidget axis.

What if you were told that a firm neither increased resources nor developed new technology, but was able to increase the output of both doodads and gidgets. How do you explain this? No doubt about it, the firm had to be producing inside its production possibilities curve before the increase in output.

We've just examined several ways that the PPC applies to microeconomic situations. Let's look now at how the PPC applies to macroeconomic situations.

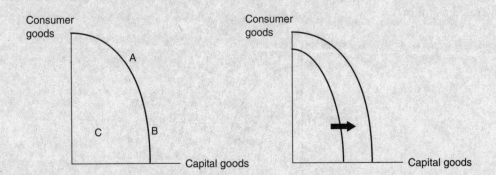

The graphs above represent larger, macroeconomic situations: They represent the output of an entire economy—not a single firm. In the graph on the left, point C represents the unemployment of the labor force and the underutilization of capital. In other words, point C would indicate that the economy was in a recession or maybe even a depression. Either way, it indicates a short-run equilibrium. Points A or B indicate full employment or long-run equilibrium, though point A represents more consumer goods and fewer capital goods. You might be asked about movement between points, indicating an economy will forgo some consumer goods in order to produce more capital goods. The message this intends to convey is that by producing more capital goods, an economy will experience more economic growth over time. Remember that the determinants of the production possibilities frontier are the availability of human resources, capital resources, and natural resources. By increasing the capital stock of the country, the economy experiences growth (the movement to the right of the long-run aggregate supply curve).

The graph on the right illustrates economic growth for an economy. Remember that in addition to an increase in the capital stock, other things can shift the PPC curve to the right, signifying economic growth: an increase in labor, natural resources, or technology.

The PPC model can also be used in the area of international economics. Assume that countries Alpha and Beta each produce wine and orange juice. Their production possibilities curves are:

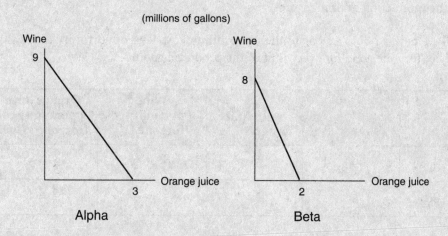

As you can see, we are using constant cost PPC graphs to compare the productive capacity of the two countries. Clearly, Alpha can produce more wine (nine million gallons) or more orange juice (three million gallons) than can country Beta. Therefore, Alpha has the **absolute advantage** in the production of both wine and orange juice (we are assuming that they both have similar resources). But should they trade?

Comparative Advantage

The question of whether the two countries should trade brings us to another important analytical model: **comparative advantage**. Comparative advantage measures the relative cost of producing a good. Cost here refers to **opportunity cost**, not to money cost. Alas, the opportunity cost is the *forgone good or service that cannot be produced if an individual, firm, or country opts to produce an alternative good or service*. (Let us not forget that scarcity forces everyone into making choices.)

> The country (or individual or firm) that has the lowest opportunity cost has the comparative advantage, and should specialize in the production of that good or service.

To calculate comparative advantage, first decide if the information given deals with comparative outputs or comparative inputs. Here, we're given various *outputs* in terms of gallons of wine and orange juice. Now, using the information from our original constant cost graph for Alpha and Beta, we can start our grid.

	Wine (gals)	Orange juice (gals)		
Alpha	9	3		
Beta	8	2		

If you're analyzing outputs, then the country with the most output for a given level of input has the *absolute advantage*. Here, Alpha has the absolute advantage in the production of wine and in the production of orange juice.

Now all we have to do is calculate the opportunity cost. The opportunity cost will be the quantity of forgone good for every unit of the produced good.

	Wine (gals)	Orange juice (gals)	Wine Opportunity cost (forgone OJ)	Orange juice Opportunity cost (forgone Wine)
Alpha	9	3	$\frac{3}{9} = \frac{1}{3}$	$\frac{9}{3} = 3$
Beta	8	2	$\frac{2}{8} = \frac{1}{4}$	$\frac{8}{2} = 4$

To calculate opportunity cost when a problem deals with different *outputs*, we divide the output quantity of the forgone good by the output quantity of the good produced. We can think of it as a fraction, with the forgone output serving as the numerator, and the produced good as the denominator.

We know that the opportunity cost for Alpha to produce one gallon of wine is the forgoing of 1/3 gallon of orange juice, and the opportunity cost for Beta to produce one gallon of wine is 1/4 of a gallon of orange juice.

The entity with the lowest opportunity cost has the comparative advantage. In the production of wine, Beta has the comparative advantage. To solve the comparative advantage for orange juice, we know that Alpha has an opportunity cost in producing orange juice of forgoing three wines, while Beta has the opportunity cost in producing orange juice of four wines. Alpha has the comparative advantage here. So to benefit the most, the two countries combine production: Beta specializes in wine and Alpha specializes in orange juice, and they trade with each other.

Even though Alpha has an *absolute advantage* in producing both wine and orange juice, Beta has a *comparative advantage* in producing wine because the opportunity cost for the production of wine (in terms of forgone orange juice) is lower for Beta than for Alpha. Similarly, Alpha has a comparative advantage in the production of orange juice because the opportunity cost for the production of orange juice (in terms of forgone wine) is lower for Alpha than for Beta.

To calculate comparative advantage when a problem deals with different *inputs*:

- Alpha needs one acre of land to produce 100 gallons of wine and three acres to produce 100 gallons of orange juice.
- Beta needs one acre of land to produce 100 gallons of wine and four acres of land to produce 100 gallons of orange juice.

In the situations above, the output (100 gallons of wine/orange juice) is held constant. What changes is the amount of inputs (resources) used to achieve the same level of output.

Inputs Required to Produce 100 Gallons (stated in acres)				
	Wine	Orange juice	Wine Opportunity cost	Orange juice Opportunity cost
Alpha	1	3	$\frac{1}{3}$ OJ	$\frac{3}{1}$ Wine
Beta	1	4	$\frac{1}{4}$ OJ	$\frac{4}{1}$ Wine

When calculating the opportunity cost of producing a good using inputs, the number of inputs in the forgone good is used as the denominator of the fraction. The entity with the lowest opportunity cost has the comparative advantage. In this set of data, too, Beta has the comparative advantage in the production of wine, while Alpha has the comparative advantage in the production of orange juice.

To calculate absolute advantage when dealing with different *inputs*, the entity that requires the least amount of input has the comparative advantage. In the problem above, neither country had the absolute advantage in the production of wine and Alpha had the absolute advantage in the production of orange juice.

> Other possible inputs could include:
> - Number of man hours or number of workers
> - Number of machine hours or number of units of capital

When dealing with comparative advantage in regard to international trade, the issue of **terms of trade** often arises. When countries specialize in the production of goods and services where they have comparative advantage, what are the acceptable terms of trade? With a grid, the answer becomes simple. A country must receive an amount greater than its opportunity cost. In the problem above, Alpha must get more than three wines for every gallon of orange juice traded; Beta must get more than 1/4 gallon of orange juice for every one traded. If the proper terms of trade are available, they both win. If they are not, they do not trade! Trade is a win–win game!

Marginal Analysis

One basic assumption that all economists make is that people pursue their own self-interest by examining the costs and benefits of their decisions. The **net benefit** of any decision is calculated by subtracting the total cost (including all opportunity costs) from the total benefit.

The **marginal benefit** is the change in total benefit by increasing by one unit the good or service that is creating the benefit. The **marginal cost** is the change in total cost created by increasing by one unit the good or service. Economists analyze decisions at the margin (marginal analysis). They perform a cost/benefit analysis by comparing the marginal benefit to the marginal cost as incrementally one more unit is added or subtracted. Any incremental change that leads to a marginal cost which is greater than the marginal benefit is *not* a good decision. We will be looking at some marginal analysis applications in later units.

Faulty Economic Reasoning

Listed below are some pitfalls to good economic reasoning. For one reason or another, these all make incorrect assumptions.

Fallacy of Composition assumes that what is true for one part also applies to the sum of the parts, and vice versa. To argue that free trade eliminates some jobs in a country and, therefore, is bad for the economy as a whole, is not a valid conclusion. Nor would it be valid to state that free trade is good for the economy and, therefore, is good for all workers.

Association Implies Causation assumes that a statistical association between two events implies that one causes the other.

Sample Selection Bias predicts behavior for an entire population from the statistical analysis of a subset of the population that is not representative of the entire population.

Faulty *ceteris paribus* assumes factors are constant that cannot logically be held constant.

Unaccounted Factors assumes that an association between two events will continue in the future, without identifying how the association depends on the stability of other factors.

KEY POINTS

- People have unlimited wants but limited resources. Scarcity creates the need for economics.

- Opportunity cost is the alternative forgone in decisionmaking.

- Market economies allow buyers and sellers to pursue their own self-interest.

- Economic efficiency exists when firms (microeconomics) or countries (macroeconomics) produce the most goods and services they can, while employing all of the resources (land, labor, and capital) available (given the current level of technology).

- The production possibilities curve (PPC) can be used to illustrate the concepts of scarcity, choice and opportunity cost, and economic efficiency. A PPC that is bowed out from the origin illustrates the concept of increasing opportunity cost. A PPC that is a straight line illustrates the concept of constant cost.

- Absolute advantage is the ability to produce more of a good or service with the same amount of resources. It can also be viewed as the ability to produce the same amount of a good or service using fewer resources.

- Productive efficiency is the ability to produce the maximum amount of a good or service using a given amount of resources.

- Comparative advantage is the ability to produce a good or service while forgoing less production of another good or service (opportunity cost) than other producers. In doing comparative advantage analysis, be careful to determine whether the problem calls for input analysis ("How many units of land, labor, or capital are required to produce a certain amount"?) or output analysis ("How much output is produced using the same amount of land, labor, or capital"?).

- Specialization is the commitment of resources to a particular task(s). What task(s) a resource should specialize in is determined by comparative advantage analysis.

- If two entities that specialize in the production of goods or services want to trade, the terms of trade must allow each entity to receive more than their respective opportunity costs used to calculate comparative advantage.

- Free trade allows the world economy to allocate resources efficiently, which results in a higher level of well being for more people.

- Eliminating trade barriers has a positive net effect on an economy, though the share of costs and benefits borne by different parties is not always equitable.

REVIEW QUESTIONS

1. Which of the following is not an economic resource?

   (A) Land
   (B) Labor
   (C) Capital
   (D) Entrepreneurship
   (E) Money

2. Opportunity cost is

   (A) the forgoing of an opportunity because it is considered unimportant.
   (B) the total value of a good and service that would be the same for all consumers.
   (C) the explicit costs of producing a good or service.
   (D) the forgoing of the next best alternative.
   (E) the sunk cost of a good that does not impact the final decision.

3. In order for a country to have the comparative advantage over another country in the production of good A, it must have

   (A) the absolute advantage in the production of good A.
   (B) lower opportunity cost in the production of the good A.
   (C) more use for the good A.
   (D) greater opportunity cost in the production of good A.
   (E) less need for the production of other goods.

4. A factory belongs to which category of the factors of production?

   (A) Land
   (B) Labor
   (C) Capital
   (D) Manufacturing
   (E) None of the above

5. If an economy could produce more consumer goods without forgoing the production of any other goods, which of the following statements would be true?

   (A) The economy is efficiently operating outside the production possibilities curve.
   (B) The economy is inefficiently operating outside the production possibilities curve.
   (C) The economy is efficiently operating inside the production possibilities curve.
   (D) The economy is inefficiently operating inside the production possibilities curve.
   (E) The economy is efficiently operating on the production possibility curve.

6. One thing that goods and services have in common is that

   (A) they both satisfy wants.
   (B) they are things we always have to pay for.
   (C) they have the same value to everybody.
   (D) they are tangible.
   (E) both are categories of the factors of production.

7. Which of the following sums up the circular flow of economic activity?

   (A) Households earn money by selling their factors of production to firms in the factor market and use that money to buy goods and services from firms in the product market.

   (B) Households earn money by selling their factors of production to firms in the product market and use that money to buy goods and services from firms in the factor market

   (C) Firms buy goods and services from other firms, who in turn buy goods and services from yet other firms.

   (D) Firms earn money by selling their factors of production to households in the factor market and use that money to buy goods and services from households in the product market

   (E) Households buy factors of production from firms and use them to produce goods and services, which they sell to other households.

8. Suppose you have the opportunity to work in the concession stand at a football game for two hours, at $5 an hour. You decide instead to go to a concert whose ticket costs $12. Which of the following is closest to your opportunity cost for going to the concert?

   (A) $10 plus the chance to work at the concession stand
   (B) $12
   (C) $20
   (D) $20 plus the chance to see the concert
   (E) $22 plus the chance to work at the concession stand

9. Suppose you can mow a lawn or wash five cars in two hours. Your neighbor, Mr. Gedye, can mow a lawn in one hour. In order for him to have a comparative advantage in mowing lawns, how many cars must he be able to wash in two hours?

   (A) More than five and fewer than 10
   (B) More than five
   (C) Fewer than 10
   (D) The number of cars he can wash is irrelevant in determining the comparative advantage.
   (E) There isn't enough information to say.

10. Doward can peel 15 potatoes or slice 20 onions in an hour. Shashawna can peel 30 potatoes or slice 25 onions in an hour. Which of the following statements is true?

   (A) Doward has a comparative advantage in potato peeling.
   (B) Shashawna has an absolute advantage in both activities.
   (C) Shashawna has a comparative advantage in onion slicing.
   (D) Shashawna's opportunity cost of peeling one potato is 6/5 of an onion.
   (E) Doward's opportunity cost of peeling one potato is 6/5 of an onion.

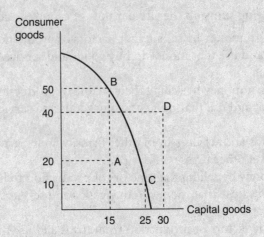

Questions 11–13

11. If the economy above were producing at point B and decided to produce at point C, its opportunity cost would be

    (A) 40 units of consumer goods.
    (B) 10 units of capital goods.
    (C) Zero, as it can change production without any additional opportunity cost.
    (D) 25 units of capital goods.
    (E) 50 units of consumer goods.

12. Which of the following would allow this economy to produce at point D?

    (A) Producing fewer capital goods.
    (B) Producing fewer consumer goods.
    (C) Developing new technology that helps the production of consumer goods.
    (D) Developing new technology that helps the production of both consumer and capital goods.
    (E) This economy will never be able to produce at point D.

13. If this economy were producing at point A,

    (A) it could produce no additional capital goods or consumer goods.
    (B) it could produce additional capital goods.
    (C) it could produce additional consumer goods.
    (D) it could produce additional capital and consumer goods.
    (E) it would be economically efficient.

Free-Response Questions

Directions: Use the information in the graph to answer the following questions. Make sure you emphasize the line of reasoning that generates your answer—it is not enough to just list the answer. Include all necessary correctly labeled diagrams.

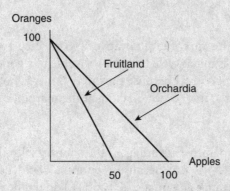

Bushels of Fruit per Acre of Land

The diagram above represents the production of fruit per acre of land for two countries, Fruitland and Orchardia.

1. (a) Which country has the absolute advantage in the production of oranges?

   (b) Which country has the absolute advantage in the production of apples?

2. (a) Which country has the comparative advantage in the production of oranges?

   (b) How do you determine who has the comparative advantage?

3. (a) What is Fruitland's opportunity cost of producing apples?

   (b) Which country should specialize in the production of apples?

4. (a) If the terms of trade are three oranges for two apples will these countries specialize and trade?

   (b) Why or why not?

5. (a) If the terms of trade are three bushels of apples for two bushels of oranges will these countries specialize and trade?

   (b) Why or why not?

ANSWERS TO REVIEW QUESTIONS

1. (E)

Money is a medium of exchange, not an economic resource. All the other answer choices are economic resources.

2. (D)

An opportunity cost is the forgone alternative. (A) is incorrect because it was not an important alternative. (B) is out as well, because the value of a good or service is not the same for all consumers. (C) is not correct because the opportunity is not the explicit cost only. And a sunk cost is not considered in decision making at the margin, so (E) is wrong as well.

3. (B)

The country with the comparative advantage is the country with the lowest opportunity cost of producing that good. (A) is out because a country could have an absolute advantage without having the comparative advantage. (C) and (E) do not deal with the opportunity cost of producing the good. (D) is not correct because greater opportunity cost would give the comparative advantage to the other country.

4. (C)

Capital is all buildings, equipment, machinery, and human skill used in producing goods and services. (A) and (B) are wrong because a factory isn't considered land or labor. (D) is wrong because manufacturing is not one of the factors of production.

5. (D)

If a country can produce more of a good without forgoing the production of other goods then the only answer that is correct is that it must be inside the PPC and not producing efficiently. Of course, a country could produce more of a good without reducing the production of other goods if it experienced economic growth (an increase in the factors of production and/or an improvement in technology) but none of the answers indicated economic growth. (A) and (B) are wrong because a country cannot be operating outside its PPC. (C) is wrong because if a country is inside its PPC it is not efficient. (E) is wrong because if a country is on the PPC, it cannot increase the production of one good without forgoing the production of another.

6. (A)

Both goods and services satisfy wants. When you want something, it's often a good (like a skateboard or a CD) or a service (like a bus ride). (B) is incorrect because there are some goods we don't have to pay for, such as air and sunlight. Goods are tangible, but services generally aren't—you can't hold an oil change or a shoe shine—so (D) is wrong as well. (E) is out too because these aren't categories of the factors of production.

7. (A)

The circular flow of economic activity tracks the economic transactions as households sell their factors of production to firms in the factor market. These factors of production include land, labor, capital, and entrepreneurial ability. Firms use these factors to make goods and services, which they in turn sell to households. Households receive money for their factors of production and use the money to buy goods and services. Firms receive money for their goods and services and use that money to buy factors of production. (C) is wrong because it neglects households. (B), (D), and (E) are wrong because they confuse who sells what in the factor and product markets.

8. (E)

Your opportunity cost is the $12 ticket price plus the $10 in lost income, or $22, plus the chance to work at the concession stand. (A), (B), and (C) have the financial part of the opportunity cost wrong. (D) does as well, plus, here, you do get to see the concert, so that can't be part of the opportunity cost. Opportunity cost is the value of the next best alternative sacrificed.

9. (C)

If Mr. Gedye has a comparative advantage in mowing lawns, he has to give up fewer washed cars than you do in the amount of time it takes you each to mow the lawn. When you mow a lawn, you give up the chance to wash five cars. Mr. Gedye can mow a lawn in one hour, so in two hours he can mow two lawns. For his opportunity cost to be less than yours, he has to be able to wash fewer than five cars an hour. So in two hours he must be able to wash fewer than 10 cars.

10. (B)

Shashawna can peel more potatoes and slice more onions than Doward can in the same amount of time. Therefore, she uses fewer resources—in this case, time—to do the job. (A) is wrong because Doward has a comparative advantage in onion slicing, not potato peeling, and C is wrong because Shashawna has a comparative advantage in potato peeling not onion slicing. Shashawna's opportunity cost of peeling one potato is 5/6 of an onion so D is wrong. E is wrong because Doward's opportunity cost of peeling one potato is 4/3 of an onion.

11. (A)

At point B, the economy is producing 50 units of consumer goods and 15 units of capital goods. At point C, it's producing 10 units of consumer goods and 25 units of capital goods. It has foregone 40 units of consumer goods to produce 10 more units of capital goods.

12. (D)

In order to produce at this level of output, new technology has to help increase the production of more capital goods. At the current level, the maximum number of capital goods that can be produced—even if no consumer goods are produced—is fewer than 30. Choice (C) would help produce more consumer goods, but not more capital goods.

13. (D)

At point A, the economy is producing 20 units of consumer goods and 15 units of capital goods. A more efficient use of resources would allow it to produce more of both. Choices (B) and (C) are partially correct, but the better answer is that it can produce more of both goods.

Free-Response Questions

1. (a) Neither country has the absolute advantage in the production of oranges. Both can produce 100 bushels an acre.

    (b) Orchardia has the absolute advantage in the production of apples. It can produce 100 bushels per acre versus 50 bushels per acre for Fruitland.

2. (a) Fruitland has the comparative advantage in the production of oranges. It has an opportunity cost of 1/2 a bushel of apples for every bushel of oranges it produces. Orchardia forgoes 1 bushel of apples for every bushel of oranges it produces.

    (b) As noted above, comparative advantage is determined by the lowest opportunity cost.

3. (a) Fruitland's opportunity cost of producing apples is two bushels of oranges for every bushel of apples produced.

    (b) Orchardia should specialize in the production of apples. It has the comparative advantage in apple production. Its opportunity cost is one bushel of oranges for every bushel of apples produced.

4. (a) Using comparative advantage we determine that Orchardia should specialize in apple production and Fruitland should specialize in orange production.

    (b) If the terms of trade are three bushels of oranges for two bushels of apples, Fruitland receives 2/3 a bushel of apples for each bushel of oranges. This exceeds Fruitland's opportunity cost of 1/2 a bushel of apples. Orchardia receives 1 and 1/2 bushels of oranges for every bushel of apples. This exceeds Orchardia's opportunity cost of 1 bushel of oranges.

5. (a) If the terms of trade are three bushels of apples for two oranges, then these countries will not trade.

    (b) Fruitland would receive one and 1/2 bushels of apples for each bushel of oranges. This is fine. But Orchardia would receive 2/3 of a bushel of oranges for one bushel of apples. This is less than Orchardia's opportunity cost of one bushel of oranges for one bushel of apples; therefore, Orchardia would refuse to trade.

SUPPLY AND DEMAND

You understand now that the basic economic questions "What to make," "How to make it," and "For whom would it be made" can be determined by **markets.** It's time for a closer look at how markets function.

Buyers and sellers come together in the marketplace to exchange goods and services. This exchange is what economists refer to as *supply* and *demand.* **Supply** is the quantity of goods or services that producers are willing to sell at different prices. **Demand** is the quantity of goods or services that consumers are willing to buy at different prices.

Two basic certainties exist for supply and demand:

Law of Supply: The amount that producers are willing to produce and sell (quantity supplied) increases when prices increase. And the amount producers are willing to produce and sell decreases when prices decrease. This is true provided everything else remains the same.

Law of Demand: The amount that consumers are willing and able to purchase (quantity demanded) increases when prices decrease. And the amount that consumers are willing and able to purchase decreases when prices increase. This is true provided all else remains fixed.

DEMAND ANALYSIS

The first thing to understand when looking at demand is that the quantity consumers are willing and able to buy at a specific price is *not* the demand; it is the **quantity demanded.** Let's look at why this distinction is important.

Consumer Demand for Roses in the Land of Zod							
A Helen		**B** Bob		**C** Sue		**D** Total Market	
P	Q^d	P	Q^d	P	Q^d	P	Q^d
$3	5	$3	4	$3	1	$3	10
$2	7	$2	6	$2	2	$2	15
$1	12	$1	9	$1	4	$1	25

The data above indicates consumer data for roses in the Land of Zod. There are three consumers in this rose market: Helen, Bob, and Sue. Column A, Helen's demand, includes the number of roses she would buy at each possible price. Helen's demand is the *quantity demanded by her at each price.* The same can be said for Bob and Sue—their individual demand is the quantity that each would be willing to buy at a particular price. Columns A, B, and C represent the individual demands of each consumer. Column D represents the total market demand for roses.

> An individual's demand is constructed from the quantity demanded at each price. The market demand is the sum of the individual demands; that is, the total quantity demanded at each possible price.

Be careful not to confuse quantity demanded with *demand,* which is the different amounts of a good that consumers are willing and able to buy at different prices. A change in the price of the product will cause a change in quantity demanded, while a change in one of the other determinants of demand will cause a change in demand.

At a price of $3 each, Helen is willing to buy five roses, Bob is willing to buy four roses, and Sue is willing to buy one rose. The demand for any given product is not the same for all consumers. The market demand for roses is the sum of all the individual demands.

The Demand Curve

The demand curve is a graphic presentation of the information provided by a table of data that relates to variables: price and quantity demanded. Let's refer back to the demand for roses in the land of Zod.

Total Market Demand	
P	Q
$3	10
$2	15
$1	25

Now we can construct our graph. In a market supply and demand graph, the *vertical axis* is always the **price**. The *horizontal axis* is always the **quantity**. Plot the coordinates of the two variables, price and quantity. Connect the dots. You now have a demand curve! Make sure to label graphs properly and completely—you will be expected to do so on the exam.

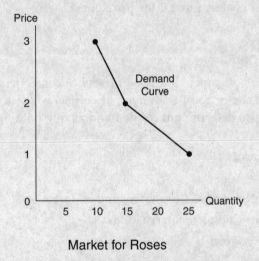

Market for Roses

As per the law of demand, there's an inverse relationship between price and quantity: *As price goes down, quantity demanded goes up,* and vice versa. As such, a demand curve will always have a negative slope—downward to the right.

Now the question arises "Why does the demand curve have a negative slope?" Another way of saying this is, "Why do consumers increase the quantity they demand as the price decreases, and vice versa?" On a common sense level you know that people will buy more of something if it has a lower price, but there are technical reasons as well.

The reason a demand curve is downward sloping is what economists call an *income effect* and a *substitution effect*. According to the **income effect**, consumers can afford to buy more as prices get lower. That's because their purchasing power (their "real income") has increased. If you have a budget of $10 per week for incidentals at school, and you enjoy a cold soda that costs $1.00, you might buy five sodas each week (spending $5). If the price of soda dropped to $.50, you would probably buy more without spending more than $5. (Even if you did not, many other students would!) The result is that as price drops from $1 to $.50, the quantity demanded increases.

The **substitution effect** says that as the price of a particular good or service goes *down* while prices of similar goods remain the same, the relative price of that good is cheaper (compared to the substitutes), and more consumers will be drawn to get that good. This increases the quantity demanded of the good.

If the price of a good goes *up* while the prices of the substitutes remain the same, consumers will turn to buying the substitutes, decreasing the quantity demanded of the original good.

One more thing that affects the slope of the demand curve is **diminishing marginal utility**. What this means is that with every additional unit of a good, the added satisfaction to consumers becomes smaller and smaller. Since consumers experience diminishing marginal utility for incremental increases of something, they place less value on acquiring additional units. Therefore, they'll only buy more if the price goes down.

Determinants of Demand

Certain things influence how much of a good or service consumers are willing and able to buy at different prices. The price of a product, of course, will determine demand for that product. But there are also **determinants of demand** having nothing to do with price. They are:

- Tastes and Preferences
- Income
- Population or the Number of Consumers in the Market
- Substitute Goods or Complementary Goods
- Expectations of Consumers

As the determinants of demand change, the demand curve shifts. If a determinant *increases* demand, then the demand curve will shift to the *right*. If the determinant *decreases* demand, then the demand curve shifts to the *left*.

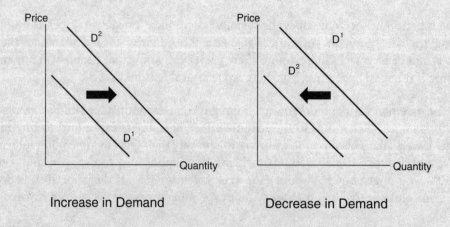

Increase in Demand   Decrease in Demand

Tastes and Preferences: This refers to anything that might change the consumer's desire for a product. It could be the result of an advertising campaign, a change in current fads, or scientific information that makes a good or service more, or less, wanted. If the American Medical Association released a report stating that Barley Crunch cereal reduced a person's chances of getting heart disease, the demand for Barley Crunch would likely increase: The demand curve then shifts to the right. If the report showed that Barley Crunch created more risk, then demand for the cereal would decrease (shift to the left).

Income: Any increases in the income of consumers would lead to increased demand of a **normal good**. Decreases in consumers' income would lead to decreased demand of a **normal good**.

The reverse is true for inferior goods: An increase in consumers' income would decrease demand of an **inferior good**, and a decrease in consumers' income would increase demand of an **inferior good.**

Population or the number of consumers in the market: If a wave of immigration were to occur in a country, then the demand for any good or service would increase (shift to the right). If a plague hit a country leaving many people dead, then the demand for any good or service would decrease (shift to the left).

Substitute goods: If two goods or services are substitutes (if consumers find that either item will satisfy a want), then when the price of one good goes up, the quantity demanded of that good drops—and the demand for the alternative good increases. Similarly, if the price of one good drops, there's an increase in the quantity demanded of that good, and a drop in demand for the alternative good.

> Make sure you are able to shift the demand curve in the appropriate direction:
> - An *increase* in demand means the demand curve shifts *right*.
> - A *decrease* in demand means the demand curve shifts *left*.

Complementary goods: Some goods tend to be consumed together, such as coffee and cream, movies and popcorn, autos and fuel, skis and ski boots, and shoes and shoelaces. If the price of coffee increased, the quantity demanded of coffee would drop. As a direct result, the demand for cream, a complementary good, would decrease, causing the demand curve to shift left. And if the price of coffee dropped, the quantity demanded of coffee would increase, as would the demand for cream.

Expectations of consumers: Expectations of future events also affect consumers' current demand for something. If the price of canned peas is expected to increase next month, people will buy more now. This increases the current demand for canned peas. Or, if they expected the price of peas to drop, they would postpone buying some peas, decreasing current demand. Similarly, if people expected a future shortage in something or a future improvement in a product, they would change their purchase behavior.

One last note on this topic: When analyzing the effect of a change in a variable, economists will invoke the conditional statement **ceteris paribus**, which means, "all other things held constant." If a country's population were to increase, we would expect the demand for goods to increase (ceteris paribus, no other variable changing). If, however, at the same time that the population increased, the scientific community discovered and revealed the dangers of a good, one could no longer conclude that demand would increase: A second variable, taste and preferences, has also changed, and will have a counterbalancing effect. In economic analysis, the intent frequently is to hold all variables constant, other than the one in question.

SUPPLY ANALYSIS

Now let's look at the supply side of the market. First, you should know that the amount that producers are willing and able to sell at a specific price is *not* the supply—it is the **quantity supplied**. Look at the following data:

Production Supply for Roses in the Land of Zod							
A		B		C		D	
Garden Spot, Inc.		Flowers R Us		Bouquets Unlimited		Total Market Supply	
P	Q^d	P	Q^d	P	Q^d	P	Q^d
$3	10	$3	8	$3	9	$3	27
$2	6	$2	4	$2	5	$2	15
$1	4	$1	2	$1	3	$1	9

Here, we're given data for the rose supply in the land of Zod. There are three producers in the rose market: Garden Spot, Flowers R Us, and Bouquets Unlimited. Column A represents Garden Spot's supply of roses; that is, the quantity that the company would supply at each possible price. The same can be said for Flowers R Us and Bouquets Unlimited: Columns B and C represent the quantities each company supplies at each price. Column D lists the total market supply for roses.

Many students confuse quantity supplied with supply. Each firm's supply is constructed from the quantity supplied at each price. At a price of $3, Garden Spot will supply 10 dozen roses, Flowers R Us will supply eight dozen, and Bouquets Unlimited, nine dozen. The quantity supplied at this price is not the same for each firm. The market supply is the sum of all individual supplies. It is the total quantity supplied at each possible price.

The Supply Curve

The **supply curve** is a graphic presentation of data that relates to the variables, *price* and *quantity supplied*. Supply refers to the quantity of a good or service a firm is willing and able to sell at different prices. Supply is not what demanders are willing and able to buy.

The shape of the supply curve reflects the fact that suppliers can only increase production at a higher per unit cost. They're willing and able to increase production only if the market price increases.

> A supply curve or schedule shows the quantity one supplier or all the firms in an industry are willing and able to sell. Make sure you know whether the graphic represents a firm's supply or industry/market supply.

Let's go back to the supply of roses in the land of Zod we saw earlier.

Total Market Supply	
P	Q
$3	27
$2	15
$1	9

Now we can construct our graph of the supply curve.

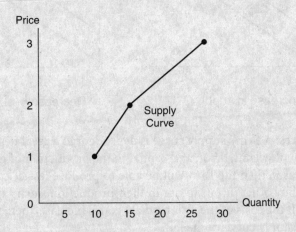

Supply curves always have a positive slope (upward to the right). This is the result of the *law of supply*: Price and quantity have a direct relationship. As price goes up, quantity supplied goes up, and vice versa.

As firms increase output, they generally face increasing costs. Therefore, they'll only increase output if the price also increases. Higher prices are necessary to make the added production worthwhile.

Determinants of Supply

Certain things in an economy determine supply. Determinants of supply are those things that influence how much of a good or service producers are willing to sell at different prices.

Product price, of course, is one determinant that affects supply. But the other nonprice factors are:

- A change in input prices
- A change in technology
- A change in producer expectations
- A change in prices of other goods
- A change in government policies, such as quotas, taxes, and subsidies
- A change in the number of suppliers

As the determinants of supply change, the supply curve shifts. If a determinant *increases* supply, then the supply curve will shift to the *right*. If the determinant *decreases* supply, then the supply curve shifts to the *left*.

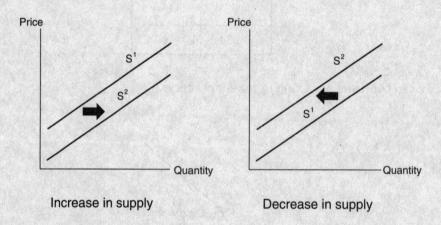

Increase in supply   Decrease in supply

Change in input prices: A firm's supply curve is dependent to a great degree upon its costs of production. Firms employ land, labor, and capital in the production of goods, and if the cost of any of these increases, then the firm will be able to produce less at each price. Firms also buy other inputs to use in their production, such as intermediate goods. If the costs of the intermediate goods increase, then, that too will shift the supply curve to the left.

> Many of us are conditioned to think of anything that goes "up" as an increase. This is a mistake when doing supply and demand curve analysis. A decrease in supply shifts the supply curve to the left and up.

Change in technology: Technology refers to how something is produced. If there is an improvement in technology, then a new, better way of doing something has been created. This leads to increased productivity (more output per manhour). Consequently it becomes less expensive to produce at each level of output. This shifts the supply curve to the right (increase in supply).

Changes in producers' expectations: If producers anticipate events in the future that would make it more profitable for them to delay production, then the supply curve will shift to the left (decrease).

Change in prices of other goods: Producers often manufacture more than one product. If a producer made tables and beds, and the price of beds rose as a result of increased demand, he could opt to make fewer tables and more beds. The price increase for beds would then lead to an increase in the quantity supplied of beds, and a decrease in the supply of tables.

Change in government policies, such as quotas, taxes, and subsidies: Government policies can affect the cost of producing goods. Taxes, for example, increase the cost of production: An excise tax on the production of tables makes it more costly for the producer to manufacture each table. The supply curve for that product will shift left. If the government reduced the tax, the supply curve would shift right. Subsidies are government payments to producers, whereby the government, in effect, pays some of the cost of production. As a result, it costs the producer less to make each product. A subsidy lowers the per unit cost to the producer, so he'll manufacture more at each price level. If a subsidy were rescinded, the producer would have to pay more of the cost, and the supply curve would shift left (decrease). Quotas restrict the number of products a foreign firm can bring into the market, so it decreases the supply of that good in the market.

Change in the number of suppliers: As more suppliers enter the market, the market supply curve will increase (shift to the right). If firms leave the market, the market supply curve will decrease (shift left).

MARKET EQUILIBRIUM AND PRICE DETERMINATION

A market is where buyers and sellers exchange goods or services for a price (unless referring to a *barter* market, where one good or service is exchanged for another). **Equilibrium** occurs at the price where the quantity demanded is equal to the quantity supplied. The **equilibrium price** is also called the **market clearing price**. The market graph (or firm's graph) is constructed from the demand and supply curves. In our previous example for the rose market in Zod, we had the following demand and supply schedules:

Total Market Demand		Total Market Supply	
Price	Q^d	Price	Q^s
$3	10	$3	27
$2	15	$2	15
$1	25	$1	9

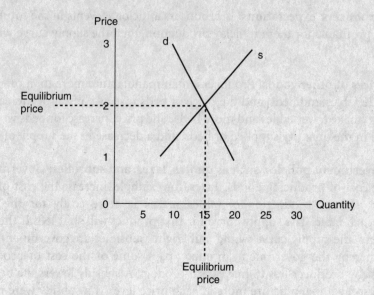

A supply and demand graph indicates the equilibrium price and quantity. The supply and demand curves intersect where quantity supplied and quantity demanded are equal. When a market is in equilibrium, the price of the good remains the same until something causes either the supply or demand to change.

As a market seeks to achieve the equilibrium price, if the quantity supplied is greater than the quantity demanded, then firms will have a surplus and the price will be lowered. On the other hand, if the quantity demanded is greater than the quantity supplied (a shortage), firms will increase production and price will be increased.

The equilibrium price and quantity discussion above assumes a market where consumers and producers are free to pursue their own self-interest. Now let's look at what happens were the government to intervene in a market's pricing mechanism.

PRICE FLOORS AND PRICE CEILINGS

A **price floor** is a minimum legal price for a good or service. A **price ceiling** is a maximum legal price for a good or service.

The graphs below illustrate the market for steak.

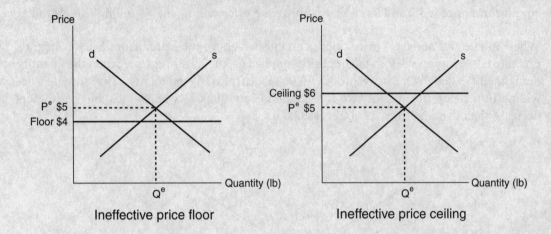

Ineffective price floor   Ineffective price ceiling

For both graphs, the equilibrium price for a pound of steak is $5. The graph on the left shows a price floor of $4. This means that the government has set a minimum legal price of $4. In other words, the price cannot be below $4. Since the equilibrium price is $5 and not below $4, the equilibrium market price will prevail and the price floor of $4 will not be in effect.

The graph on the right shows a price ceiling of $6: The government has set a maximum legal price of $6. Since the equilibrium price of $5 is not above the legal maximum of $6, it will prevail, and the price ceiling of $6 will not be in effect.

For price floors and price ceilings to be effective (to have an impact on price) a price floor must be above the equilibrium price, and a price ceiling must be below it, as in the graphs below.

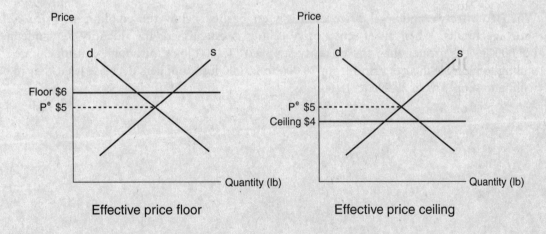

Effective price floor   Effective price ceiling

If a price floor is established above the equilibrium price, the price floor will be effective. In the graph on the left, a price floor of $6 is established. Since the equilibrium price of $5 is below that amount, the $6 price floor will prevail.

Similarly, if a price ceiling is established below the equilibrium price, it will be effective. In the graph on the right, the market cannot have a price above $4 (the price ceiling). The equilibrium price is $5, and since that is above the price ceiling, the $4 ceiling will prevail.

When an effective and legal price floor is established above the equilibrium price, a **surplus** is created. In the graph below, the quantity supplied (25,000 lbs.) is greater than the quantity demanded (15,000 lbs.). The result is a 10,000 lb. surplus. At the higher price, suppliers are willing to increase the quantity from the equilibrium 20,000 to 25,000 lbs, but consumers decrease their demand from 20,000 to 15,000 lbs.

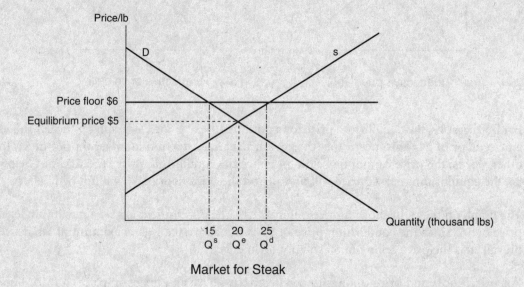

Market for Steak

The surplus created by the effective price floor is 10,000 lbs. But the price floor has increased the quantity supplied by 5,000 lbs., and decreased the quantity demanded by 5,000 lbs.

When an effective and legal price ceiling is established below the equilibrium price, a **shortage** results. When an effective price ceiling is established, the quantity demanded (25,000 lbs.) is greater than the quantity supplied (15,000 lbs.). Although consumers are willing to increase their demand from 20,000 to 25,000 lbs., suppliers decrease what they're willing to supply from 20,000 to 15,000 lbs.

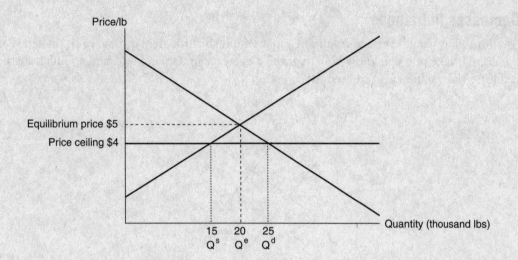

The quantity demanded has increased by 5,000 lbs., and the quantity supplied has decreased by 5,000 lbs. The effective price ceiling has created a shortage of 10,000 lbs.

SHIFTS IN DEMAND AND SUPPLY

Now that we have looked at the determinants of demand and supply, we need to examine how shifts in demand and supply affect equilibrium price and quantity.

Increases in Demand

Anything that would cause an *increase in demand* would shift the demand curve to the right.

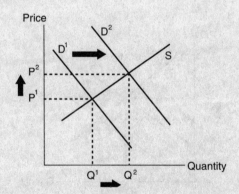

This graph illustrates an increase in demand, *ceteris paribus* (holding all other variables constant). The resulting effects on equilibrium price and equilibrium quantity are:

- Price increase from P^1 to P^2
- Quantity increase from Q^1 to Q^2

> The effects on equilibrium price and quantity are created by shifts in the demand or supply.

Decreases in Demand

Anything that would cause a *drop in demand* would shift the demand curve to the left. For the exam, make sure you know how to graph a decrease in demand and how to illustrate the resulting change in price and quantity.

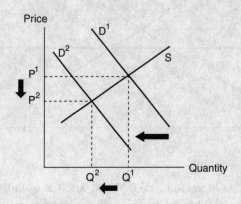

> Assuming no other changes, anytime there's an increase in demand, both equilibrium price and quantity will increase. Similarly, whenever there's a decrease in demand, both equilibrium price and quantity will decrease.

This graph illustrates a decrease in demand (shift to the left) holding all other variables constant. The resulting effects on equilibrium price and quantity are:

- Price decrease from P^1 to P^2
- Quantity decrease from Q^1 to Q^2

Increases in Supply

Anything that would cause an *increase in supply* would shift the supply curve to the right.

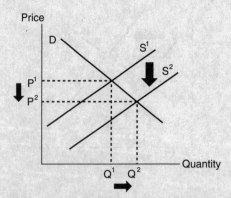

The graph here illustrates an increase in supply (supply shifts to the right), holding all other variables constant. The resulting effects on equilibrium price and equilibrium quantity are:

- Price decrease from P^1 to P^2
- Quantity increase from Q^1 to Q^2

Decreases in Supply

Anything that would cause a *decrease in supply* would shift the supply curve to the left.

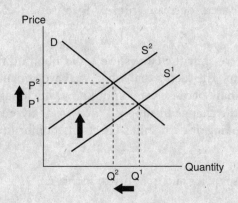

The graph above illustrates a decrease in supply, holding all other variables constant. The resulting effects on equilibrium price and quantity are:

- Price increase from P^1 to P^2
- Quantity decrease from Q^1 to Q^2

> Given no other changes, when supply increases, the price will decrease and the quantity will increase. When supply decreases, the price will increase and the quantity will decrease.

Concurrent Shifts in Supply and Demand

On the AP exam, you will be expected to analyze concurrent shifts in the supply curve and the demand curve. Be careful not to study the effects of demand and supply curve shifts solely with graphic analysis—this could be problematic. That is because one tends to make assumptions on how much of a shift occurs to both curves. If we knew that there was an increase in demand and an increase in supply, we could graph it as follows:

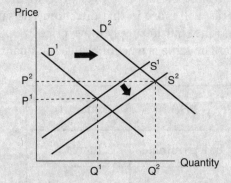
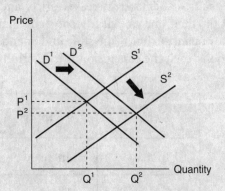

Notice that both graphs indicate an increase in demand (shift to the right from D^1 to D^2), and an increase in supply (shift to the right from S^1 to S^2).

The graph on the left illustrates a greater increase in demand than in supply. The result is that the equilibrium price increases from P^1 to P^2, and the equilibrium quantity increases from Q^1 to Q^2. The graph on the right illustrates a greater increase in supply than in demand, causing the equilibrium price to decrease from p^1 to p^2, and the equilibrium quantity to increase from Q^1 to Q^2.

Depending on how much we shift the curves, we could obtain different results. The price could go either down or up. The fact is that when we have concurrent shifts, the price or quantity will be **indeterminate** because we do not know which has the greater influence—the change in demand or the change in supply. When we analyze the effects of concurrent shifts, we are better off looking at each shift's effect on equilibrium price and equilibrium quantity.

An *increase in demand* causes price and quantity to increase:

P↑   Q↑

A *decrease in demand* causes price and quantity to decrease:

P↓   Q↓

An *increase in supply* causes price to decrease and quantity to increase:

P↓   Q↑

A *decrease in supply* causes price to increase and quantity to decrease:

P↑   Q↓

If the shift in demand increases price, and the shift in supply moves price in the same direction, then one can clearly conclude that price will move in that direction. The same is true for quantity. But if the shift in demand and the shift in supply move price in opposite directions, then the conclusion is indeterminate. The same is true for changes in quantity.

Demand	Supply	Price	Quantity
Increase	Increase	Indeterminate	Increase
Increase	Decrease	Increase	Indeterminate
Decrease	Increase	Decrease	Indeterminate
Decrease	Decrease	Indeterminate	Decrease

ELASTICITY

Elasticity can be explained as how responsive the quantity demanded or quantity supplied is to changes in price. Changes in income also affect percent change with regard to quantity demanded. The four measures of elasticity are:

1. Price elasticity of demand: $\dfrac{\Delta\% \ Q^d}{\Delta\% \ P}$

Price elasticity of demand measures how much the quantity demanded changes, when the price of a good changes. Economists have classified demand elasticity into three types:

> Elasticity measures the direction of change of total revenue or expenditure in response to changes in price.

Elastic: When the ratio of changes, $\dfrac{\Delta\% \ Q^d}{\Delta\% \ P}$, is greater than one

Inelastic: When the ratio of changes is less than one

Unit Elastic: When the ratio of changes is equal to one

Note: Since price and quantity demanded move in opposite directions, what we are considering here is the absolute value of these changes.

In determining the significance of elasticity, it is important to look at the result of a price change on total revenue (or total expenditure). The following matrix is useful in analyzing problems that consider the responsiveness of consumers to price changes. It also reminds us that elasticity does not defy the law of demand: It measures the direction of change of total revenue or expenditure in response to changes in price.

Price	Quantity Demanded	Total Revenue (Expenditure)	Elasticity
↑	↓	↑	Inelastic
↑	↓	↓	Elastic
↑	↓	→ (no change)	Unit Elastic
↓	↑	↑	Elastic
↓	↑	↓	Inelastic
↓	↑	→	Unit Elastic

The arrows indicate the direction of change for price, quantity demanded, and total revenue or expenditure. The changes in price and quantity always go in *opposite* directions (the law of demand). When the changes in price and total revenue go in the same direction, the demand is inelastic. If they go in opposite directions, the demand is elastic. If the price changes and there's no change in total revenue, the demand is unit elastic.

The main determinants of the elasticity of demand for a good or service are:
- The number of substitutes available
- The proportion of income required to purchase the good
- The amount of time a consumer has to respond to the price change
- The need of the good by the consumer, in terms of whether it is a necessity

2. Cross price elasticity of demand: $\dfrac{\Delta\% \ Q^d \text{ of good A}}{\Delta\% \ P \text{ of good B}}$

Cross price elasticity of demand measures how a price change in one good affects the quantity demanded of another good.

If goods are substitutes, then if the price of one goes up, the quantity demanded for the other will also go up. If the price of one drops, then the quantity demanded for the other will also drop. Thus, the cross price elasticity for substitutes is always positive.

If the goods are complements, then if the price of one goes up, the quantity demanded for the other will drop. If the price of one drops, then the quantity demanded for the other goes up. Hence, the cross price elasticity of demand for complements is negative.

3. Income elasticity of demand: $\dfrac{\Delta\% \ Q^d}{\Delta\% \ \text{Income}}$

Income elasticity of demand measures how changes in income affect the quantity demanded of a good or service. Remember that we have recognized the difference between normal goods and inferior goods.

If the good is a normal good, demand will go up as income increases, and will decrease as income drops. If it's an inferior good, demand will drop as income rises, and will increase as income drops. So, for normal goods, income elasticity of demand is a positive number, and vice versa for inferior goods.

4. Price elasticity of supply: $\dfrac{\Delta\% \ Q^s}{\Delta\% \ P}$

Price elasticity of supply compares the change in quantity supplied to a change in price. In other words, it measures the responsiveness of suppliers to a price change. The more elastic the supply, the greater the change in supply with respect to a price change. The more inelastic the supply, the smaller the change in supply with respect to a price change.

The main determinants of the elasticity of supply for a good or service are:

- Substitutability: If the factors of production can be easily used or substituted from the production of one good to the production of an alternative good, then the supply for the first good is fairly elastic.

- Time: If a supplier has more time to respond to a change in price, supply is more elastic.

Elasticity and Graphs

Visually, one can recognize the relative elasticity of supply or demand by the steepness or shallowness of the curves.

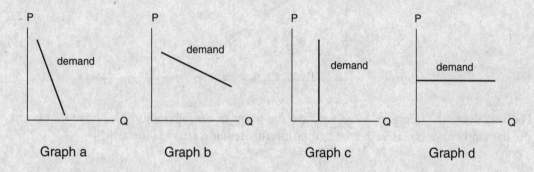

Given that the scale of the demand curves is the same, the demand in graph a is more inelastic than graph b. In graph a, the change in quantity demanded is less for a measured change in price than in graph b. That is why graph a is steeper.

Graph c illustrates a perfectly vertical demand curve. There is no change in quantity demanded as price changes, so this is a perfectly inelastic demand curve. Graph d illustrates a perfectly horizontal demand curve: There is an infinite quantity demanded at a single price. This demand curve is perfectly elastic.

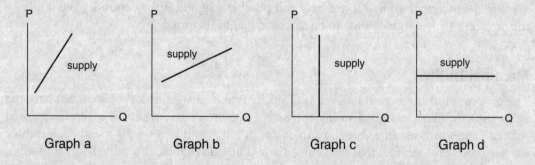

Here, given that the scale of the supply curves is the same, graph a illustrates a supply that is more inelastic than graph b. In graph a, the change in quantity supplied is less for a measured change in price then in graph b.

In any sloped straight-line demand curve, demand is elastic on the upper portion, and inelastic on the lower portion.

Graph c illustrates a perfectly vertical supply curve, that is, a perfectly inelastic supply curve. Graph d illustrates a perfectly horizontal supply curve, which is a perfectly elastic supply curve.

Another point to remember is that in any straight-line demand curve, demand is elastic on the upper portion, and inelastic on the lower portion.

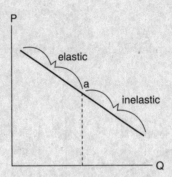

Halfway down the demand curve, we have the point of unit elasticity (a). Above that point, the demand curve is elastic. Below that point, the demand curve is inelastic.

CONSUMER CHOICE

In a market system, a consumer will buy a good or service if he perceives its price to be equal or less than the pleasure he would get from the good. What we refer to here as *pleasure* is called *utility* by economists. Utility can also be viewed as a consumer's willingness to pay.

Total utility is the total satisfaction a person receives from consuming a good or service. As a rule, as additional units are consumed, the consumer experiences less utility. And as we discussed earlier, the decline a consumer experiences as an additional unit is consumed is the *diminishing marginal utility*. Consumers will purchase a good if they consider the utility of the next unit (the marginal unit) to be at least equal to the price.

Marginal Utility

The concept of utility is abstract. A unit of utility is also called a **util.** People do not have the same total utility or marginal utility for each good or service. Utility is a very individual matter. Economists assume that consumers are rational, and that they'll spend their money on the goods and services that maximize their utility. Let's look at a table of information, which provides data on Joan's utility for soda.

Cans of Soda		
Total Cans	Total Utility	Marginal Utility
0	0	....
1	50	....
2	90	....
3	120	....
4	145	....
5	140	....

The total utility increases until Joan consumes the fifth can of soda. At that point, Joan experiences negative marginal utility. Perhaps the fifth can makes her ill.

For the AP exam, you will be expected to calculate the marginal utility from data of this sort. The marginal utility of each additional soda consumed by Joan is computed by calculating the change in total utility divided by change in number of cans consumed:

Cans of Soda		
Total Cans	Total Utility	Marginal Utility
0	0	....
1	50	50
2	90	40
3	120	30
4	145	25
5	140	−5

The marginal utility for Joan's second can of soda is 40, for the third can, 30, and for the fourth can, 25. As noted above, the marginal utility for the fifth can is negative. For the second, third, and fourth cans, marginal utility is diminishing.

Now let's look at Joan's utility schedule for slices of pizza.

Slices of Pizza		
Total Slices	Total Utility	Marginal Utility
0	0	....
1	120	120
2	210	90
3	270	60
4	300	30
5	309	9

And now let's compare Joan's marginal utility for soda with her marginal utility for pizza.

Slice/Can	Soda Marginal Utility	Pizza Marginal Utility
0	0	....
1	50	120
2	40	90
3	30	60
4	25	30

It's evident that Joan's marginal utility for the first slice of pizza is greater than that for a can of soda. But when determining which one Joan would buy first, you must also consider the price of each item. It is assumed that a rational consumer will maximize utility based on the marginal utility received for each dollar spent.

Marginal Utility per Dollar Spent (MU/P)

For analysis, we have to calculate the marginal utility of pizza per dollar spent versus the marginal utility of soda per dollar spent. We do this by dividing the marginal utility by the price of the good. In our example, Joan has to pay $1 for a can of soda and $3 for a slice of pizza.

Slice/Can	Soda Marginal Utility	MU/P Price $1	Pizza Marginal Utility	MU/P Price $3
0	0	....	0	....
1	50	50	120	40
2	40	40	90	30
3	30	30	60	20
4	25	25	30	10

Now that we have calculated the marginal utility per dollar, we can determine how Joan would spend her money on soda and pizza. The first thing that she would buy would be the first can of soda: Her marginal utility per dollar is 50 compared to 40 for the first pizza slice. Her second purchase would be the second soda or the first slice of pizza. Since the MU/P of both is 40, either item would satisfy Joan.

Do not make the mistake in thinking that Joan would buy the pizza since she already has a soda. If that were the case, her marginal utility for the first slice of pizza would have been greater than it is.

Let's assume she buys the second soda. Now when she makes the third purchase, she'll buy the first slice of pizza. The third can of soda provides her with a MU/P of 30, which is less than the MU/P of 40 for the first slice.

If Joan had additional money to spend on soda and pizza, she would continue to make her decisions at the margin, acquiring in sequence the good that provided her with the most MU/P. This is what economists refer to as **rational maximizing**.

When determining if a consumer has maximized her utility when buying two or more goods, analyze at the margin. If she has maximized utility, the marginal utility of each should be equal (or close to equal, given budget constraints).

David is a consumer who buys corn and beans. If he has maximized his purchases, the marginal utility per dollar of corn (the last corn purchased) will equal the marginal utility per dollar of beans (the last beans purchased). The equation used to denote this is:

$$\frac{MU_c}{P_c} = \frac{MU_b}{P_b}$$

However, if David finds that his last purchase of corn has a higher marginal utility per dollar than his last purchase of beans, he should buy more corn and less beans.

$$\frac{MU_c}{P_c} > \frac{MU_b}{P_b}$$

Remember that marginal utility is diminishing. As David buys more corn, the marginal utility per dollar of the last corn purchased will go down. As he buys less beans, the marginal utility per dollar of the last beans purchased will go up. He should continue buying more corn and less beans until he has allocated his resources so that:

$$\frac{MU_c}{P_c} = \frac{MU_b}{P_b}$$

This is called the **law of equal marginal utility per dollar**. That is, a consumer will maximize his/her purchases when the marginal utility per dollar of the last unit purchased of good A is equal to the marginal utility per dollar of the last unit purchased of good B.

If David had no budget restraints in the buying of corn and beans, he would optimize his utility by buying corn and beans until:

$$\frac{MU_c}{P_c} = \frac{MU_b}{P_b} = 1$$

The household income, wealth and product prices impose limits on household consumption choices. These limits we call the **budget constraint**.

Marginal Utility and Price

A consumer's marginal utility for a product determines the price she is willing to pay for that product. If her perceived marginal revenue per dollar (MU/$), is satisfied by the price, then a purchase will occur. If her marginal utility for one more product doesn't justify paying the price, then she will not be part of the demand at that price.

Marginal Utility and the Demand Curve

The marginal utility a consumer has for a good determines his demand curve for that product. We know that in the **law of diminishing marginal utility, a** consumer's marginal utility for additional units of a product is decreasing. This allows us to construct a downward sloping marginal utility curve:

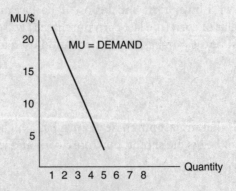

An individual's demand curve

Remember that the market demand is the sum of all consumer demand. We can now identify consumer surplus in a market demand curve.

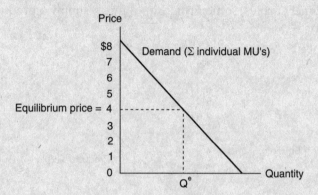

The equilibrium price is $4, yet the demand curve illustrates that there are consumers who would be willing to buy the product at higher prices. For these consumers, their individual demands are such that their marginal utility is greater than the price of $4 (MU > P). This is consumer surplus.

Consumer Surplus

If a consumer's marginal utility for a good is such that he would be willing to pay more than the market price, then he has consumer surplus. Consumer surplus can be describes as marginal utility greater than price (MU > P). If a person were thirsty and willing to pay $1.00 for a cold drink, but bought the drink for 75 cents, that consumer has 25 cents worth of consumer surplus.

To graphically identify the consumer surplus, look for the triangle formed by the vertical axis above the equilibrium price, the demand curve above the equilibrium price, and the base line formed from the vertical axis at the equilibrium price to the demand curve. In our example, consumer surplus is the triangle formed by the points: $4, $8, and c.

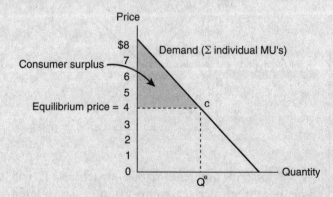

Producer Surplus

Let's look again at the market's supply side to identify producer surplus. Similar to what we've just seen for consumer surplus, some firms are willing to supply a product at a price below the equilibrium price.

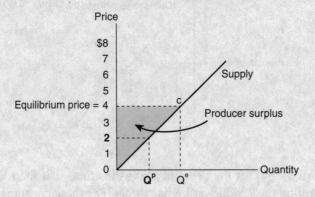

As per this supply curve, some firms are willing to supply the product at a lower price. At a price of $2, firms would provide the quantity, Q^p. However this quantity is provided at a price of $4, the equilibrium price. This is a part of the producer surplus that is defined as the quantity that would be supplied at a lower price than the equilibrium price, but is not.

Graphically, the producer surplus is the area of the triangle formed by points: 0, $4, and c.

Total Surplus

We can now look at the combined consumer and producer surplus. In the graph below, the area of triangle A is the consumer surplus. The area of triangle B is the producer surplus. The combined surpluses, A plus B, is the total surplus.

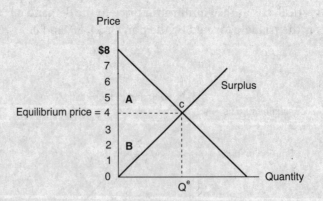

> When markets are inefficient, there's "deadweight loss," (loss of total surplus), indicating that output is not at its efficient level. Perfect competition is considered the ideal model because it delivers the greatest amount of total surplus.

As we look at different market structures, it will serve us well to remember that perfect competition is considered the ideal model because it delivers the greatest amount of total surplus. When markets are imperfect or impeded, there is "deadweight loss." Deadweight loss is the loss of total surplus.

KAPLAN

KEY POINTS

- Demand is the quantity of a good that consumers are willing and able to purchase at various prices during a given period *ceteris paribus*. The law of demand states the inverse relationship between price and quantity demanded. *As the price rises, the quantity demanded decreases, and as the price falls, the quantity demanded increases,* ceteris paribus.

- A change in the price of a good has two effects on consumers: the income effect and the substitution effect. When the price increases, the same amount of money can buy less of the good, so consumers buy less. And, when the price increases, the relative price of an alternative good decreases, so consumers buy less of the first good and more of the alternative good.

- Since demand is the relationship between price and quantity demanded, a change in price is shown by movement along the same demand curve to a new quantity demanded—a new point on the same demand curve.

- Determinants of demand are those things that determine how much of a good consumers are willing and able to buy at different prices. The most important determinants of demand are: *tastes/preferences, income; population,* or *the number of consumers in the market; substitute or complementary goods;* and *expectations of consumers.*

- When the demand curve shifts to the right, demand has increased. When the demand curve shifts left, demand has decreased. If the price of a good changes in the current period, the demand does not shift. The change in price results in a change in quantity demanded. This is a movement along the demand curve.

- Supply is the quantity of a good that a firm is willing and able to sell at different prices, holding everything else constant. It can also indicate how much of a good all the firms in an industry are willing and able to supply at different prices.

- The supply curve shows a positive, direct relationship between the price and the quantity of a good supplied. An increase in the market price will lead to an increase in the quantity of a good supplied, and a decrease in the market price will lead to a decrease in the quantity of a good supplied, *ceteris paribus.* A change in price is shown as a movement along the supply curve to a new quantity supplied—a new point on the same supply curve.

- Suppliers generally face increasing costs as they increase production, so they'll only increase production if the price increases. Higher prices are necessary to make increased production worthwhile.

- Determinants of supply are those things that determine how much of a good suppliers are willing and able to supply at different prices. The most important determinants of supply are: a change in input prices; a change in technology; a change in producer expectations; a change in the prices of other goods; a change in government policies, such as quotas, taxes, and subsidies; and a change in the number of suppliers.

- When both demand and supply change, the effects on equilibrium are partly indeterminate. For example, if both demand and supply decrease, the change in the equilibrium price is indeterminate, but the equilibrium quantity decreases.

- Price elasticity of demand measures how much the quantity demanded changes when the price changes. Economists often refer to this as *the sensitivity of consumers to price changes*. The elasticity of the demand for a good or service is measured by comparing the percentage change in price to the percentage change in quantity demanded. If demand is elastic, the percentage change in quantity demanded is larger than the percentage change in price. This means consumers respond strongly to a price change. If demand is inelastic, the percentage change in quantity demanded is smaller than the percentage change in price. This means consumers respond very little to a price change.

- Demand is unit elastic if the percentage change in quantity demanded is equal to the percentage change in price. Demand is perfectly inelastic when the quantity demanded does not respond at all to a price change.

- The three main determinants of the elasticity of demand for a good are: the number of substitutes available; the proportion of income the good requires in order to be purchased; the amount of time a consumer has to respond to the price change; and the consumer's need for the good, in terms of necessity. To calculate the price elasticity of demand, divide the percent change in quantity demanded by the percent change in price. Percent change in quantity demanded equals the change in quantity divided by the average of the two quantities. Similarly for the percent change in price.

- Economists have classified demand elasticity into three types: elastic (when it's greater than one), inelastic (when it's less than one), and unit elastic (when it equals one).

- Price elasticity of supply compares the change in quantity supplied to a change in price. Economists often refer to this as *measuring the responsiveness of suppliers to a price change.*

- The more elastic the supply, the greater the change in quantity supplied will be compared to the change in price. The more inelastic the supply, the smaller the change in quantity supplied compared to the change in price.

- The first determinant for supply elasticity is *substitutability*. If the factors of production can be easily used or substituted from the production of one good to the production of an alternative good, then the supply for the first good is fairly elastic. The second determinant for supply elasticity is *time*. If a supplier has more time to respond to a change in price, supply is more elastic.

- Income elasticity of demand measures how the demand for a good changes as a result of a change in income. Cross-price elasticity of demand measures the responsiveness of demanders to a change in the price of another good.

- Utility, the satisfaction a person obtains from consuming a good, is measured in arbitrary units called utils. Marginal utility is the increase in utility he gains from consuming an additional unit, while total utility is the total satisfaction he receives from consuming the good. As a general rule, as each additional unit of a good is consumed, it generates less utility. This is called *diminishing marginal utility*, and explains why the demand curve is downward sloping.

- Consumer surplus is the difference between what consumers actually pay for a good and the maximum amount they would have been willing to pay. It can also be described as the amount that a consumer's marginal utility for a good exceeds the price paid. In other words, it is the difference between the total value consumers place on a good and what they pay for the good. Graphically, it is the area under the demand curve down to the market price.

- Producer surplus is the difference between what price firms would sell a quantity of goods for and the market price. Graphically, it is the area above the supply curve up to the market price.

REVIEW QUESTIONS

1. A period of inclement weather destroys a significant portion of Georgia's Vidalia onion crop. What effect will this have on the Vidalia onion market?

   (A) Market price will decrease and the market quantity will decrease.
   (B) Market price will increase and the market quantity will increase.
   (C) Market price will decrease and the market quantity will increase.
   (D) Market price will increase and the market quantity will decrease.
   (E) The market price will increase and the market quantity will be indeterminate.

2. Technology has helped to increase the productivity of workers in the truck industry. What effects will this technology have on price and quantity in the truck industry?

   (A) Market price will decrease and the market quantity will decrease.
   (B) Market price will increase and the market quantity will increase.
   (C) Market price will decrease and the market quantity will increase.
   (D) Market price will increase and the market quantity will decrease.
   (E) Market price will increase and the market quantity will be indeterminate.

3. The *Journal of American Medicine* releases a study that indicates the consumption of prunes has a definite positive effect on an individual's health. How will this news affect the prune industry?

   (A) Market price will decrease, and market quantity will decrease.
   (B) Market price will increase, and market quantity will increase.
   (C) Market price will decrease, and market quantity will increase.
   (D) Market price will increase, and market quantity will decrease.
   (E) Market price will increase, and market quantity will be indeterminate.

4. The economy is doing extremely well and to accommodate the need for workers, a large influx of immigrants is allowed into the country. None of the new immigrants will work in the milk industry. What will be the effect on price and quantity in the milk market?

   (A) Market price will decrease and the market quantity will decrease.
   (B) Market price will increase and the market quantity will increase.
   (C) Market price will decrease and the market quantity will increase.
   (D) Market price will increase and the market quantity will decrease.
   (E) Market price and market quantity will be indeterminate.

5. The price of energy increases dramatically. How will this increase affect market prices and quantity in the clothing industry?

   (A) Market price will not change and the market quantity will decrease.
   (B) Market price and market quantity will increase.
   (C) Market price will decrease and the market quantity will increase.
   (D) Market price will increase and the market quantity will decrease.
   (E) Market price will be indeterminate and the market quantity will decrease.

6. If the price of hamburgers increases from $2 to $2.50, what will happen to the hamburger market?

    (A) The demand for hamburgers will decrease.
    (B) The supply of hamburgers will increase.
    (C) The quantity demanded for hamburgers will increase.
    (D) The quantity demanded for hamburgers will decrease.
    (E) There will be a movement down the demand curve for hamburgers to achieve new equilibrium.

7. In an effort to support family orange growing businesses, the government sets a minimum price of $6 a gallon of orange juice. In this situation, the government has created a

    (A) Subsidy
    (B) Price ceiling
    (C) Price floor
    (D) Demand
    (E) Grant

8. In an effort to support family orange growing businesses, the government sets a minimum price of $6 for a gallon of orange juice. The current market price for orange juice is $7 for a gallon. The government's action will have what effect on the orange juice market?

    (A) It will create a surplus.
    (B) It will create a shortage.
    (C) It will have no effect.
    (D) It will cause a decrease in total revenue.
    (E) It will cause an increase in total revenue

9. The government establishes an effective price ceiling for a gallon of milk. What will be the result of this ceiling?

    (A) It will create a surplus.
    (B) It will create a shortage.
    (C) It will have no effect.
    (D) It will cause an increase in demand.
    (E) It will cause an increase in supply.

10. A firm increases the price of its product and finds that its total revenue increases. Which of the following best describes why this has happened?

    (A) The firm's supply has increased.
    (B) The firm has an elastic demand.
    (C) The firm has a unit elastic demand.
    (D) The firm has an inelastic demand.
    (E) The firm has decreased its quantity supplied.

11. If a firm faces an elastic demand for its product and the price of the product drops, the firm can expect that

    (A) the quantity sold will decrease and the total revenue will increase.
    (B) the quantity sold will increase and the total revenue will increase.
    (C) the quantity sold will decrease and the total revenue will decrease.
    (D) the quantity sold will increase and the total revenue will decrease.
    (E) the quantity sold and the total revenue will not change.

12. If a firm faces a relatively inelastic demand for its product and the price of the product rises, the firm can expect that

    (A) total revenues will increase and profit will increase.
    (B) total revenues will increase and profit will decrease.
    (C) total revenues will decrease and profit will increase.
    (D) total revenues will decrease and profit will decrease.
    (E) total revenues will decrease and the effect on profits are indeterminate without additional information.

13. John finishes a 10-mile run, and in order to quench his thirst, decides he would be willing to pay $1.00 for a cold drink. Once he finds a drink stand, though, he finds that he only has to pay 75 cents for a drink. An economist would conclude that

    (A) John has a profit.
    (B) John is lucky.
    (C) John has consumer surplus.
    (D) John is not a rational maximizer.
    (E) John has a unit elastic demand.

14. Helen receives a large raise at work and as a result, begins to buy fewer macaroni and cheese dinners. We can conclude that

    (A) Helen's demand for macaroni and cheese is not price sensitive.
    (B) Helen's demand for macaroni and cheese is price elastic.
    (C) Helen's demand for macaroni and cheese is not predictable.
    (D) For Helen, macaroni and cheese is a normal good.
    (E) For Helen, macaroni and cheese is an inferior good.

Questions 15–21

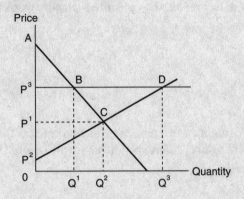

15. Using the above graph, if the market for frankfurters is left unregulated the market clearing price and quantity will be:

(A) P^3, Q^1
(B) P^1, Q^2
(C) P^3, Q^3
(D) P^1, Q^3
(E) P^2, Q^2

16. If the government were to establish an effective price floor, and the graph above illustrates the price floor, the market price and the quantity supplied would be

(A) P^3, Q^1
(B) P^1, Q^2
(C) P^3, Q^3
(D) P^1, Q^3
(E) P^2, Q^2

17. If the government were to establish an effective price floor as indicated in the graph, the result would be a

(A) Shortage equal to Q^1 minus Q^2
(B) Market clearing price of P^3
(C) Surplus equal to Q^3 minus Q^1
(D) Shortage equal to Q^2 minus Q^1
(E) Shortage equal to Q^3 minus Q^1

18. If the government were to establish an effective price floor as indicated in the graph, the result would be a(n)

(A) Shortage of Q^1 minus P
(B) Increase of quantity supplied equal to Q^3 minus Q^2
(C) Surplus of Q^3 minus Q^2
(D) Shortage of Q^2 minus Q^1
(E) Increase of quantity supplied equal to Q minus Q^1

19. If there were no government interference in this market, and the market equilibrium price and quantity were to prevail, the consumer surplus would be the area

    (A) A, C, P^2
    (B) P^1, C, P^2
    (C) A, C, P^2
    (D) A, C, 0
    (E) A, C, P^1

20. If there were no government interference in this market and the market equilibrium price and quantity were to prevail, the producer surplus would be the area

    (A) P^2, A, C
    (B) P^3, B, Q^1
    (C) A, B, P^3
    (D) P^1, C, P^2
    (E) A, C, P^1

21. If there were no government interference in this market and the market equilibrium price and quantity were to prevail, the total surplus would be the area

    (A) A, C, P^2
    (B) A, B, P^3
    (C) A, C, P^1
    (D) A, C, 0
    (E) C, D, Q^3

Free-Response Questions

1. Assume that the market for roses is in equilibrium, and that carnations are a close substitute. One day, a disease strikes the carnations, though the roses remain unharmed.

   (a) Using two well-labeled graphs, one for the carnation industry and one for the rose industry, indicate the market equilibrium before the effects of the disease.

   (b) (i) Determine what will happen to the price and quantity in the carnation market as a result of the carnation disease.
       (ii) Illustrate using your graph

   (c) (i) Determine what will happen to price and quantity in the rose market as a result of the carnation disease.
       (ii) Illustrate on your graph.

   (d) Now suppose that a fertilizer is developed that will improve productivity in the rose market, using a new graph for the rose market.
       (i) Determine what will happen to price and quantity in the rose market. (ii) Illustrate on your graph how you determined the effects of the fertilizer.

   (e) (i) Show how the introduction of the fertilizer will affect consumer surplus in the rose market.
       (ii) Show how the introduction of the fertilizer will affect producer surplus in the rose market.

2. If the price of Buster sneakers drops from $50 to $40 a pair, the number of sneakers that the Buster company sells increase from 10,000 pairs to 11,000 pairs.

   (a) (i) Is demand for Buster sneakers elastic or inelastic? (ii) Show how to determine the elasticity, without reference to total revenue or expenditures. (iii) Show how to determine elasticity using the total revenue approach.

   (b) Now assume that Brown Company sneakers are the only close substitute for Buster sneakers, and that the Brown Company manufacturing capacity and all of its inventory is destroyed.
      (i) What will happen to the price and quantity sold of Buster sneakers? Explain why.
      (ii) What will happen to the relative elasticity of demand for Buster sneakers? Illustrate this change on a graph.

3. It is customary for companies in the widget industry to also produce gadgets. The companies use many of the same inputs to make both products. These inputs are available in limited supplies. If the demand for gadgets increases and Acme's profit in the gadget industry also increases, explain what is likely to happen to the industry price and quantity in the widget and gadget markets. Use two correctly labeled graphs.

ANSWERS TO REVIEW QUESTIONS

Questions 1–10 deal with changes in supply or demand or price floors and price ceilings. The best way to answer these types of question is to draw the supply and demand curves and analyze the result. Use margin space next to the question to do your analysis.

1. (D)

Destruction of a significant portion of the Vidalia onion crop would decrease the supply of Vidalia onions. The decrease in supply increases the equilibrium price from P^1 to P^2 and decreases the equilibrium quantity from Q^1 to Q^2.

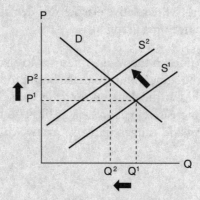

Market for Vidalia onions

2. (C)

An increase in productivity in the truck industry would cause the supply to increase. This would shift the supply curve to the right. The increase in supply decreases the price and increases the quantity (P^1 to P^2 and Q^1 to Q^2).

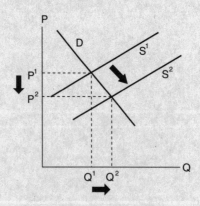

Market for trucks

3. (B)

An increase in demand for prunes increases equilibrium price from P^1 to P^2, and increases equilibrium quantity from Q^1 to Q^2.

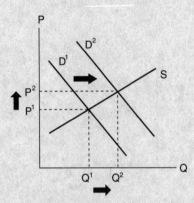

Market for prunes

4. (B)

This questions gives information that would lead to an increase in demand. Since it states that none of the new immigrants will work in the milk industry, supply will not change. The result is an increase in equilibrium price from P^1 to P^2, and in equilibrium quantity from Q^1 to Q^2.

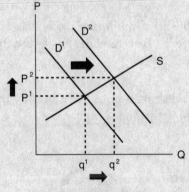

Market for milk

5. (D)

The decrease in supply increases the equilibrium price from P^1 to P^2, and decreases the equilibrium quantity from Q^1 to Q^2.

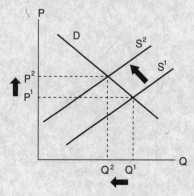

Market for cloths

6. (D)

The price change for the current period does not result in a shift of demand or supply. The increase in price will cause the quantity demanded to decrease or the quantity supplied to increase.

7. (C)

When the government establishes a minimum price, it is creating a price floor. The price cannot legally go below this price. Be careful of (A). A subsidy is a payment.

8. (C)

Here, the government is establishing a price floor, but the market equilibrium price is not below the price floor. Therefore, the floor is ineffective.

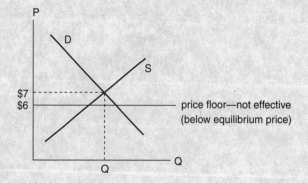

9. (B)

In this question, it is stated that the price ceiling is effective. Therefore it must be below the market-clearing price.

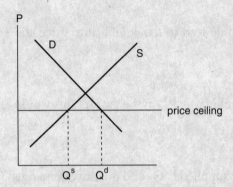

In the case of an effective price ceiling, the quantity demanded, Q^d, is more than the quantity supplied, Q^s. This means that a shortage is created in this market. Notice that what has changed is the quantity demanded and the quantity supplied.

10. (D)

An increase in price and in total revenue can result from an inelastic demand (price increases and total revenue increases). (A) would lead to a lower price. (B) would lead to a lower total revenue. (C) would lead to no change in total revenue. And (E) would defy the law of supply.

11. (B)

The law of demand states that at a lower price, quantity demanded increases, and an elastic demand means that if price drops, total revenue will increase. (A) defies the law of demand. (C) and (D) defy the definition of elasticity. (E) defies both the law of demand and the definition of elasticity.

12. (A)

If a firm has a relatively inelastic demand, it means that if price increases, total revenue will increase. Since the demand is not perfectly inelastic, the quantity demanded will decrease (law of demand). If the firm produces less (quantity supplied has decreased at the new equilibrium), the firm's costs will go down. This should result in more profit, or less loss if the firm was already incurring a loss.

13. (C)

Because John is willing to pay more than the price he ultimately pays, his marginal utility is greater than the price. This defines consumer surplus. Choice (A), profit, is not relevant here. (B) may be true but it would not be the economist's conclusion. (D) would be true only if John paid more than he was willing to pay. And (E) does not relate to the situation.

14. (E)

An inferior good is a good for which demand decreases as income increases. Choices (A) and (B) are irrelevant because a price change is not at issue. (C) is out because her demand is predicable. (D) is also wrong because if macaroni and cheese were a normal good for Helen, she would consume more as her income increased.

15. (B)

An unregulated market would lead to the equilibrium price and equilibrium quantity at P^1 and Q^2.

16. (C)

An effective price floor would be at P^3 on the graph. This would lead to a quantity supplied of Q^3.

17. (C)

At the price floor, quantity supplied is Q^3 and quantity demanded is Q^1. Thus, the surplus is the difference between quantity supplied and quantity demanded.

18. (B)

This questions asks the same thing as question 17, except the appropriate surplus of $Q^3 - Q^1$ is not an answer choice. What has happened as a result is that the quantity supplied has increased to Q^3 from the equilibrium quantity supplied before the floor of Q^2.

19. (E)

We are asked to describe the consumer surplus at the unregulated market equilibrium. This can only be the area of the triangle A, C, P^1.

20. (D)

Here, we must describe the producer surplus at the unregulated market equilibrium. This can only be the area of the triangle P^1, C, P^2.

21. (A)

The total surplus at the unregulated market equilibrium is the area that combines both consumer and producer surplus.

Free-Response Questions

1.　(a)　The graphs below illustrate the original equilibrium at P^1, Q^1 for both markets.

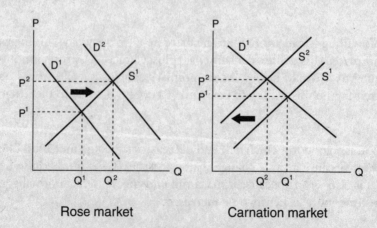

Rose market　　　　Carnation market

(b) As a result of the carnation disease, the supply curve in the carnation market will decrease from S1 to S2, changing price from P^1 to P^2, and changing quantity from Q^1 to Q^2.

(c) Since carnations are a substitute for roses, the drop in demand for carnations will result in an increased demand for roses. Rose demand shifts from D^1 to D^2. The equilibrium price and the equilibrium quantity increase to P^2, Q^2.

(d)

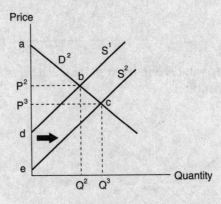

Rose market

The development of the new fertilizer shifts the supply curve for roses from S1 to S2. The price moves from P^2 to P^3 and the quantity moves from Q^2 to Q^3.

(e) (i) The new fertilizer will change consumer surplus from the area P^2,a,b to the area P^3,a,c.

  (ii) The producer surplus will change from d,P^2,b to e, P^3,c

2. **(a) (i)** Demand for Buster sneakers is inelastic.

  (ii) Change in price 20 percent decrease; change in quantity 10 percent increase. $\frac{10\%}{20\%} = {<}1$

  (iii) At a price of $50, total revenue = $50 X 10,000 = $50,000. At a price of $40, total revenue = $40 × 11,000 = $44,000. Price has decreased and total revenue has decreased.

 (b) (i) The price and quantity sold for Buster sneakers will increase because the demand for them will increase.

(ii)

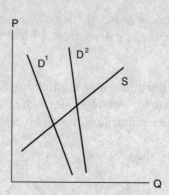

The relative elasticity will become even more inelastic, from D^1 to D^2, as a result of the loss of the only close substitute.

3.

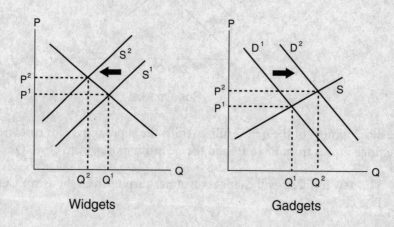

Widgets   Gadgets

As the demand for gadgets increases from D^1 to D^2, price and quantity increases from P^1 to P^2 and Q^1 to Q^2, respectively. Since resources shift from widgets to gadgets, the widget supply will decrease from S^1 to S^2. Price will increase from P^1 to P^2 and quantity will decrease from Q^1 to Q^2.

MACROECONOMICS

MACROECONOMIC VARIABLES

Macroeconomics looks at the larger picture of economic activity in an economy. Instead of looking at the demand for a particular product as is done in microeconomics, macroeconomics looks at the aggregate demand for all products. And instead of looking at the production by a firm or industry, it looks at the aggregate supply of all firms and industries. The study of macroeconomics examines what is going on with the **real variables**: labor, capital, natural resources, and output.

Although the major concern in macroeconomics is the total number of automobiles, chairs, computers, medical services, legal services, haircuts, etc., in an economy, it is impossible to account for every unit of every good and service produced at a given time. Consequently we use the total value expressed in dollars. We can refer to a $10 trillion value of GDP. (Imagine listing every unit of good and service included in this $10 trillion of output!). It is not the dollar amount that is important, but rather the actual goods and services. If your father paid $5 for a haircut 25 years ago, and you pay $15 for the same haircut today, it is still the one haircut that counts. In order to account for price increases, we refer to the current value of GDP or wages or interest rates as **nominal**. When the inflation rate is factored out, we get the **real** figures: real GDP, real wages, and real interest rates.

Real GDP is given in terms of dollar value, and builds in a correction for inflation. That way, we can get a better picture of whether the units produced and consumed have in fact increased. Nonetheless, it is the actual units of goods and services produced and consumed that is important.

Macroeconomics divides the economy into four sectors. Each sector participates in both the production and the consumption of goods.

1. **Households** are individuals who live together and make collective economic decisions. The number of people is irrelevant: If a person lives alone, he is a household. If a family (in the broadest sense) comprises 10 individuals, then that family is a household. Households provide the labor, capital, and natural resources to businesses for the production of goods and services. Households also consume most of the goods and services produced. Invariably they consume 67 percent of the total output of the country.

2. **Businesses** are private producers of goods and services. Businesses can be sole proprietorships, partnerships, or corporations. Businesses organize the factors of production and make most of the goods and services available in the economy. Businesses also consume capital stock (factories and equipment).

3. **Government** includes all the political units of a country. In the United States, the government refers to the federal government, the state governments, county governments, and municipal governments. Government purchases some of the output of a country, employs some of the factors and also provides some of the goods and services available to the economy.

4. **Foreign (International)** refers to all of the economies outside the economy under study. Other economies buy U.S. goods and services (exports), and also sell their goods and services to the United States (imports). Financial capital also flows between economies. The more "open" an economy, the more significant the international economies are. If one were to examine Canada's economy, then the United States would be part of the foreign sector.

In chapter 2, Basic Economic Concepts, we looked at the circular flow model. It is important to remember that all sectors wear two hats: They *buy* and they *sell*.

In macroeconomics, there are three important markets to understand: the *product market*; the *factor market*; and the *financial market*. We will focus here on the product and factor markets.

In the **product market**, a market in which finished goods and services are exchanged, households *buy* about 67 percent of the total output. Other sectors acquire the balance (33 percent). In the **factor market**, (a market in which resources and semifinished products are exchanged), households *sell* labor (human resources), capital (capital resources), and land (natural resources). Of course, some of the economic capital supplied to businesses is done indirectly through an intermediary—the **financial market**.

Government also supplies some goods and services that may not be provided efficiently by the private markets. In return, government collects taxes or fees. If this is not enough revenue, the government will also borrow from the capital market. Whether the private sector (business) could, or even should, provide some goods and services provided by government may be a normative issue that we will not address here.

Economics has three key goals: economic growth, full employment, and price stability. **Economic growth** is the economy increasing its capability to produce more goods and services. **Full employment** is the economy providing jobs for those who want to be employed. **Price stability** allows us to coordinate the resources of the economy. In order to be most efficient, we must get clear and dependable signals. Without price stability, consumers and producers are less likely to make good decisions that will benefit the overall economy.

ECONOMIC GROWTH AND GROSS DOMESTIC PRODUCT

Gross domestic product (GDP) is one of the best measures we have of an economy's well-being. It measures the goods and services available to an economy, as well as the income created that can be used to buy those goods and services. (An even better measure of an economy's well-being is **real GDP per capita**, which divides the population into the GDP.)

When the **potential real GDP** of an economy increases, we have economic growth. The potential real GDP is the amount of goods and services that could be produced if all of the factors of production were fully and efficiently employed. When real GDP is increasing, more goods and services are available, more jobs are created, and more income is created. When it is decreasing, fewer goods and services are being produced, more jobs are lost, and less income is available.

Businesses receive revenues from selling output, which are in turn used to pay for the costs of producing. Thus, most revenues are returned to households as factor payments. This is how the households can "pay" for the consumption of the GDP. There is one exception to the payment of costs: *depreciation*. **Depreciation**, also called *capital consumption allowance*, is an expense for the "wear and tear" of buildings and equipment. No money is actually paid out for depreciation. Think of it as a fund that a business establishes, so that when the building or equipment finally wears out, the business will be able to purchase **replacement investment** with the initial cost it had set aside.

Of course, revenues that are not used for the cost of producing are used for taxes or profits. Taxes go to the government, which uses the money to "pay" for government purchases. Once businesses have made factor payments and tax payments, they're left with profits. The profits are actually claimed by the households since, as shareholders, they own the sole proprietorships, partnerships, or corporations. Profits—if they're distributed at all—become the last factor payment. There is one exception: Some firms may keep some or all of the profits in order to fund the expansion of the firm. Profits that are not returned to the shareholders are called **retained earnings**.

Now we can see that the entire value of the goods and services sold is returned to households (factor payments) or the government (taxes), or it is kept by the businesses (depreciation and retained earnings). This is true for **closed economies** with no foreign sector. **Open economies** need to also consider the **net foreign factor income**. People within the country supply resources to other countries, and vice versa: People outside supply resources to the given country. Therefore, payments are made to resource providers outside the economy. Payments are also made by other economies to households inside the country. The net foreign factor income is an adjustment to account for this fact. It is the income that comes into this country minus the income that leaves this country.

> The GDP is the value of all final goods and services produced in an economy in *one year*. Sometimes we look at GDP per quarter, but unless otherwise noted, it refers to the aggregate output for a year.

While the GDP is the value of all final goods and services produced in one year by factors of production located within a country, GNP (or **Gross National Product**) is the value of all final goods and services produced in one year by factors of production owned by a country's citizens, regardless of where the output is produced. **Net National Product** is the gross national product minus the capital consumption allowance. **National income** is the total income (wages, interest, rents, profits) earned by factors of production owned by a country's citizens.

GDP and Expenditures

We have shown how GDP measures the final output of an economy and provides funds to the various sectors of the economy. Now we'll look at the expenditures of the various sectors to buy the output. The expenditures are:

1. Consumption (C)
2. Investment (I)
3. Government Purchases (G)
4. Net Exports (X)

GDP will always equal expenditures:

$$GDP = C + I + G + X$$

GDP also equals total income. Therefore,

$$Total\ Income = C + I + G + X$$

Consumption (C) is the expenditures by households for goods and services (both durable and nondurable).

Investment (I) is the expenditures by business for capital stock (buildings and equipment) and inventory. It also includes new housing that is purchased by households. New housing is not considered a part of consumption; rather, it is treated as an asset. Unlike the business assets, buildings and equipment, we do not have to deal with the depreciation of new housing.

Investment in the expenditure model refers to *gross investment*. If we want to compute *net investment*, we must subtract the capital consumption allowance from the gross investment.

Government Purchases (G) are the expenditures by government for goods and services. It does not include transfer payments, those payments sent by government to households which use these funds for consumption (C).

Net Exports (X) are exports minus imports. That is, the payment that comes in for goods leaving the country minus the payments that leave for goods coming into the country.

So, now coming back to our original equation, GDP = C + I + G + X, how do we calculate the GDP? We can add up C + I + G + X. Alternatively, we can add up the factor payments (national income) plus depreciation plus indirect taxes.

Why do we include only the final goods and services in computing the GDP? The output that is not a final product is an **intermediate product.** An intermediate product is one that is used by a business in the production of a final product. When a computer company buys circuit boards to build into its computers, the value of the circuit boards is included in the value of the final computers. If we accounted for the value of the circuit board plus the value of the final computer, we would be incorrectly duplicating the value of the circuit board.

What GDP Doesn't Measure

While GDP is one of the best measures we have of an economy's well-being, it isn't perfect. First, it doesn't necessarily measure quality of life. It doesn't tell us about the economic environment or address other important issues. Second, GDP measures only the goods and services produced in the legal marketplace, not those in an illegal or underground market. This is usually a bigger factor in less well-developed economies. And third, GDP doesn't measure the goods and services that people provide for themselves, such as the service a housewife provides for the household when she cooks, cleans, or takes care of the children.

The Business Cycle

The business cycle is the upward and downward movement of overall economic activity over many years. It's the pattern over time in which increases in real GDP are followed by decreases in real GDP, and decreases are followed by increases. The upward movement involves economic expansion, where jobs are created and goods/services are produced. At some point, inventory builds up because not everything is being consumed. When that happens, there's a slow-down period (the downward movement), where production is cut back and labor is laid off. Most of us have seen illustrations of the business cycle in economic and history books. It looks like this:

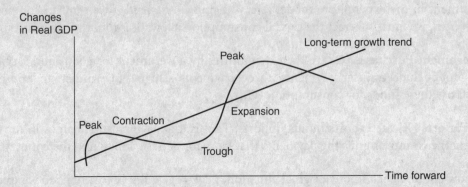

Think of various points in the cycle as changes in real GDP at a specific time. When the economy is contracting, real GDP is decreasing. If the contraction is serious enough, it is a recession, and at an extreme, a depression. When the cycle is expanding, real GDP is increasing and jobs are being created. At the peak, the real GDP is producing at or near full employment level.

> The formal definition of **recession** is that *the GDP has shown negative growth for two successive quarters.* Recently, some people have taken exception to this definition, but it is still useful.

The straight line indicates the long-term growth trend. Factors that contribute to long-term growth are:

• Technology

• Increases in the Labor Force

• Increases in Capital

• Increases in Human Capital (increased schooling and training of the workforce)

Leakages and Injections

Since we understand the circular flow model where the value of output will equal the value of income, we now ask how it is that fluctuations occur in the flow of expenditure. The first thing that causes fluctuations is *leakages*. **Leakages** are uses of household income not used for consumption of the GDP.

Leakages *from* the flow of expenditure include: *taxes*, *savings*, and *imports*. They're not used for consumption: **Taxes** are sent to the government. **Savings**, by definition, means nonconsumption. **Imports** are income created by one economy to purchase output from another economy.

The second thing causing fluctuations is **injections**. Injections are expenditures by government, business, or foreign sectors on domestic goods or services, including government purchases, investment, and exports. In other words, they're injections *into* the flow of expenditure.

The government can spend the taxes it collects by making **government purchases**. These purchases are part of expenditures. Business spends on **investment**. Business has retained some profits and capital consumption allowances for investment. If the government spends more on government purchases than it has collected in taxes, or if business spends more on investment than it has in depreciation and retained earnings accounts, they then borrow the "savings" of households. Thus, the offset to household savings would be the borrowing of business and government for G or I.

Exports also inject income back into the economy. This is the income created from other economies buying the products of this economy. (It can also be the income from this economy that is sent to households outside this economy, called *foreign factor income*, but we will not address that here.)

An economy grows when injections are greater than leakages. It shrinks when leakages are greater than injections.

FULL EMPLOYMENT

Full employment is another key goal of the economy. The following terms are associated with employment. Make sure you understand them for the exam.

1. **Unemployed**: Any person who is not working but actively looking for a job. If someone is not even looking for a job, he is not considered unemployed.

   Cyclical unemployment results from fluctuations in the business cycle. *Frictional unemployment*, considered temporary, results from life decisions made by people who are between jobs for personal reasons. Perhaps they have moved and so are looking for a new job. College students who are undergoing interviews are classified under frictional unemployment. *Structural unemployment* results from job seekers not having the skills to obtain the jobs that are available.

   There has been some criticism about how the unemployment statistic is measured. Critics claim that it does not account for "discouraged workers," people who have given up trying to find a job after unsuccessful searches, though they'd like one. Nor does it account for workers who want a full-time job but only have a part time job: These people are not considered unemployed.

2. **Employed**: Any person who has a job is considered employed. Even if someone works part time but would prefer full-time employment, she is still considered employed.

3. **Labor force**: The group of people who are employed or who qualify for being unemployed. They must be at least 16 years of age, not retired, not full-time students, and not in the military.

4. **Full employment**: This is the level at which no one in the labor force is cyclically unemployed. When the economy is at full employment, it is considered to be in the long run. If the economy is not at full employment, it is not producing its potential real gross domestic product.

As defined above, full employment is consistent with an economy that is producing efficiently. Graphically we can illustrate full employment as follows:

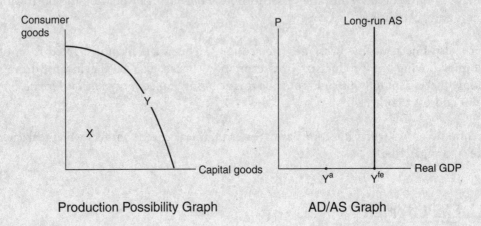

Production Possibility Graph   AD/AS Graph

The production possibilities curve illustrates the economy at full employment. If the economy is at point Y, then there is full employment. At point X, the economy is not at full employment.

The AD/AS graph on the right shows the long-run aggregate supply curve (Long-run AS). It is vertical because at point Y^{fe}, the real GDP is at its potential—the economy is producing as much as it can. Therefore, there is no cyclical unemployment. At point Y^a, the economy is not at full employment, and there is cyclical unemployment.

PRICE STABILITY

Important to the successful long-run performance of any market economy is *price stability*. **Price stability** means that there's very little price inflation or deflation. If prices are not dependable, we start making decisions based on fighting inflation or deflation rather than on the most efficient ways of producing products, investing savings, or maximizing consumption.

Inflation

Inflation is a general increase in prices throughout an economy. It is possible to have inflation and experience a decrease in some prices, and it is possible to have an increase in some prices without having inflation. The price level is the weighted average of all prices in an economy. This is an abstract notion: If we were to compute all the prices of all the goods and services produced in an economy, and derived an average price by accounting for all the units of each product, we would get the price level. Inflation is the increase of this general price level.

Inflation creates problems because an economy depends on prices to coordinate resources efficiently. When there is uncertainty about inflation, it becomes more difficult and more costly to plan. The uncertainty that results makes for a less efficient economy.

Earlier in this discussion we noted that the gross domestic product was a measure of the total output on an economy. We also differentiated between real GDP and nominal GDP. If the real GDP is less than the nominal GDP, the difference is inflation.

Demand–pull inflation occurs when consumer demand for goods and services increases faster than economy can produce these extra goods and services. If one imagines an auction with only a few items available and many consumers wanting to buy, one can understand how demand that outpaces supply will bid up the price.

Cost–push inflation occurs when businesses supply fewer goods and services because of increasing costs, and so the price level rises. The increasing costs could result from higher input costs or because businesses expect prices to go up and so produce less currently.

Who is Hurt by Inflation?

Inflation reduces the purchasing power of the dollar. As the price level rises, each dollar can buy less. If the inflation has not been expected, it can be very damaging to lenders such as banks: The money paid back for a loan will have less real value than the money that was originally provided. If a homeowner borrowed $200,000 to buy a house, and in the time it takes to repay the loan, unexpected inflation occurs, the borrower will pay back with cheaper dollars. If the inflation had been expected, the bank would have built an inflation premium into the interest rate. The additional interest paid would compensate for the lower value of the dollar.

Savers are also hurt by unanticipated inflation. Households that have been saving money as a nest egg for the future are left with dollars that have diminished purchasing power. But if the inflation is expected, savers would be compensated for the loss of dollar value by receiving a greater rate of return. The return of their savings would have an expected inflation premium.

> Unanticipated inflation wreaks more havoc than anticipated inflation.

Inflation is not a problem if prices and incomes rise at the same rate. But if prices rise faster than incomes, consumers will not be able to buy as many goods and services as they did before. People living on fixed incomes are particularly hurt: The cost of living (buying the goods and services) would increase while their fixed incomes would not. The net result would be a decrease in living standard. Of course if the income had a **cost of living adjustment** (COLA), then the living standard would not be affected. Social Security benefits have a cost of living adjustment. The COLA increases the income received by the inflation rate, thereby providing an income that will maintain the same standard of living.

Expecting inflation becomes a self-full-filling prophecy. When consumers expect prices to rise, they buy more in the current period, creating demand–pull inflation. Suppliers expecting prices to rise will decrease the supply, creating a higher price level.

How to Measure Inflation

There are three price indexes used to measure inflation:

1. Consumer Price Index
2. Producer Price Index
3. GDP Deflator

The **Consumer Price Index** (CPI) measures the cost of a market basket of goods that a consumer typically buys. It is intended to show the cost of the purchases of an "average" household and the overall change in prices of these purchases. To do so, the U.S. Bureau of Labor Statistics (BLS) collects thousands of prices every month and compares them to prices from the previous month. The BLS creates a "basket" of these goods, and the typical quantity of each. Each item is weighted to reflect its relative importance.

The formula for constructing the CPI includes a base year. The base year is the year selected to measure prices by. Periodically, the base year will change, but it always has an index of 100.

$$\text{Consumer Price Index} = \frac{\text{Cost of Basket in Current Year}}{\text{Cost of Basket in Base Year}} \times 100$$

Suppose the cost of the basket in the base year were $200. The formula would be:

$200 ÷ $200 = 1 × 100 = 100

Now suppose that in the following year (year two), the basket cost $220. The index formula would be $220 ÷ 200 = 1.1 × 100 = 110. And if, in year three, it were $240, the index would be $240 ÷ $200 = 1.2 × 100 = 120. We have constructed the following price index:

Year 1 (base year):   100

Year 2:   110

Year 3:   120

Note: The **inflation rate** for a given year is the change in price level from the previous year. It is not the change in index number. To compute the inflation rate from year two to year three using the information above, take the change in index from year three to year two, and divide that by the year two index: 120 – 110 = 10. The index changed 10 points. The previous index was 110. So the inflation rate is 10/110 = approximately 9 percent (.0909).

Although the CPI is an important index for computing inflation, it isn't perfect. Many economists believe that it overstates inflation by as much as one percent. Some specific criticisms of the CPI are:

1. The CPI market basket is based on the spending patterns of consumers, but not all consumers have the same spending habits. Spending patterns change over time. The government does try to adjust for some of these problems but there's still room for error.

2. The quality of products changes over time. The personal computers we buy today are superior to the personal computers we bought 15 years ago. The government tries to adjust for this as well but it's a difficult problem.

3. Price changes for some products can lead consumers to substitute other goods. The fixed market basket does not account for this substitution.

The **Producer Price Index** (PPI) is an index of goods used in the production process. It is calculated like the consumer price index, only the "basket" changes. The PPI is considered an early indication of inflation because the higher prices paid for inputs by producers will likely lead to cost–push inflation.

The **GDP Deflator** measures the changes in prices of all goods and services produced in the economy. This is the more accurate index to use when converting nominal GDP to real GDP.

$$\textbf{Real GDP} = \textbf{Nominal GDP} \times \frac{\textbf{GDP Deflator (base year)}}{\textbf{GDP Deflator (current year)}}$$

Assume that for the year 2001, the nominal GDP was $10 trillion and the GDP deflator 1.08 (base year 1996). What was the real GDP for 2001 based on the 1996 prices?

$$\textbf{Real GDP 2001} = \textbf{\$10 trillion} \times \frac{\textbf{1.0}}{\textbf{1.08}} = \frac{\textbf{\$10 trillion}}{\textbf{1.08}} = \textbf{\$9.26 trillion}$$

When we convert the nominal GDP to real GDP based on 1996 prices, we have a real GDP of $9.26 trillion.

In determining the real GDP, we have arbitrarily picked a year to establish base prices. Here, the real GDP of $9.26 trillion for 2001 is based on 1996 dollars. If we were to calculate this figure based on a different year, we would get a different number. Our conclusion measures the real GDP in the prices of the base year.

We began this unit by noting that in macroeconomics, what's important is how the factors of production are used to produce actual goods and services. We also noted the use of prices to establish the value of resources and output. Changes in price levels are adjusted for price changes by using one of the indexes to factor out inflation.

> While the examples used here look at indexes with a single base year, it is common to encounter indexes based on chained based data. In these cases, an average or 'rates over successive years' is used.

MEASURING CHANGES IN REAL GDP, REAL WAGES, AND REAL INTEREST RATES

The inflation rate measures the increase in overall prices. If the price of a good or service increases, that is not necessarily inflation; it is only inflation when the general price level increases. Once we have the inflation rate expressed in a percentage (such as 3 percent for the year), we can calculate the real rates of GDP growth, wage growth, and interest rates by simple subtraction.

GDP

For GDP, the equation is as follows:

Increase in Nominal GDP – Inflation Rate = Real Change in GDP

For instance, if nominal GDP increases by five percent over the previous year's nominal GDP, but the inflation rate for the year was four percent, the increase in real GDP is one percent: Five percent minus four percent equals one percent.

Or, if nominal GDP last year was $10 trillion, and it's $11 trillion this year alongside a six percent inflation rate, the nominal increase in GDP would be $1 trillion ($11 t – $10 t). The GDP increased by $1 trillion dollars. That's a 10 percent increase ($1 t/$10 t). So the nominal GDP increased by 10 percent, but since the stated inflation rate is six percent, the real change in GDP is four percent (10 percent minus six percent). There was a four percent real change in GDP.

Wages

If the nominal wage increases seven percent, but the inflation rate for the year was eight percent, the real change in wages is negative one (-1) percent. While workers' wages increased, the purchasing power of those wages decreased by one percent.

$$7\% - 8\% = -1\%$$

Interest Rates

The interest rate is the "price" of borrowing and lending of household savings. The study of macroeconomics involves many references to the interest rate. Most of us are accustomed to seeing different interest rates: prime rate, mortgage rate, credit card rate, etc. Regardless of which one we're dealing with, they all have a common base rate.

The **nominal interest rate** is made up of different components. It includes a real, risk-free rate (no inflation premium or risk premium), plus an expected inflation premium (anticipated inflation) plus default premium (*default risk* is the risk the lender takes that the borrower might not repay the loan) plus maturity premium (premium for future uncertainty).

The expected inflation premium affects all interest rates. The default premium is the added amount charged to account for lending risk. It is this factor that creates the difference in rates. Credit card rates are always more expensive because so many borrowers default. The added interest that is charged to the "nondefaulting" borrowers covers the cost of the defaulting borrowers.

Now, returning to the generic, macroeconomic interest rate: If the nominal interest rate is 10 percent and the inflation rate is six percent, the real rate is 10 – 6 = 4 percent.

Because lenders include a premium into the interest rate for expected inflation, they may not be hurt by inflation when it occurs. But if the inflation is unexpected, we can assume that the lenders were not able to include sufficient premium into the interest rate, and will therefore, lose.

Computing the real interest rate using the inflation rate:

Nominal Rate – Inflation Rate = Real Rate

If the nominal interest rate were seven percent, and the inflation rate were four percent, then the real interest rate would be 7 – 4 = 3 percent real rate of interest.

KEY POINTS

- In a market economy, there are three markets: a product market (where businesses supply goods and services to consumers); a factor market (where households supply resources to businesses); and a financial market (where savings is made available to businesses and government). And within a market economy, there are four sectors: households, businesses, the government, and foreign (other economies). These sectors are responsible for the following expenditures: consumption, investment, government purchases, and net exports (export–imports).

- The three key goals of the economy are *economic growth* (the increase of real, potential output); *full employment* (no cyclical unemployment); and *price stability*. Economic growth occurs because of increases in the factors of production, increases in technology, and increases in human capital.

- The circular flow model of the economy equates output with income.

- Gross domestic product (GDP) is the value of the total output of the economy. It can be calculated by adding up the expenditures (C + I + G + X), or by adding up all of the income generated. When calculating the GDP, only the final goods and services are used; this avoids double counting.

- The *inflation rate* is the difference between real GDP and nominal GDP. A change in real GDP indicates a change in output, while a change in nominal GDP indicates a change in prices (though it could also indicate a change in both prices and output if the nominal change is different from the inflation rate).

- The types of unemployment are cyclical, structural, and frictional. Full employment does not mean zero unemployment, but rather zero cyclical unemployment. If the economy is not producing at the maximum real potential output, it will not be at full employment.

- Inflation is the change in price levels. There are two types of inflation: demand–pull and cost–push. To determine inflation, three popular methods are used: *consumer price index* (CPI), the *producer price index* (PI), and the *GDP deflator*.

- Real wage (nominal wages minus inflation) is most important because it reflects the true purchasing power from the price received for supplying labor.

- The real interest rate is the nominal interest rate minus the inflation rate.

- An increase in real GDP is not necessarily economic growth. If the economy is not at full employment, an increase in real GDP will be a movement toward the potential GDP (full employment GDP). Economic growth refers to the increase in potential real GDP. We can illustrate economic growth by an outward movement of the production possibilities curve or a rightward shift of the long run aggregate supply curve.

- The business cycle indicates short-run fluctuations of output and employment. The long-run trend is an increase in output and employment, averaging about three percent per year.

REVIEW QUESTIONS

1. Frictional unemployment is

   (A) associated with general downturns in the economy.
   (B) the same as structural unemployment.
   (C) present in any dynamic economy.
   (D) long-term unemployment.
   (E) associated with the long-term decline of specific industries.

2. If top government officials claim that more people are working now than ever before, which of the following must be true?

   (A) The unemployment rate is lower now than ever before.
   (B) The number of people employed is higher now than ever before.
   (C) The employment rate is higher now than ever before.
   (D) The number of people in the labor force is higher now than ever before.
   (E) The number of people unemployed is lower now than ever before.

3. Economic growth requires either technological advances or expansion of

   (A) the resources available.
   (B) the federal budget deficit.
   (C) the amount of foreign aid a country contributes.
   (D) imports.
   (E) consumption.

4. Declining population in an economy

   (A) may increase economic growth.
   (B) may cause lower living standards, even if GDP increases.
   (C) could contribute to higher real GDP per capita.
   (D) increases the rate of savings in an economy.
   (E) increases real GDP.

5. Full employment indicates a zero percent

   (A) cyclical unemployment rate.
   (B) frictional unemployment rate.
   (C) structural unemployment rate.
   (D) seasonal unemployment rate.
   (E) aggregate unemployment rate.

6. Investment spurs growth of potential output because it increases

   (A) consumption expenditures.
   (B) capital stock for future use.
   (C) tax rates and absorbs savings.
   (D) government expenditures.
   (E) firms' production.

7. The best measure of the rise in the average standard of living is the increase of

 (A) Consumption
 (B) Savings
 (C) Real GDP
 (D) Real GDP per capita
 (E) Government spending

8. If the nominal GDP is $10 trillion dollars and the GDP deflator is .9, the real GDP is approximately

 (A) $9 trillion
 (B) $11.1 trillion
 (C) $1 trillion
 (D) $9.9 trillion
 (E) $10.9 trillion

9. Given the following data, what is this country's gross domestic product?

Consumption	$14
Investment	4
Government Purchases	7
Exports	5
Imports	8

 (A) $38
 (B) $25
 (C) $28
 (D) $22
 (E) $31

10. If the nominal interest rate is 12 percent and the inflation rate is 7 percent, the real interest rate is

 (A) 12 percent
 (B) 19 percent
 (C) 5 percent
 (D) 7 percent
 (E) 10 percent

Free-Response Questions

1. Suppose that the economic data for year X indicates that:

   • GDP is $10 trillion
   • Consumption is $6.5 trillion
   • Investment is $2 trillion
   • Government Purchases equal $2 trillion
   • Imports equal $2 trillion

   (a) (i) What is the value of net exports?
       (ii) What is the value of exports?

   (b) If the $2 trillion of Investment includes $.5 trillion of unplanned Investment,
       (i) Explain what the unplanned investment is.
       (ii) Explain what will happen to output in the near future as a result of this unplanned investment.

   (c) If the capital consumption allowance (CCA) for the year is $.5 trillion dollars,
       (i) What is the net domestic product?
       (ii) What is the net Investment?

2. Sally's job pays $50,000 a year, and she has just received a five percent raise for next year. She currently pays mortgage interest of eight percent on her condominium. If the Consumer Price Index this year is 120, and next year it rises to 126,

   (a) What will be the inflation rate next year?
   (b) What will be Sally's real wage increase?
   (c) What will be the real interest rate that Sally pays on her mortgage next year?

ANSWERS TO REVIEW QUESTIONS

1. (C)

People will always move, change careers, or look for better opportunities. (A) would be true for cyclical unemployment. (D) is the opposite of what is true; that is, frictional unemployment is short term.

2. (B)

As more people start working, the number of people employed increases. If population increased dramatically, a nation could have more people working than ever before and still have a large unemployment rate, so (A) is wrong. (C) is out because if the size of the labor force changes, the employment rate may decrease. Changes in unemployment rate depend on changes in the number of people working and the number of people in the labor force. (D) is incorrect, since an increase in the labor force does not necessarily mean more people will be working. It could be an increase in unemployment. (E) is wrong because the number of people unemployed can be higher, even though the number of people working is increasing. If the labor force is increasing and more people start looking for a job, the number of unemployed people may go up.

3. (A)

Changes in the factors of production can change the quantity of production possible in a year. (B) is wrong since an increased budget deficit can discourage economic growth. (D) and (E) are not necessarily correct, since both could use funds that would otherwise be used for investment.

4. (C)

Real GDP per capita equals real GDP divided by the population. Changes in real GDP per capita measures whether the production per person in the economy is increasing or decreasing. If real GDP stays constant during a population decline, the real GDP per capita goes up. Population and the rate of savings are unrelated, so (D) is wrong. And we wouldn't necessarily know how a declining population would affect the real GDP, though it's most likely to result in a decreased work force and therefore decreased production. That means (E) should be eliminated as well.

5. (A)

If the economy is at full employment, the cyclical unemployment rate is zero. It doesn't mean that the unemployment rate is zero. Full employment is the highest level of real GDP an economy can maintain without an increase in prices. At full employment, cyclical unemployment is zero, but structural and frictional unemployment still exist. An economy needs some level of frictional unemployment to keep inflationary pressures in check, so (B) is wrong. And structural unemployment is inherent in a dynamic society, so it's not zero at full employment, making (C) out as well.

6. (B)

Investment generates some economic growth today, but it generates significantly more economic growth in the future. This is because investment is purchases of capital goods. And more capital results in an increase in the PPF for an economy. (A) can be eliminated because it has an opposite effect on investment: When consumption expenditures increase, there's less money available for investment.

7. (D)

To adjust for the population issue in calculating real GDP, we use real GDP per capita. Changes in real GDP per capita show whether the production per person in the economy is increasing or decreasing. Therefore it's a better measure of economic growth of average standard of living. (C) can be eliminated, too: A change in real GDP doesn't show if the production per person is increasing or decreasing, since it isn't adjusted for population. There's a better measure of the growth of average standard of living.

8. (B)

The formula we need is: Nominal GDP $\times \dfrac{\text{Base Year Deflator}}{\text{Current Year Deflator}}$ or $\dfrac{\text{Nominal GDP}}{\text{Current Year Deflator}}$

so, $\dfrac{\$10}{.9} = 11.1$

9. (D)

GDP = C + I + G + NX (exports-imports), so GDP $= 14 + 4 + 7 + (5 - 8) = 22$.

10. (C)

Nominal rate minus the inflation rate equals the real rate. So 12 percent minus 7 percent is 5 percent.

Free-Response Questions

1. (a) (i) GDP = C + I + G + X, so we can set up the equation:

$10 trillion = 6.5 t + 2 t + 2 t + ?

$10 t = 10.5 t + X, so X must be -$.5 trillion. Net exports are -.5 trillion.

(ii) If net exports are -$.5 trillion while imports are $2 trillion, then exports minus imports = net exports. We can set up the equation:

? – $2 trillion = -$.5 t

Exports must be $1.5 trillion.

(b) (i) Unplanned investment is the unintended increase in inventories.

(ii) Since businesses will have high unexpected inventory levels, output will be reduced, and the economy will slow down.

(c) **(i)** GDP minus CCA = Net Domestic Product. So net domestic product is:

$10 trillion – $.5 trillion = $9.5 trillion

(ii) Net investment is gross investment minus replacement investment. If the given gross investment is $2 trillion, and the CCA is $.5 trillion, net investment will equal $1.5 trillion. The CCA can be used as the replacement investment dollar value.

2. **(a)** Computing the inflation rate from the Consumer Price Index, we need the change in the index divided by the prior year's index. 126 minus 120 equals 6. The index has increased six points.

$$\frac{6}{120} = 5\%$$

The inflation rate next year will be five percent.

(b) Sally's raise is five percent. Five percent minus inflation is the real wage increase.

5% – 5% = 0

Sally will have no real wage change.

(c) Eight percent minus inflation is the real interest rate.

8% – 5% = 3%

Sally will pay a three percent real interest rate on her mortgage next year.

AD/AS MODELS

CHAPTER FIVE

We have already looked at the gross domestic product, expenditures, employment, and price levels. This chapter will explore these topics in greater depth and review the necessary graphic analysis.

GDP is determined by the aggregate demand and aggregate supply equilibrium, where the quantities of AD and AS are equal. If this equilibrium occurs where the economy is at full employment, then the economy is at long-run equilibrium. If it does not, then the economy is in the short run, and unemployment is a problem.

AGGREGATE DEMAND (AD)

The **aggregate demand** is a schedule of the quantity of output that the economic sectors (households, businesses, government, and foreign) are willing to purchase at various price levels. At each price level, aggregate demand will equal the expenditures: consumption, investment, government purchases, and exports (or net exports).

> *Exports* are purchased by people outside the country. *Net exports* are exports minus imports, which in effect reduces the potential consumption. One can use either term in economic analysis.

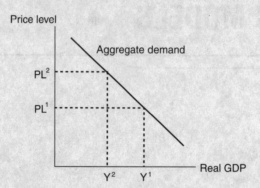

The graph above may look like a microeconomic demand graph but it is not! The vertical axis measures the price level, not price. The horizontal axis measures real GDP or real output. It represents the output of all industries, not a single industry. The downward sloping curve is the **aggregate demand**, that is, the demand for all products and services. When you label this graph, make sure the vertical is labeled **price level**, and the downward sloping curve is labeled **aggregate demand**.

As the price level increases from PL^1 to PL^2, the quantity of total goods and services demanded drops from Y^1 to Y^2. Conversely, if the price level drops from PL^2 to PL^1 the quantity demanded increases to Y^1 from Y^2. Changes in the price level change the quantity of aggregate demand!

As price level changes, there is movement along the aggregate demand curve. The aggregate demand curve is downward sloping (negative slope) for several reasons. All of these reasons are related to changes in price:

- **Real interest rate effect**: An increase in the price level increases the need for money for transactions, which in turn leaves less money saved. This reduces the money supplied to the loanable funds market and increases interest rates. The higher interest rates discourages investment spending and consumer spending. Conversely if prices drop, more money will enter the loanable funds market and interest rates will drop, encouraging investment and consumer spending.

- **Real balances effect:** An increase in the price level decreases the purchasing power of financial assets. This will reduce the quantity demanded. Conversely, if price level drops, the purchasing power of financial assets will increase and the quantity demanded will increase.

- **Net exports effect:** An increase in the price level makes domestic goods and services relatively more expensive than foreign goods and services. Thus we will export less and import more. Conversely a decrease in the price level will lead to more exports and less imports.

What shifts the demand curve? Anything that shifts spending patterns, other than changes in price level. An increase in consumption (C), investment (I), government purchases (G), and exports (E) will shift the aggregate demand curve to the right (increase), while a decrease in these things will shift it to the left (decrease).

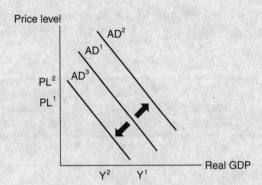

Here, an increase in aggregate demand would shift the AD curve right, from AD^1 to AD^2, while a decrease would shift it left, from AD^1 to AD^3.

Components of Aggregate Demand

Consumption

The largest component of aggregate demand is consumption. Consistently from year to year, consumption will equal approximately 67 percent of all expenditures on the goods and services that are produced. The production of goods and services provides the income flow to households, who in turn will spend this income buying the goods and services that are produced.

Consumption is dependent on the **disposable income** of households. Disposable income is what is left of income after adjusting for:

- Depreciation
- Undistributed corporate profits
- Corporate taxes
- Social security taxes
- Personal taxes
- Adding back transfer payments that go from the government to households

If disposable income increases, we can expect consumption to increase; if it decreases, consumption will likely drop. This tendency to spend more as income increases is dependable.

The **marginal propensity to consume (MPC)** is the fraction of an increase in disposable income that is consumed. In other words, it is the portion of one additional dollar of disposable income spent on consumption. It is the change in consumption divided by the change in disposable income. $\Delta C/\Delta DI$: There is also some portion of consumption that is not dependent on income. This is called **autonomous consumption**.

The **average propensity to consume** (APC) measures total consumption divided by total income: C/Y. Given the following table, we can compute the marginal and average propensities to consume.

	Income (billions)	Consumption (billions)	Average Propensity to Consume	Marginal Propensity to Consume
Year 1	$1000	$750	.75	
Year 2	1100	840	.76	.9

The average propensities to consume for years 1 and 2, respectively, are .75 (750/1000) and .76 (840/1100). For year 1, the MPC cannot be computed, since, with no previous period data, one cannot measure the change. For year 2, it's .9 (90/100).

If disposable income is not consumed, it is saved:

Consumption + Household Savings = Disposable Income

If the marginal propensity to consume is .9, then the **marginal propensity to save (MPS)** must be .1. If the average propensity to consume is .75, then the average propensity to save is .25. MPC + MPS = 1 and APC + APS = 1.

The marginal propensity to consume allows us to calculate the spending multiplier. The spending multiplier allows us to calculate the change in total GDP (or income) that results from an initial change in one component of aggregate demand. If government purchases increased from $2,000 billion to $2,100 billion, what would be the final impact on the economy given a marginal propensity to consume of .75?

> In our spending multiplier formula, the denominator is 1 - MPC. This is also the marginal propensity to save. Therefore, we can achieve the multiplier by using the formula: 1 ÷ MPS.

The formula for the spending multiplier is: $\dfrac{1}{1 - MPC}$

So, using the information above:

$$\frac{1}{1 - .75} = \frac{1}{.25} = 4$$

The spending multiplier is four. The $100 billion increase in government purchases will lead to a total increase of GDP and income of $400 billion.

This simplified version of the spending multiplier overstates the actual multiplier, but it is helpful at the principles level. In actuality, this multiplier has leakages such as taxes and imports.

Now we can see that any changes in savings patterns can have both an initial effect on demand and an effect on the spending multiplier.

Investment

What changes the investment (I) component of aggregate demand? First, there's the businessman's view of **future cash flows** (**profitability**): Investment includes new factories and new equipment (the **capital stock** of the economy). Increasing the capital stock means increasing output capabilities. In order for a business to expand its productive capabilities, it must be optimistic that the additional output will sell and pay back the cost of the investment. If the business is investing in capital stock to produce the same quantity but at a lower cost, it will still need to be optimistic that the output will sell and the additional cost of investment will be worth it. In times of recession, depending on investment as a stimulus to aggregate demand (in the short run) and aggregate supply (in the long run) can lead to disappointment.

The second thing affecting an increase in investment is the **interest rate**. The interest rate is the cost of borrowing. When a business wants to build factories and buy equipment, it frequently needs to borrow money to accomplish the increase in capital stock. Of course, the business has depreciation funds to replace equipment, but replacement equipment does not add to the capital stock of the economy. The business also has retained earnings (undistributed corporate profits), but this may not be enough. The interest rate determines the cost of the capital stock expansion. The higher the interest rate, the greater the cost that needs to be recovered. The greater the cost, the more optimistic the firms have to be about future profitability.

Businesses can also raise funds by selling stock. Buying stock is a form of savings for households. Investors expect higher returns from investing in equities (stocks) because it is a riskier investment than investing in bonds. Thus, investors expect the going interest rate plus a risk premium (market premium). The interest rate affects all forms of raising money to buy capital stock or inventory. It influences the demand for new housing, which is also a part of investment (I).

Government Purchases

Increasing government purchases is dependent on the collective will and the political process. If the government pursues an expansionary program, G increases and the aggregate demand curve shifts to the right. Whether the government should pursue expansionary or contractionary policies can be a normative issue: It may depend on which philosophy prevails at the time.

Exports

Increasing exports depends on several factors. If the income in other economies were to increase, the demand for exports would increase. If the value of the dollar vis-à-vis another currency were to appreciate, exports would become more expensive and would therefore decrease. If the price level in the economy were to decrease while it stayed the same in other countries, export goods would become relatively less expensive and exports would therefore increase. If productivity were to increase, lowering the price level, exports would increase.

AGGREGATE SUPPLY (AS)

Aggregate supply is a schedule of the quantity of output that an economy will supply at various price levels in the short run. It is also the total potential output that an economy can supply in the long run.

First let's look at the long-run aggregate supply curve.

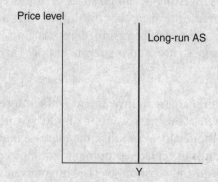

The long-run supply curve is vertical because there is no possibility at that time to produce more. Real GDP is maximized. Any changes in AD will affect only the price level.

In the long run, prices and wages are **flexible**. This means that if products don't sell and employees become unemployed, the market will **self-correct** in the following ways:

- Firms will lower their prices to sell off inventory
- Workers will take lower wages, thus leading to re-employment by the firms

The economy self-corrects to full employment output. Price and wage levels will change but these will be nominal changes. Moreover, these changes will offset each other and purchasing power will remain the same. This is the **classical view of macroeconomic equilibrium**. Flexible prices and wages are broadly accepted among economists looking at the long run. The key question is, how long do these adjustments take? If we are not at full-employment (potential) output, then we are in the short-run.

> Economic growth is illustrated by a shift to the right of the aggregate supply curve or by an outward shift of the production possibilities curve.

Sticky Price Model

In this model, the short-run prices and wages are **sticky**. This means that firms do not quickly adjust their prices, and workers do not quickly adjust their wages. This may mean that the economy will not self-correct quickly.

How quickly the economy self-corrects and what role the government should play in the short run is a subject of debate. For the AP exam, it is only necessary to understand the models.

KAPLAN

Short-Run Aggregate Supply

In the short run, the economy is not producing at the potential, full-employment output. There will be some cyclical unemployment. The short-run aggregate supply will not be vertical.

Two graphs exist for illustrating short-run aggregate supply:

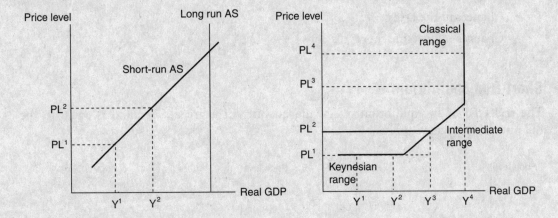

The graph on the left indicates that output can be increased from Y^1 to Y^2, but that the price level will change from PL^1 to PL^2. The graph on the right also indicates that output can be increased, but it has three segments: The horizontal segment is the Keynesian segment. Since it's horizontal, a movement from Y^1 to Y^2 would increase output and employment, but wouldn't result in an increased price level. Movement from Y^2 to Y^3 would increase output and employment. Once we are into the intermediate segment, the price level also increases from PL^2 to PL^3. Here, an increase in real GDP will increase the price level. Once the AS curve is in the classical range (full employment), there can be no increase in output or employment: Any change can only change the price level.

The supply curve is dependent on the cost of production. Anything that lowers the real cost of production will shift the aggregate supply curve to the right.

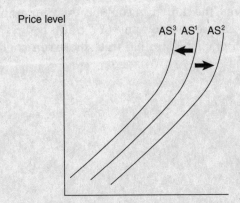

This graph illustrates a decrease in the cost of production that will shift the AS curve from AS^1 to AS^2 This is an increase in aggregate supply. An increase in the real cost of production will shift the AS from AS^1 to AS^3, illustrating a decrease in aggregate supply.

The nonprice level factors that will change the aggregate supply are:
- Changes in technology
- Changes in the real cost of resources
- Changes in the taxes
- Changes in government regulations

Short-Run Equilibrium

The real GDP is in equilibrium when the quantity of aggregate demand is equal to the quantity of aggregate supply.

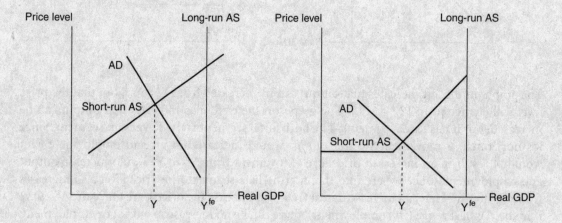

Real GDP at any given time will be where the AD curve intersects the short-run AS curve. At this point, the quantity of AD equals the quantity of AS. GDP equals C plus I plus G plus X.

In order to properly illustrate the short-run equilibrium, your graph must include the long-run AS curve, and the equilibrium output (Y) must be less than the long-run full employment output. Both graphs above illustrate short-run conditions because there are unemployed resources.

Long-Run Equilibrium

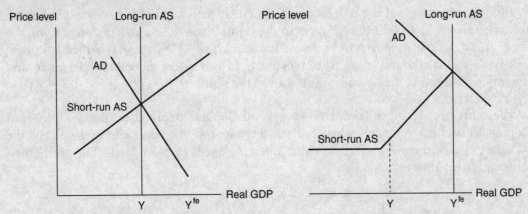

In both graphs above, the aggregate demand curves intersect the aggregate supply curves on the vertical long-run supply. At this level of real GDP, the quantity of aggregate supply is equal to the quantity of aggregate demand at the full employment (potential) gross domestic product. GDP = C + I + G + X at a level of output that is fully employing the resources of the country.

Supply Shocks

Let's look at what happens if the aggregate supply were adversely affected by an energy shortage or horrendous weather—the type of event that would impact many industries. The aggregate supply curve would shift left because overall production of the economy would be impeded. An energy shortage would drive up the cost of energy: All industries depend on energy, so the supply curve would shift as follows:

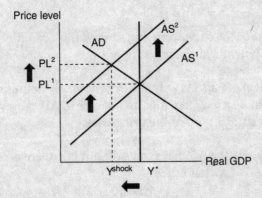

As a result of the "supply shock," the economy faces more unemployment as the real GDP drops from Y^* to Y^{shock} and the price level rises from PL^1 to PL^2. When the economy faces both increasing unemployment and increasing inflation, it is experiencing **stagflation**. In order to eliminate the economic condition of stagflation, the aggregate supply curve must shift right.

Concurrent Shifts

Within the framework of the AD/AS model, when an economy is experiencing stagflation, the only solution is to shift the AS curve to the right. If the AD curve has shifted right, the result will be less unemployment but more inflation. If the AD curve has shifted left, there will be less inflation and more unemployment. In order to reduce both the price and unemployment levels, the AS curve must shift to the right.

In the short-run AD/AS model with an upward sloping supply curve and a downward sloping demand curve, the following occurs: If there are simultaneous shifts in the AS and the AD, we can determine the effect on either unemployment or price level—but not both—without further information.

	Increase AS	Decrease AS	Increase AD	Decrease AD
Price level	Down	Up	Up	Down
Unemployment	Down	Up	Down	Up

If both AS and AD increase, the economy will experience less unemployment, but the impact of these concurrent shifts on price level will be indeterminant because of opposing influences. If they both decrease, the economy will experience an increase in unemployment, but the change in price level will be indeterminant.

If AS increases while AD decreases, the economy will experience a drop in price level but the impact on unemployment will be indeterminant. If AS decreases and AD increases, there will be a rise in price level, but the change in unemployment will be indeterminant.

Long-Run Shifts

In the long run, only the AD curve can shift unless the economy experiences economic growth (increase in the potential aggregate supply).

A change in aggregate demand affects only the price level. By definition, in the long run, the aggregate supply is at full capacity. Therefore, an increase in AD causes a rise in the price level, while a decrease in AD causes a drop in the price level.

In the long run, the only way the AS curve can shift out is if there is economic growth, and a new long-run potential GDP is established.

Real GDP versus Economic Growth

The difference between an increase in real GDP and in economic growth in the AD/AS model is that real GDP can increase if the economy is not at full employment, without increasing the potential GDP. Economic growth occurs when the potential GDP increases, and the long-run AS curve shifts to the right.

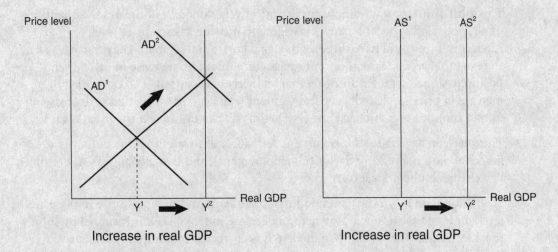

Increase in real GDP   Increase in real GDP

The graph on the left illustrates an increase in aggregate demand from AD^1 to AD^2. Initially the economy was in equilibrium at Y^1, a short-run equilibrium. Movement to Y^2 shows an increase in real GDP, but it is not economic growth, because the potential (full capacity) output did not change.

The graph on the right illustrates a change in potential GDP from Y^1 to Y^2, illustrating economic growth. The long-run aggregate supply curve has shifted to the right.

KEY IDEAS

- Aggregate demand (AD) is the quantity of all the goods and services that consumers would purchase at various price levels. The components of AD include Consumption, Investment, Government Purchases, and Net Exports (C + I + G + X).

- The AD curve has a negative slope because of the real interest rate effect, the real balance effect, and the net exports effect. A change in any of the components will shift the AD curve: An increase will shift it right, while a decrease will shift it left.

- Consumption is primarily dependent on one's income. The percentage of additional disposable income that will be used for consumption is called the *marginal propensity to consume* (MPC), while the percentage to be used for savings is called the *marginal propensity to save* (MPS). MPC + MPS = 1. Changes in consumption—and therefore savings—can shift the AD curve, as can consumer expectations.

- Changes in investment are dependent on business optimism regarding future profitability and the interest rate.

- Changes in government purchases are dependent on political decisions to conduct expansionary or contractionary fiscal policy.

- Changes in exports (and imports) are dependent on relative prices in the international market, the value of the currency on the foreign exchange, and changes in incomes in different countries.

- The short-run aggregate supply curve is positively sloped. It illustrates the quantity of all goods and services business is willing to provide at each price level. Alternatively, it could have three segments: a horizontal segment (Keynesian) showing that an increase in output can occur without an increase in price level; a positively sloped segment showing that an increase in output is accompanied by an increase in price level; and a vertical segment (classical) showing that an increase in output cannot occur and that any changes in AD can only affect the price level.

- The long-run aggregate supply curve is vertical. It illustrates that the output is at potential output (full capacity or full employment), and that a change in AD results in a change in the price level.

- Stagflation is an economic condition that includes both inflation (a rise in the price level) and increase in unemployment (a decrease in real GDP). It is caused by supply shocks that shift the AS curve to the left. It is corrected by shifting the AS curve to the right.

- An increase in real GDP does not necessarily signify economic growth. Economic growth occurs when the potential aggregate supply shifts to the right.

- If both the AS and AD curves shift at the same time, one can predict the result of a change either in the price level or in output (unemployment)—but not both—unless additional information is provided.

REVIEW QUESTIONS

1. In a nation, the current level of investment

   (A) shifts the production possibilities frontier inward.
   (B) is half the current level of consumption.
   (C) has no effect on economic growth.
   (D) affects future capacity to produce.
   (E) is not affected by consumption.

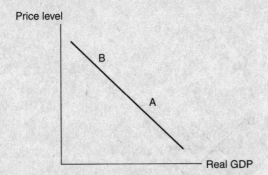

2. Moving from A to B on the above graph represents

   (A) a decrease in aggregate demand.
   (B) an increase in aggregate demand.
   (C) a decrease in the aggregate quantity demanded.
   (D) an increase in the aggregate quantity demanded.
   (E) no change in the aggregate quantity demanded.

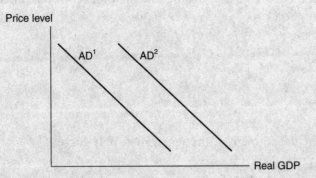

3. In the graph above, movement from AD^1 to AD^2 indicates

   (A) an increase in the aggregate quantity demanded.
   (B) an increase in aggregate demand.
   (C) a decrease in the aggregate quantity demanded.
   (D) a decrease in aggregate demand.
   (E) the price level increased.

4. Technological improvement causes

    (A) the AS curve to shift to the right.
    (B) the AS curve to shift to the left.
    (C) the AS curve to remain unchanged.
    (D) production costs to increase.
    (E) decreases in production.

5. Which one of the following will not cause a shift in aggregate demand?

    (A) Consumption
    (B) Investment
    (C) Imports
    (D) Exports
    (E) Prices

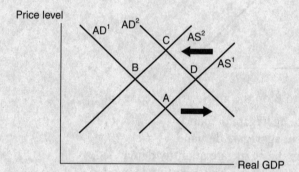

6. In the above graph, the economy begins at AD^1 and AS^1 (in equilibrium at point A). If the country experiences an oil embargo at the same time that it goes to war, then equilibrium in this economy will

    (A) Remain at point A
    (B) Shift to point B
    (C) Shift to point C.
    (D) Shift to point D
    (E) None of the above

7. When an economy is on the flat segment of the aggregate supply curve,

    (A) the economy is near full capacity.
    (B) small changes in the price level have little or no effect on the amount of production in the economy.
    (C) attempts to increase the output of the economy will result in inflation.
    (D) the economy is well below full capacity.
    (E) There is no relatively flat portion of the AS curve.

8. There are three reasons the aggregate demand curve is downward sloping. When a higher price level decreases the purchasing power of money saved, this is an example of the

(A) Income effect
(B) Interest rate effect
(C) Net exports effect
(D) All of the above
(E) None of the above

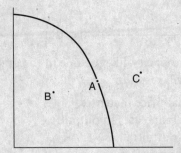

9. In the PPF above, which point might mark full capacity?

(A) point A
(B) point B
(C) point C
(D) All the points could represent full capacity.
(E) No point could represent full capacity.

10. What is the primary difference between AD/AS equilibrium graphs in the short run and in the long run?

(A) Short-run AS is downward sloping.
(B) Long-run AD is upward sloping.
(C) Long-run AS is vertical.
(D) Short-run AS is steeper than long-run AS.
(E) There is no difference between long-run and short-run equilibrium.

11. Let's say that consumer confidence hits its highest level in 30 years. This means consumers expect good economic times in the future. What effect will this have on aggregate demand?

(A) A rightward shift in the AD curve
(B) A leftward shift in the AD curve
(C) A rightward movement along the AD curve
(D) A leftward movement along the AD curve
(E) It will have no effect on aggregate demand

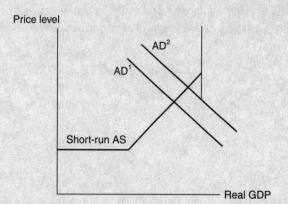

12. If an economy is operating near full capacity, like the one in the graph above, a further increase in AD (from AD^1 to AD^2) will result in

(A) much higher output and minimal price increases.
(B) much higher prices and minimal increases in output.
(C) minimal increases in prices and output.
(D) large increases in output and prices.
(E) Aggregate demand cannot increase beyond equilibrium levels.

Free-Response Questions

1. The economy in the country Oz is currently experiencing high unemployment.

   (a) Using an AD/AS graph, illustrate the current economy in Oz.
   (b) What are the four components of aggregate demand in Oz?
   (c) In the short run, what will happen if the government decides to increase government purchases? Illustrate and explain.
   (d) After the government has increased purchases, what will happen to consumption (C) in Oz? Explain.

2. An energy crisis has just occurred, and it creates a significant aggregate supply shock.

   (a) (i) Illustrate on a graph the result of this energy crisis.
        (ii) What will happen to the price level and employment?
   (b) Subsequent to the above, the government (G) reduces energy taxes (shifting the AS curve to the right), and increases spending (increasing the AD curve). What will be the effect on the price level and on unemployment?

ANSWERS TO REVIEW QUESTIONS

1. (D)

Investment is purchases of capital goods. More capital results in an increase in production for an economy in the future. Therefore investment in capital goods affects future capacity to produce. (A) is out because investment doesn't decrease the PPF; it shifts it outward, meaning an increase in the PPF. (E) can be ruled out because consumption affects the level of savings in the economy. The total amount of investment in the economy is equal to the total amount of savings in the economy, so it also affects the level of investment.

2. (C)

Movement along an aggregate demand curve represents a change in the aggregate quantity demanded. In this case, the movement is in response to a price increase and represents a decrease in the aggregate quantity demanded. (A) and (B) are wrong because the aggregate demand curve did not shift. When aggregate demand decreases or increases, the entire curve shifts. (D) is wrong because while it's true that movement along an aggregate demand curve represents a change in the aggregate quantity demanded, this is not an increase in aggregate quantity demanded. When prices rise, aggregate quantity demanded falls; when prices fall, aggregate quantity demanded rises.

3. (B)

A shift in the demand curve indicates that the aggregate quantity demanded at every price level has changed. In this case, it increased. (A) and (C) are wrong because an increase or decrease in aggregate quantity demanded is represented by movement along an aggregate demand curve. In this case, the entire curve shifted. (E) is wrong because the AD curve shows the relationship between the aggregate quantity demanded and the price level. An increase in the price level is a movement along an AD curve, not a shift of the curve. When the AD curve shifts to the right it represents an increase in aggregate demand.

4. (A)

Technological improvements cause production costs to decrease, shifting the AS curve to the right and increasing output. Technological improvements are a main source of growth in an economy.

5. (E)

A shift of the AD curve (also called a *change in aggregate demand*) is caused by changes in the level of consumption, investment, government expenditures, exports, or imports that aren't caused by a change in the price level. A change in the price level causes a change in aggregate quantity demanded and thus a movement along the AD curve.

6. (C)

An oil embargo would shift AS to the left (moving equilibrium from A to B). War would shift AD to the right (moving equilibrium from B to C). Note that the order of these events doesn't matter, meaning if AD shifted first, equilibrium would shift from A to D to C, and the final result is the same.

7. (D)

The AS curve is flat on the left side (where output is low), then curved, then nearly vertical on the right side (where output is high). When the economy is in the flat section, it is well below full capacity, and small changes in the price level cause large changes in the amount of production in the economy. A small increase in price level will lead to a large increase in RGDP. This couldn't happen when the economy was near full capacity because full capacity is the maximum amount of RGDP the economy can produce.

8. (A)

The higher price level decreases the purchasing power of money saved, so consumption falls and aggregate quantity demanded falls. This is called the *income effect*. (B) is wrong because according to the interest rate effect, which mainly affects businesses buying capital, when the price level increases, the prices of capital (and other goods too) increase. So to make purchases, business owners need to borrow more money than they needed previously to buy the same number of capital goods. Assuming that the supply of dollars available in the loanable funds market is fixed, the increase in demand for loans drives up the interest rate, causing an increase in the cost of borrowing, therefore less investment and less aggregate quantity demanded. (C) is wrong because the net exports effect arises from changes in relative price levels between domestic and foreign goods, so it's not illustrated by a change in the purchasing power of savings.

9. (A)

All the points on the PPF represent maximum possible production. Of course, they represent different combinations of production. One of these points represents the production combination with the highest possible value of production as measured by real GDP (that's full capacity). We don't have enough information to know which one, but full capacity is definitely one of the points on the curve. It would be impossible for points B or C to be full capacity: If the economy is producing at point B, it could produce more, and the economy can't produce at point C. Therefore, by process of elimination, it's point A.

10. (C)

The long-run AS curve is a vertical line, which is very different from the upward-sloping AS curve of the short-run AD/AS model. In the short-run, AS is price sensitive, but in the long-run, it's price insensitive, so (E) is out. And AS is always upward sloping, while AD is always downward sloping, no matter if they're in the short or the long run, so (A) and (B) are out as well.

11. (A)

Shifting the AD curve represents a change in aggregate demand. An increase in aggregate demand is a shift to the right; a decrease in aggregate demand is a shift to the left. Increasing consumer confidence will increase consumption and therefore increase aggregate demand. (B) would reflect a decrease in consumer confidence. (C) and (D) would represent changes in the quantity of aggregate demand. This is caused only by price level changes.

12. (B)

When an economy is near full capacity, it is near its maximum possible output with the resources available. Increasing AD in this situation leads to large increases in the price level for increasingly small increases in output. Near full capacity, increases in AD yield inflation as wages and prices are pushed upward. Near full capacity, the economy has very few unused resources. This makes it increasingly difficult to increase output too much.

Free-Response Questions

1. **(a)**

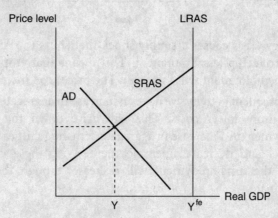

(b) The four components of aggregate demand are: consumption, investment, government purchases and net exports.

(c)

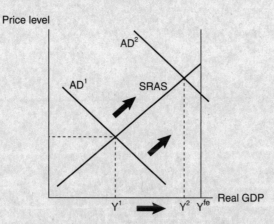

As the government increases G (a component of aggregate demand), the AD curve shifts to the right. The real GDP increases from Y^1 to Y^2. Because the increase in G creates more jobs and incomes, consumption will also increase.

(d) When the government increases its purchases, more goods and services will have to be produced. Additional labor is needed, so household incomes increase. When household income increases, households will spend more on consumption.

2. **(a)**

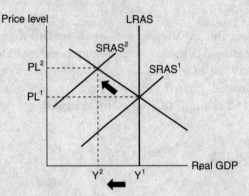

The energy crisis causes a supply shock that shifts the AS curve left. The economy now is producing less Y^2 than Y^1. This means that employment will decrease (or rather, unemployment will increase). The price level increases from PL^1 to PL^2.

(b) In the subsequent activity, we have an increase in aggregate supply (shift to the right), resulting from lower costs. This will drive down the price level and decrease unemployment. An increase in aggregate demand (shift to the right) will drive up the price level and decrease unemployment. With these concurrent shifts, we can conclude that unemployment will decrease, though the effect on price level is indeterminate.

Fiscal Policy

Fiscal policy refers to the decisions that government makes to increase or decrease transfer payments, government purchases, and taxes. Any and all of these decisions will affect macroeconomic activity.

Governments spend money. For our purposes, we can put this spending into one of two categories: *transfer payments* or *government purchases*.

Transfer payments are those payments that government makes to households. They include social security payments, unemployment compensation, welfare payments, etc. Transfer payments increase the disposable income of a household—that income is used for consumption or savings.

Government purchases (G), refer to all of the other spending that government makes to provide for national defense, education, police protection, roads, etc. Transfer payments are not included in government purchases. To pay for government purchases, government has several options. It could:

- Tax
- Borrow
- Print more money

Government could also sell government assets such as land, or charge various fees to pay for spending, though neither of these is significant for our purposes.

The government operates on a fiscal year in which a fiscal budget is created. **Debits** are the funds spent, while **credits** are the revenues raised from taxes.

Debits	Credits
• Transfer payments • Government purchases	• Revenues from taxes
Total spending	Total revenue

In any given year, if government's total spending exceeds the total revenue, there is a *deficit*. A **deficit** means that the government did not raise enough funds to pay for the spending that year, and had to borrow the difference. The **national debt** is the accumulation of deficits over many years—less any retired debt (paid off).

Revenues – Spending = Deficit

If the government runs a deficit, then it competes with the private sector to borrow funds. We can illustrate this using a graph of the **"loanable funds" market**:

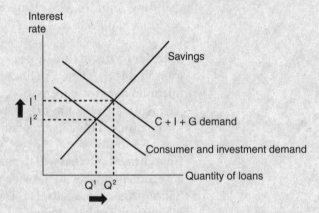

Loanable funds market

Government borrowing adds to the demand for savings, and also raises interest rates. This is the **"crowding out"** effect: Not only is there less savings available for the private sector, the government also puts claims on resources that will no longer be available to the private sector, thereby decreasing investment.

If the government raises enough money to pay for all of its spending, then it has a **balanced budget**.

Tax Revenues – Government Spending = 0 = Balanced Budget

If the government raises more money than it spends, then it has a **surplus**. Surpluses are a part of national savings.

Tax Revenues – Government Spending = Surplus

Governments that pay for spending by printing money create serious **inflationary problems** that have an adverse affect on the macroeconomy. More money in circulation chasing after the same output will drive up prices.

KEYNESIAN ECONOMICS

During the 1930's, the Great Depression struck most of the economies in the world. The economic systems of many countries appeared to be broken. Classical economists had focused on the long run, and on the "laissez-faire" policy that advocated no government intervention in the marketplace.

> Fiscal policy works on the premise that government can minimize short-run hardships. While not everyone supports its use to "stabilize the economy," you should know for the exam how it can be implemented.

It was at this time that British economist John Maynard Keynes advanced his own theory on the problem: He recommended government involvement in the economy during recessions and depressions. In his book, *The General Theory of Employment, Interest and Money*, and other writings, Keynes developed much of the analysis that is part of macroeconomic theory today: the expenditure model, spending multiplier, propensity to consume, etc. Though today some of his ideas have been questioned or improved upon, Keynes proposed that:

a. Households have a marginal propensity to consume that is between zero and one. The MPC indicates the proportion of a change in income that is consumed. This propensity to consume gives us the spending multiplier. Even though Alpha has an absolute advantage in producing both wine and orange juice, Beta has a comparative advantage in producing wine, as the opportunity cost for the production of wine (in terms of forgone orange juice) is lower for Beta than for Alpha. Similarly, Alpha has a comparative advantage in the production of orange juice because the opportunity cost for the production of orange juice (in terms of forgone wine) is lower for Alpha than for Beta.

b. The marginal propensity to consume should decrease as income increases, and consequently, the average propensity to consume will decline. The empirical evidence does not support a decline in the average propensity to consume.

c. Current income plays a role in determining consumption, as do expectations of future income and future wealth.

d. Sticky wages and prices will render the economy unable to quickly reach long-run equilibrium. Businesses will not necessarily drop prices quickly, sell off inventory, or increase orders, nor will wages rapidly adjust downward to keep labor fully employed. Today, sticky prices and wages are still at the root of a lot of short-run theory, though other reasons have now been added to short-run analysis.

For the test, you should know that Keynesian economics influenced the debate over the role of fiscal policy in dealing with short-run fluctuations. You should also be familiar with the models for sticky prices and wages versus flexible prices and wages. The Keynesian premise is that the *main cause of short-run instability is the lack of spending*. In other words, it is a demand problem, and demand needs to be stimulated. The government is in the best position to stimulate demand through deficit spending if necessary.

Before Keynes, the prevailing theory of classical economists was based in part on Say's Law: *Supply creates its own demand*. This belief was founded on the notion that production created output that had value—and that this value would equal income. Therefore, the income would purchase the output, and the full-employment level of output would be sustained. One drawback to Say's Law was the problem of savings. If households did not use all of the income generated to buy back the output, then not all goods would be purchased, workers would become unemployed, and income would fall. But the classical economists responded by saying that the drop in demand caused by this situation would be offset by the following cycle:

a. Lower interest rates would occur, because the additional household savings would shift the supply of loanable funds to the right—leading to lower interest rates.

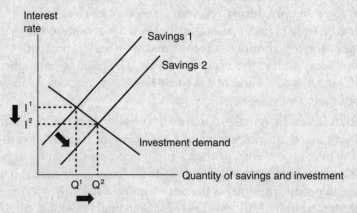

Loanable funds market

b. Lower interest rates would lead to an increase in the quantity of investment, which would offset the decrease in consumer demand.

c. Businesses who experienced a surplus of products would reduce prices, which would create an increase in consumer demand.

d. Workers who lost their jobs would be willing to take lower wages, which businesses would find profitable.

Thus, the mechanisms of lower interest rates and flexible wages and price would return the economy to full employment.

The problem with Say's Law, though, according to Keynes, was that the short run could last a significant amount of time. Prices and wages were sticky and did not quickly respond to short-run fluctuations. The demand for goods was dependent on *income*, not on production. He argued that lower interest rates alone would not necessarily lead to increased investment. If businessmen were pessimistic about the profitability of additional investment, they wouldn't necessarily respond to lower interest rates. Thus, there might not be investment to offset the demand gap created by less consumption (resulting from less income). Since households could not increase consumption with lower incomes, and businesses might not increase investment in response to lower interest rates, the economic equilibrium below full employment could last a long time.

Today, **investment** is no doubt the most volatile component of aggregate demand. Not only is it a product of interest rates and future profitability optimism, it's also a product of current profitability. Many businesses fund a good percentage of new investment with **retained earnings**, that is, those profits that do not get returned to stockholders (undistributed corporate profits). In times of recession and depression, most companies experience greatly diminished or even nonexistent corporate profits.

Keynes felt that government itself could provide the solution: By increasing its purchases, the government could create the additional demand needed to pull the economy back to full employment. In an economy experiencing unemployment, government could make the political decision to "deficit spend," in order to increase government purchases and thus, increase aggregate demand. Keynes called this **"priming the pump,"** as is done with a manual water pump: A water seeker puts a few cupfuls of water into the pump's vacuum to start the flow of water. Once the water begins to flow, there's no longer a need to continue priming the pump. Using the analogy for government intervention, creating demand through government purchases and tax reduction would get the flow of income going—which would lead to additional consumption and income.

When the economy is not at full employment, governments can increase spending to improve the economy. The **spending multiplier** is used to determine the effect of additional government purchases on the economy. If the marginal propensity to consume is .75, then the spending multiplier is 4 (1/1-.75). This means an additional $40 billion of government spending will lead to $160 billion of additional income. The **Keynesian Cross** (45 degree line) was used by the Keynesians to illustrate the impact of government spending on the economy, and though this model is not commonly seen in basic macroeconomic courses today, it is still worth knowing.

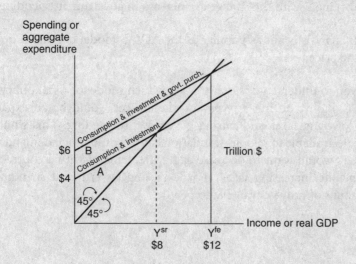

In the Keynesian model of government stimulus (also called the *aggregate expenditure* (AE) model), the Keynesian Cross is an important graph for students to grasp. The vertical axis is labeled *spending* or *aggregate expenditures*. The horizontal axis is labeled *income* or *real GDP*. The 45-degree line divides equally the axes that form a right triangle (90 degrees). So any point on the 45-degree line represents equilibrium, where spending equals income, or where aggregate expenditures equal real GDP. Lines A and B represent levels of aggregate expenditures. The line is sloped upward because of the consumption function $(X + {}_mY)$, where X is autonomous consumption, $_m$ is the marginal propensity to consume, and Y is income. The autonomous spending is illustrated where lines A and B intersect the vertical axis. The marginal propensity gives the slope of the aggregate expenditure line.

> During a recession, fiscal policymakers would want an expansionary fiscal policy to "stabilize" the economy. This type of policy would encourage more spending and boost the economy. If inflation caused by too much demand is the problem, they'd want to use a contractionary policy, which would reduce the level of demand in the economy, and help to reduce inflation.

In the example above, the aggregate expenditure line including consumption and investment has autonomous spending of $4 trillion and an equilibrium real GDP of $8 trillion. The full employment real GDP is $12 trillion. There is a recessionary gap of $4 trillion. Adding $2 trillion in government purchases (spending) brings us to the new equilibrium of $12 trillion that is full employment.

The reason why $2 trillion of additional autonomous spending creates $4 trillion of additional income and real GDP is because the spending multiplier is two. The change in real GDP (horizontal axis) divided by the change in aggregate expenditure (vertical axis) gives us the multiplier. Four divided by two equals two. If the multiplier is two, the marginal propensity to consume would be .5. In the example, we used line A with AE, including consumption and investment, and line B with AE, including consumption, investment, and government purchases. In fact, we could have used C + I + G for line A, and for line B with the change an increase in government spending.

Keynesian Cross analysis is not as popular as the AD/AS model because it does not account for changes in the price level.

What's key for you to understand is that if asked which model of fiscal policy could be used to stabilize the economy during a recession, the answer would be an expansionary fiscal policy, such as lowering taxes and raising government spending. This would increase the amount of income available to people. If inflation cause by too much demand is the problem, then policymakers would want to decrease aggregate demand with a contractionary policy, which would include increasing taxes and decreasing government spending. This would decrease the amount of money available to people.

	Policy	Policy	Goal
Expansionary	Increase G spending	Decrease taxes	Fight recession
Contractionary	Decrease G spending	Increase taxes	Fight inflation

Let's look at it another way. Which of the following fiscal policies would have the greatest effect on income—a $10 billion increase in government purchases or a $10 billion decrease in taxes? Answer: the increase in government purchases, because that would create a $10 billion increase in spending in the initial round, before the spending multiplier kicked in. The $10 billion tax decrease would lead to *less* initial spending. If the marginal propensity to consume were .9, then the $10 billion tax cut would lead to a $9 billion increase in spending in the initial round before the spending multiplier kicks in.

Government Spending Multiplier = 1/1 - MPC or 1/.1 = 10

Tax Cut Multiplier = MPC/1 - MPC or .9/.1 = 9

Note: As was mentioned at the beginning of this chapter, there's a danger of "crowding out," if, during a recession, the government starts with a balanced budget but then engages in an expansionary fiscal policy. Tax revenues are down during a recession, so unless a surplus exists, an increase in government spending would have to be financed by borrowing.

Automatic Stabilizers

We have just discussed how the government can pursue expansionary or contractionary policies to fight recession or inflation. These are **discretionary policies**. These are not the only ways to fight recession: There are other ways, already built into the system. Two examples are:

- The existing tax rate
- Unemployment compensation

Suppose a business decides to cut back on production and lay off people after there has been a build-up of inventory. It reduces output by $10 billion, and soon income decreases by $10 billion. Will consumption decrease by $10 billion? No! If the tax rate were 20 percent, then disposable income drops by $8 billion. Already we see that consumption will not drop by as much as the drop in output.

Now suppose the government will send $2 billion in unemployment compensation to the laid-off workers. The decrease in disposable income becomes $6 billion. Output decreased by $10 billion, but demand decreased by $6 billion. This will ease the downward cycle and keep the recession from becoming more severe.

FISCAL POLICY AND THE AD/AS MODEL

For the AP exam, you will be expected to analyze the effects of fiscal policy by using AD/AS graphs. Let's look at how we should illustrate expansionary and contractionary fiscal policies.

Fiscal Policy and the Short Run

If government elects to increase G and/or cut taxes, that will increase disposable income and thus, consumption, and the aggregate demand will increase. The graph below illustrates the effect of an **expansionary fiscal policy**.

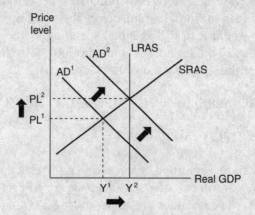

Remember, an increase in C, I, G, or NX will increase aggregate demand, shifting the AD curve right, from AD^1 to AD^2. Output will increase from Y^1 to Y^2. Unemployment will decrease as more workers are hired to produce the added output. The price level will rise to PL^2 from PL^1.

In this case, the increase in aggregate demand shifted equilibrium to the long run. Given the information, it is not necessary to shift the aggregate demand all the way to long-run equilibrium. Shifting to the right is what is important. In either case, real GDP increases, and (in this graph), price level rises.

If the government pursued a **contractionary fiscal policy**, the aggregate demand would decrease in the short run, shifting the AD curve left. This will result in a decrease of real GDP, an increase in unemployment, and a decrease in the price level.

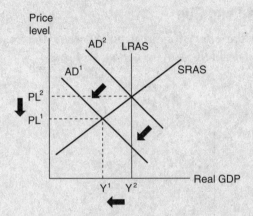

When using the short-run aggregate supply curve with three segments (where the horizontal segment is Keynesian, the upslope is intermediate, and the vertical is classical), we reach different conclusions, depending on how much to the right an expansionary fiscal policy shifts the AD curve. If we were in a severe recession and the economy were in short-run equilibrium at Y^1, an expansionary fiscal policy would shift the AD curve to the right. If you opt to show the increase in aggregate demand as a shift to AD^2 with equilibrium at Y^2, then the results are an increase in real GDP, an increase in employment (decrease in unemployment), and no change in the price level.

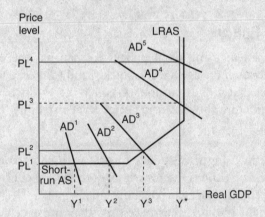

If, however, the increase in aggregate demand caused by an expansionary fiscal policy shifts from AD^1 to AD^3, real GDP shifts from Y^1 to Y^3. There's a resulting increase in real GDP and in employment. But we now also show an increase in price level, from PL^1 to PL^2. If the expansionary fiscal policy shifts the aggregate demand to AD^4 or AD^5, full employment equilibrium is restored, and there's an increase in both employment and price.

To illustrate a contractionary fiscal policy, we shift our AD curve left, from AD^4 to AD^3. In this case, we have a decrease in real GDP from Y^* to Y^3, which means we have a drop in employment and in price level. A contractionary fiscal policy that shifts the real GDP from Y^2 to Y^1 would illustrate a decrease in output and in employment, but no change in the price level.

Fiscal Policy and the Long Run

If we want to illustrate the effects of fiscal policy when the economy is already at full employment, we use a vertical long-run AS curve as follows:

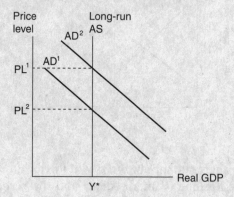

The graph above illustrates the long run equilibrium at Y^*. If the government pursues an expansionary fiscal policy, the AD curve will shift from AD^1 to AD^2. What is the result? Output and employment cannot increase because we began at the full-employment level. The only possibility is an increase in price level. The real GDP hasn't changed, but the nominal GDP has increased.

Criticisms of Fiscal Policy

Some people are opposed to using fiscal policy to "manage" the economy. They believe strongly that "flexible prices and wages" work quickly, and so there's no need to worry about the short run. They feel that any expansionary policy merely increases aggregate demand from AD^1 to AD^2 in the picture above, causing price-level instability. They are not supporters of demand-side policies.

Even those who believe in using fiscal policy to deal with short-run fluctuations must be concerned with *lag time*. **Lag time** is the time it takes to see the effect of fiscal policy once it has been decided. If the country faces a recession, and lawmakers decide that a stimulus (say, an increase in government purchases) is necessary, they must debate the issue, vote, and decide to put it into effect in the budget for the coming year. All of this takes time. If the economy self-corrected in the interim, the result of the expansionary policy would be inflation.

In examining the kind of impact fiscal policy will have in the long run, you must first remember that, whether expansionary or contractionary, fiscal policy will shift the AD curve in the short run. Some fiscal policy may have long-run implications. If the government decides to increase spending on training and education, it can be argued that this would increase human capital and human productivity. Increases in productivity shift the long-run aggregate supply curve to the right.

It could also be argued that increases in government funding of research and development or in the infrastructure of the economy would increase productivity shifting the long run aggregate supply curve to the right.

Fiscal policy that reduces business taxes or creates investment tax credits could also shift the AS curve to the right, as long it encouraged investment which included an increase in the capital stock of the economy.

KEY IDEAS

- Fiscal policy is government's policy on increasing or decreasing government purchases and taxes. This type of policy may be used to alleviate short-run fluctuations, but there are different opinions on the efficacy of using it for the long-run.

- Changing G and taxes are discretionary policies. On the other hand, automatic stabilizers are part of the existing system and are not discretionary: They serve as a governor on recessionary or inflationary pressures.

- Expansionary fiscal policies increase G or decrease taxes, shifting the AD curve to the right. Contractionary policies decrease G or increase taxes, shifting the AD curve to the left. When graphing, fiscal policy effects determine the impact on real GDP, unemployment, and price level.

- Government spending for goods and services affects the G component of aggregate demand.

- Government must pay for purchases and transfer payments by collecting taxes. If tax revenues are less than government spending, then the government budget has a deficit. If tax revenues exceed government spending, then the government budget has a surplus. If the government spending equals the tax revenues, than the budget is balanced.

- Government debt is the accumulated deficits over all the years of budgets, minus any payment toward the debt. Government deficits can lead to the crowding out effect.

- Today, wages and prices are considered sticky in the short run and flexible in the long run.

- The government spending multiplier is greater than the tax cut multiplier in the short run.

- The Keynesian Cross graph can be used to illustrate the effects of autonomous spending and the multiplier effect.

REVIEW QUESTIONS

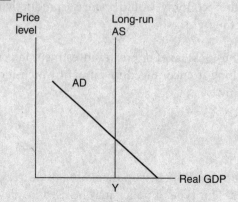

1. If an economy begins in long-run equilibrium as in the illustration above, an increase in government expenditures will have what effect on long-run equilibrium?

   (A) No effect
   (B) Increase in the price level
   (C) Decrease in the price level
   (D) Increase in output
   (E) Decrease in aggregate output

2. Suppose that taxes decrease by $100 billion. If everything else stays constant and the marginal propensity to consume is 0.8, the value of equilibrium output increases by

   (A) $100 billion
   (B) $80 billion
   (C) $500 billion
   (D) $320 billion
   (E) $400 billion

3. Which of the following does not characterize the classical view of the economy?

   (A) An economy automatically moves to equilibrium at the full-employment level of GDP.
   (B) Prices and wage variations are the mechanisms for short-run adjustments leading to long-run equilibrium.
   (C) The economy will stay out of equilibrium only for short periods.
   (D) The level of production determines the short-run economic equilibrium.
   (E) Prices and wages do not automatically adjust in the short run.

4. When an economy is on the flat segment of the AS curve, then

   (A) increases in real GDP can occur only with correspondingly large increases in the economy's price level.
   (B) real GDP can increase with very little or no effect on the economy's price level.
   (C) the price level and real GDP will be unaffected if aggregate demand changes.
   (D) there is a negative relationship between real GDP and the price level.
   (E) the price level can increase without affecting real GDP.

5. In the section of the AS curve with a somewhat upward slope (the intermediate range), when aggregate demand increases,

   (A) both real GDP and the price level rise.
   (B) real GDP increases, but the price level does not change.
   (C) real GDP decreases, and the price level rises.
   (D) real GDP increases, and the price level falls.
   (E) there is no change in real GDP or the price level.

6. An expansionary fiscal policy would be the one that

   (A) lowers both government spending and taxes.
   (B) raises both government spending and taxes.
   (C) raises government spending and/or lowers taxes.
   (D) raises tax rates.
   (E) lowers government spending.

7. Aggregate demand reflects the willingness and capability of which of the following, to purchase a quantity of goods and services at any price level?

   (A) Households
   (B) Households and businesses
   (C) Households and government
   (D) Households, businesses, and government
   (E) Households, businesses, government, and foreign consumers

8. An increase in the price level will

   (A) Increase demand
   (B) Increase employment
   (C) Shift aggregate demand to the left
   (D) Decrease the quantity demanded
   (E) Increase aggregate supply

9. An increase in investment will lead to economic growth if it includes

   (A) An increase in replacement investment
   (B) An increase in inventories
   (C) An increase in new housing
   (D) An increase in the money supply
   (E) An increase in the capital stock

10. Sticky price theory in the short run supports

    (A) A vertical supply curve
    (B) A negatively sloped demand curve
    (C) A horizontal or upward sloping supply curve
    (D) Self-correcting mechanisms
    (E) Full employment GDP

11. Keynesian economists believe that short-run fluctuations are caused by

    (A) flexible prices and wages.
    (B) too much profit.
    (C) a lack of sufficient aggregate demand.
    (D) a surplus of aggregate supply.
    (E) too little inventory.

12. During a period of demand-pull inflation, fiscal policymakers should

    (A) cut taxes and increase G spending.
    (B) cut taxes and decrease G spending.
    (C) raise taxes and increase G spending.
    (D) raise taxes and decrease G spending.
    (E) increase the money supply.

Free-Response Questions

1. The economy is currently experiencing eight percent unemployment. The government currently has a balanced budget. Using a sticky price model,

   (a) Draw an AS and AD graph that illustrates this situation.

   (b) Identify two policies that fiscal policy makers could pursue to address the situation and explain how each would change the status of the economy.

   (c) Explain how the policy could affect investment.

2. The economy is currently experiencing an eight percent unemployment rate and a nine percent inflation rate.

   (a) Describe the above economic condition and illustrate it with a correctly labeled graph.

   (b) Identify two policies that fiscal policy makers could pursue to address the situation and explain how each would change the status of the economy.

   (c) Explain how the policy could affect the long-run aggregate supply.

ANSWERS TO REVIEW QUESTIONS

1. (B)

An increase in government spending, G, will increase aggregate demand. This will cause a rise in the price level, but not an increase in output in the long run. An output increase is possible in the short run, but in the long run it's not. In the long run, the economy returns to the full-employment level of output. Graphically, this is a shift of the AD curve to the right. In the long run, the economy adjusts to the full-employment level of RGDP, where the new AD curve intersects the LRAS curve at a higher price level.

2. (E)

$400 billion. The value of equilibrium output will increase by $400 billion. To figure the increase in output, you first need to calculate the tax multiplier by using the MPC. When MPC is equal to 0.8 the tax multiplier will be equal to MPC/(1 – MPC) = 0.8/(1 – 0.8) = 4.

3. (E)

Prices and wages do not automatically adjust in the short run. The classical view says two things: prices and wages automatically adjust to create equilibrium, and equilibrium is determined by the quantity of production the economy is capable of. Classical economists believe the economy automatically adjusts to full employment. Their argument depends on the flexibility of prices and wages. In a world where prices and wages are completely flexible, everything produced will be purchased. Except for short-term fluctuations in the economy, the economy automatically moves to equilibrium at the full-employment level of GDP.

4. (B)

Real GDP can increase with little or no effect on the economy's price level. Let's see what happens when aggregate demand increases in the flat segment of the AS curve. Suppose aggregate demand increases. This is shown as a shift of the AD curve to the right. The new equilibrium point is to the right of the original equilibrium. The equilibrium level of real GDP increases, but is there any significant change in the price level? The price level increases only slightly, but real GDP increases a lot. When we're on the flat segment of the AS curve, an increase in spending will cause a large increase in real GDP, but only a small increase in the price level. Therefore the flat segment of the aggregate supply curve shows that real GDP can increase without affecting the economy's price level significantly.

5. (A)

Both real GDP and the price level rise. (B) and (E) are wrong because in the intermediate segment of the AS curve, a change in the AD affects both the price level and the real GDP. (C) and (D) are wrong because in the middle segment of the AS curve, a change in the AD affects both the price level and the real GDP in the same direction.

6. (C)

An expansionary fiscal policy would be one that raises government spending and/or lowers taxes. If the government spends more money, it's buying more goods and services. Those purchases create income for the sellers. These sellers then turn around and purchase other goods and services, which creates more income, and so on. Increases in spending create increases in real GDP. Lowering taxes is also expansionary. If the government decreases taxes, households will have more income to buy goods and services. If households pay less in taxes, they'll have more disposable income. They buy more, so there is more income for others, and even more spending, and so on. Therefore decreases in taxes increase real GDP. (A) is wrong because lowering government spending is contrary to expansionary fiscal policy. (B) is wrong because raising taxes isn't expansionary. If taxes increase, the government is taking away the ability to buy goods and services from the households. If households pay more in taxes, they have less disposable income. Therefore they buy less, so there is less income for others, and even less spending, and so on. Similarly, (D) is out. And (E) is wrong because it is a contractionary policy.

7. (E)

The components of aggregate demand include all the sectors of the economy.

8. (D)

An increase in the price level will decrease the quantity demanded.

9. (E)

Investment can include increases in inventories, replacement capital, and new housing, but none of these will lead to economic growth (shift to the right of the long run aggregate supply curve). Only if the increase in Investment leads to an increase in the capital stock (net result more factories or equipment), will it mean economic growth.

10. (C)

Sticky prices and wages are associated with the short run, and that means an aggregate supply curve that is either horizontal or upward sloping but not vertical. (A), the vertical supply curve is associated with the long run and flexible prices and wages. (B), a downward sloping demand curve is associated with either the short run or the long run and the shape of the demand curve does not change whether we are dealing with sticky or flexible prices and wages.

11. (C)

Keynesian economics is demand side economics. According to Keynes, short-run instability is caused by a lack of aggregate demand.

12. (D)

If fiscal policymakers wanted to curb inflation caused by too much aggregate demand, they would decrease the aggregate demand by increasing taxes (reducing consumption) and decreasing government purchases.

Free-Response Questions

1.

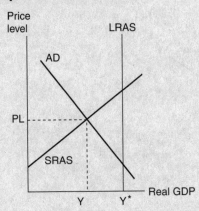
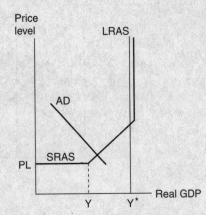

(a) Either graph above would represent the economy's equilibrium described in the question. Eight percent unemployment indicates that the economy is not at full employment. There may not be any precise identification of what the full employment unemployment rate should be, but between five and six percent is a pretty good benchmark. Clearly eight percent unemployment would include some cyclical unemployment. The current equilibrium is Y and this must be stated. In order to clearly show that the economy is in a short-run equilibrium, the long-run equilibrium should be shown on the graph. The presence of the long-run AS and the long-run equilibrium Y* illustrates this correctly.

(b) Two policies would be (i) Cut taxes, which would increase disposable income and thus, consumption. This will increase aggregate demand, and shift the aggregate demand curve to the right—increasing total output and employment. (ii) Increase government purchases. This would increase aggregate demand, shifting the curve to the right—increasing total output and employment.

(c) Since the budget is currently in balance, a decrease in tax revenues or an increase in government expenditures would lead to a budget deficit. It is possible to argue that an increase in government borrowing resulting from the deficit would "crowd out" the private sector by increasing the short-run interest rates. This would discourage investment. It is also possible to argue that despite the higher interest rates, the fiscal policies could encourage business optimism and investment, because the projected cash flows would outweigh the higher interest rates.

2.

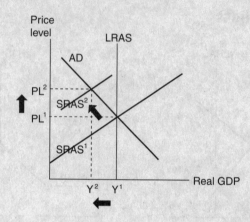

(a) The economic condition described is stagflation. Both the unemployment rate and the inflation rate are problematic. The above is a correctly labeled graph, or you could use a three-segment short-run AS curve. The short-run AS curve has shifted to the left, creating the condition of stagflation. As you write out an answer like this, you must make it clear that Y^2 represents the condition described.

(b) Government must use policies that would shift the short-run AS curve to the right. Reducing business taxes would be one possibility, since they would decrease the cost of production, shifting the short-run AS curve right. Reducing government regulations that are costly to production would also work.

(c) If the government policies also encouraged increased net investment in the capital stock of the country, it would also shift the long-run AS curve to the right.

Money and Monetary Policy

CHAPTER SEVEN

Money. What is it? We have all been using money since we were children, yet most of us don't fully understand what it is. Sure, having it is a good thing. The more money we have, the more goods and services we can get, and the more investments we can make. But is it the *amount* of money that counts or is it the claim on goods and services or resources? Given our basic understanding of economics, we know that what's important is the claims on goods, services, or resources. If we have $100 and it costs us $100 for groceries for the week, are we less well off than we would be if we had $200 and it cost $200 for weekly groceries? No! The only change is in the nominal values.

We value money:

- For what it can buy us
- Because it gives us an understanding of relative value through the pricing system
- Because it facilitates transactions

Without money, the economy would have to depend on barter. **Barter** depends on the exchange of one good or service for another good or service—trade without the use of money. In an economic exchange, it would require our finding someone who had what we wanted, and who wanted what we had. In other words, a **coincidence of wants**. Imagine how few economic activities would occur if this were the case. It is much easier to work for a day's pay and then take the money to buy groceries than it is to find someone who wants our labor and has groceries to exchange for it.

MONEY

Money has three functions: medium of exchange, unit of account, and store of value. When money is used as a **medium of exchange**, it is replacing the barter system. We exchange a day's labor for a day's pay—not for groceries. The grocer sells us groceries for a certain amount of money. No coincidence of wants is needed.

As a **unit of account**, money is used to determine relative prices. If we're paid $100 for a day's labor, and groceries for a week cost us $100, we understand that weekly groceries are equivalent to a day's labor. If a winter coat is $100, we understand that a day's labor, a week's groceries, and a winter coat all have the same value. We use prices expressed in terms of money to give us information of the relative value of resources and output.

The use of money as a **store of value** refers to the fact that we can postpone some exchanges. Instead of bartering a day's labor for groceries, we can take the value of our labor for a day in the form of money and exchange that at later date for groceries. Of course, this works best when prices are stable. If, in July, we exchange a day's labor for $100 and "store" the $100 to buy groceries in November, but prices then double so that it costs $200 for the same groceries that were $100 in July—we have a problem.

> When referring to a dollar, the term *buck* comes from colonial times, when one buckskin sold for a Spanish dollar. When dollars were scarce, people used deer pelts.

There are two types of money that we need to be aware of. **Commodity money** is money that has an intrinsic value. Gold as currency is one example, as a precious metal that has value. People want it because they can use it in jewelry, among other things. **Fiat money** is used today. A fiat is a decree by government that orders some rule into effect. Today, that decree says that paper money is to be accepted as a medium of exchange. It is accepted because the government has decreed it to be money. After all, a one-hundred dollar bill has very little intrinsic value. (What else can it be used for?)

Money Supply

One of the main goals of the economy is price stability. We do not want too much inflation or deflation affecting the purchasing power of the dollar, because that creates havoc with the pricing system that efficiently coordinates economic activity. We have already established that the value of money is what you can buy with it, so we can see a relationship between the money supply and the real gross domestic product.

But how do we define money supply? Is it just the cash in circulation? Money in checking accounts? Money in bank accounts?

We measure different types of money by their **liquidity**; that is, how soon they can be converted to cash. The term *cash* here means any form of money that can be spent immediately, whether it's dollar bills or checks. When talking about liquidity, we'll hear terms such as near money, types of money stock, and money aggregates. But when analyzing the money supply, we must focus on specific types of money. Some definitions:

M1: Currency in circulation, demand deposits (checking accounts), and traveler's checks

M2: Everything in M1 plus small saving accounts and money market accounts

M3: Everything in M2 plus large time deposits and repurchase agreements

> *Liquidity* measures how easily an asset can be turned into cash without significant loss of value. Currency can be used immediately, so it is liquid.

The list can go on to M4, M5, M6 and so on. As we go from M1 and M2 to additional levels, we are adding near monies that are less liquid. In other words, it takes more time to convert them to cash.

At the principles level, we can focus on M1 and M2 as the components of money supply. For analysis, we can simply refer to the *money supply*.

The money supply of a country is controlled by its central bank. If the central bank is independent and is free from political pressure, it can exercise its prerogative. If it is not independent, then it will be subject to more political pressure in terms of controlling the money supply.

The Central Bank

In the United States, the central bank is the **Federal Reserve (the Fed)**, located in Washington, D.C. There are 12 banks in the Federal Reserve system, located across the country. The **Board of Governors**, with seven members, administers the Fed; each member is appointed by the U.S. president and approved by the U.S. Senate. Governors serve for a 14-year nonrenewable period, and terms are staggered so that a new person is appointed every two years. This committee is responsible for the money supply policies and the banking system.

One member of the Board of Governors is selected by the president to serve as chairperson. The chair is the principle spokesperson and has significant influence over policy.

The **Federal Open Market Committee** (**FOMC**) is made up of the Board of Governors members and five of the presidents of the Federal Reserve banks. It is this committee that establishes monetary policy and directs open market operations (the buying and selling of government bonds).

The Fed does not print currency. Rather, it assures that there are sufficient amounts in circulation to meet the needs of the economy. It does this by:

- Controlling the money supply
- Clearing checks
- Supervising and regulating banks
- Controlling the availability of currency
- Serving as the bank for the government

Money Demand

> Do not confuse credit cards with money. Credit cards are a form of debt, not money. Debit cards, on the other hand, are a form of money. They're just like checks. Using a debit card means money is taken from your checking account for payment.

There are various reasons that people want to hold money in their wallets or in their checking accounts. We have already noted that money is a medium of exchange. As such, people need it to pay bills and to take care of "out-of-pocket" expenses like movies, dinners, and gifts. In this manner, it is for a **transaction demand**. People also keep money on hand for possible emergencies. This is for **precautionary demand**.

Lastly, people hold money as a store of value. People may not want to put all their wealth into stocks and bonds at one given time, preferring to keep some money on hand so they can purchase investments at a better time in the future. This is for **speculative demand**.

We can graph the money market as follows:

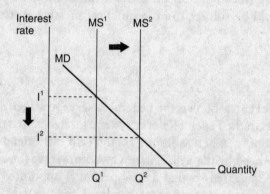

The opportunity cost of holding money is the **interest rate**. If the interest rate is high, people will have a higher opportunity cost of holding money. The quantity of money will decrease. As interest rates go down, the opportunity cost of holding money is less and the quantity demanded is more.

If the supply of money is increased, then the money supply curve (MS^1) will shift right to MS^2, and the interest rate will fall from I^1 to I^2. The money supply is vertical because it is the quantity of money supplied by the Federal Reserve at a given time, and as such is assumed to be fixed.

Money Creation and Fractional Reserve Banking

How is money created? In addition to currency that is printed by the government and put into circulation by the Fed, money is created through the **fractional reserve banking** system. When banks receive a deposit from a customer, they will keep some of that money in reserve and lend the balance. Banks are required to keep a certain amount in **required reserves (RR)**. Any additional reserves are **excess reserves**.

To understand the fractional reserve banking system we need to understand a **T account**. The T account is a basic tool of accounting. Shaped like a T, it divides transactions into two columns: The column on the left is for assets, and the column on the right is for liabilities and equity. Every transaction requires an entry in the left column and in the right column. This is called **double-entry accounting**.

Let's follow a $10,000 customer deposit. We'll assume a 10 percent reserve requirement. The T account for the bank will look like this:

Assets	Liabilities
• Required reserves $1,000 • Excess reserves $9,000	• Checkable deposits $10,000

The bank will now have a liability to the customer of $10,000. It will also have required reserves of $1,000 and excess reserves of $9,000. It can choose to make a loan of $9,000 with the excess reserves. Let's take a look at what happens if the bank makes that loan.

Assets	Liabilities
• Required reserves $1,000 • Excess reserves $ 0 • Loans $9,000	• Checkable deposits $10,000

Now, what happens to the $9,000 that is lent to another customer? Let's assume that that customer deposits the $9,000 into her bank and creates the following change in the T account for that bank:

Assets	Liabilities
• Required reserves $ 900 • Excess reserves $ 0 • Loans $8,100	• Checkable deposits $9,000

We have assumed that the bank has made loans with the full additional $8,100 available from excess reserves. This process will continue in the **banking system** (all of the individual banks) until there is no more to lend from the initial deposit. We can calculate the entire amount of money created from the initial deposit by using the **banking** or **money multiplier** formula:

$$\text{Money Multiplier} = \frac{1}{\text{Reserve Requirement}}$$

Our reserve requirement is 10 percent. The money multiplier is $1/.1 = 10$. The initial deposit of $10,000 will lead to a total of $100,000 in money supply.

Bonds are not money: They are I.O.U.'s. As a rule, consumers do not purchase groceries with bonds: They use currency or checks.

Now here's where we need to be careful: Since the original $10,000 was already a part of the money supply, the additional amount of money created by the banking system is $100,000 minus the original $10,000. In other words, $ 90,000.

If the original $10,000 came from the Fed, then the total amount of money created would be $10,000. That's because money at the Fed is not part of the money supply.

The full force of the banking multiplier is dependent on two things. First, that banks do not keep any excess reserves. If excess reserves are kept, then all of the loans possible are not occurring. Second, it assumes that consumers deposit all of the money they borrow into another account. If they don't deposit it all, there will be less money for the banks to lend.

When one or both of the conditions are not met, the money supply won't increase as much as the simple money multiplier (1/RR) would indicate. Thus, the two **leakages from the money (banking) multiplier** are:

- Banks keeping excess reserves
- Borrowers keeping currency and not redepositing the amount of the loan.

Tools of the Fed

How does the Fed affect the money supply? By adding or subtracting money from the banking system. The Fed uses certain tools to conduct either an expansionary (easy money) policy or a contractionary (tight money) policy. These tools are: open market operations, discount rate, and the reserve requirement

When the government needs to borrow money, it issues bonds for the first time. The Fed itself will buy some of these bonds, and sell the rest to banks and individuals. These bonds then become marketable securities that can be bought and sold again. In addition to this initial float of government bonds, the Fed will buy and sell bonds in a secondary market. These are bonds that have already been issued, and now the bondholder—not the government—will receive the money from their sale.

1. **Open market operations** is the buying and selling of bonds by the Fed to increase or decrease the money supply, not to fund government debt. In other words, it is the purchase or sale of government securities by the Fed in the open market. When the Fed buys bonds from banks or other bondholders, it is introducing money into the money supply. If the banks use this money to create loans, then the money supply is affected by the original amount and the banking multiplier effect.

   When the Fed sells bonds to banks and other bondholders, it's taking money out of the money supply. The money multiplier can work both ways, expanding or contracting the money supply. The money supply will decrease by an amount greater than the total sale of bonds because of the money multiplier effect.

2. The **discount rate** is the rate of interest that the Fed charges banks for borrowing money. When this interest rate is low, banks are more inclined to borrow money and create loans to customers. When the discount rate is high, banks are less inclined to borrow money to create customer loans. So when the Fed wants to increase the money

supply, it will decrease the discount rate, encouraging banks to borrow money to put into the banking system. If the Fed wants to decrease money supply and discourage banks from borrowing, it will increase the discount rate.

3. The **reserve requirement (RR)** is the amount of required reserves that banks have to keep. The banking multiplier is 1/RR, so if the reserve requirement increased, it would dampen the multiplier effect. If it is decreased, it would increase the multiplier effect. For example, if the RR were 20 percent, the money multiplier would be 1/.2, or 5. If it were 10 percent, the money multiplier would be 1/.1, or 10.

Now let's see how the Fed can implement an expansionary money policy (increase the money supply) or a contractionary money policy (decrease the money supply).

	Expansionary	Contractionary
Open market operations	Buy bonds	Sell bonds
Discount rate	Lower the rate	Increase the rate
Reserve requirement	Lower the RR	Increase the RR

Of the three tools, the one most often used is open market operations. Least used is changing the reserve requirement. Keep in mind that while the Fed tries to influence the money supply, it's not a perfect science. There are still markets at work. Banks may choose not to lend excess reserves, and businesses/consumers may choose not to borrow. Banks are financial intermediaries, and disintermediation can occur when people choose to withdraw their money to hold more cash. Thus, the supply and demand of money can be affected by people's—and banks'—behavior.

MONETARY POLICY

Why would the Fed want to pursue an expansionary or contractionary monetary policy? One simple answer is that it may wish to deal with short-run fluctuations in the money supply, assuring some stability in the banking system.

A more complex motive for changing the money supply would be to promote growth in the gross domestic product or to fight impending inflation. Economists are not in agreement about whether the Fed should engage in activist stabilization policies. For our purposes here, we need to understand how the models work. *Should the Fed use discretionary decisions or should it follow a rule?*

First let's simplify the choices that the Fed has in determining the money supply. There are two choices: *Money aggregates*, or *interest rates*.

Money Aggregates

Money aggregates refer to the various definitions of money: M1, M2, and M3. The question here is, What percentage should the chosen aggregate change? One percent, two percent, three percent, etc.? Of course in determining the change, the central bank needs to decide on what it will base the decision. Will it be the potential GDP or some other nominal variable, such as nominal income? We don't have to worry about *which* variable at this juncture of our economic education. What we need to understand is the two main views on how the central bank should conduct policy.

Classical Theory of Monetary Policy

The classical economists believed that there was a clear connection between the money supply and prices. The classical position is that a change in money supply changes aggregate demand and that, in turn, affects prices, real GDP, and employment. However, this view, called the **classical transmission mechanism**, holds that flexible wages and prices will self-correct and automatically eliminate any recessions, and return the entire economy to long-run equilibrium (where output is at full employment). Therefore, increases in the money supply that are greater than the real growth rate will cause price levels to rise.

A good model to illustrate this effect is the **equation of exchange:**

$$M \times V = P \times Q$$

where M equals quantity of money, V equals velocity of money, P equals price level, and Q equals quantity of goods and services produced (real GDP).

Because Q represents the real GDP, you'll occasionally see this algebraic equation written as $M \times V = P \times Y$, since Y is the letter symbol used for income and output.

We can use M1 or M2 or any money aggregate to represent M. What we need to know is the significance of the equation of exchange and at this time not worry about which M is being used.

Velocity is the average number of times that a dollar is used to purchase final goods and services over a period of one year. We can solve for velocity with the following equation:

$$\text{Velocity} = \frac{\text{Nominal GDP } (P \times Q)}{\text{Money supply } (M)}$$

Price level is the same abstract idea of an average price of all goods and services that we use as the vertical axis of the AD/AS model.

The real variable in this equation is Q, the actual goods and services produced (real GDP). P times Q is the **nominal GDP**. We have already seen the classical view state that the economy would self-correct to full employment GDP. Therefore, any increase in the money supply would only lead to an increase in real GDP, to the extent that real growth in GDP was possible. Money supply changes that exceeded the potential growth rate of GDP would lead to inflation.

The classical position on equilibrium is that the self-correcting mechanism of flexible prices and wages will return equilibrium to the full-employment level. In other words, the long-run AS curve is the model to measure by. Not inconsistent with this was the idea that increasing the money supply beyond the potential for growth (a shift in the long-run AS curve to the right) could only increase prices. After all, if an economy is producing as much as it possibly can, what else can happen if the money supply increases? The **classical quantity theory of money** argues that velocity and real output are fairly constant. Therefore, changes in the money supply are directly related to changes in price level. It is one of the oldest theories on inflation.

Monetarist Theory of Monetary Policy

The *monetarists* (a subschool of the classical view) led by Milton Friedman, argued that Fed shouldn't focus on interest rates, but rather on a monetary policy that matched the money supply's growth rate to the potential growth rate in real GDP. This is an example of a **monetary rule**; it eliminates the Fed's discretion to change monetary policy in reaction to short-run instability problems. The monetarists claimed that while this rule wouldn't solve all short-run problems, it would prevent the central bank from adding to the problems, and at that point, the self-correcting mechanisms could take effect (flexible prices and wages).

If we look again at the equation of exchange, $M \times V = P \times Q$, we can see that monetarism is predicated on the fact that velocity (V) is constant. So if real GDP (Q) has the potential to grow at three percent, and the central bank increases (M) by three percent, then (P) does not change.

$$M \uparrow 3\% \times V^{constant} = P \times Q \uparrow 3\%$$

What if velocity isn't constant? Then pegging the money supply to potential growth can lead to unexpected problems. Changes in velocity can leave the money supply at less than desired and insufficient to keep the economy at full employment, or at more than desired and encourage inflation. In the short run, velocity is not constant. But is the short-run important? This goes back to the short run, sticky prices versus long run, flexible prices debate. We don't have to decide if the short run is important; we just have to know both sides of the argument. Remember that in the flexible prices and wages model, an increase in the money supply beyond the potential increase in growth will lead to inflation.

Whether the Fed should increase the money supply according to a rule or according to its own discretion (targeting interest rates) is a debate that continues. Not all of those who advocate the use of rules assume constant velocity or full employment. Some assert that it's predictable, and that money aggregates should be pegged to some variable such as potential GDP or nominal income.

Keynesian Theory of Monetary Policy

Keynesians believe that changes in the money supply affect the interest rates first, and that this in turn affects the aggregate demand. They explain the process in this way: A change in monetary policy leads to a change in money supply, which leads to a change in interest rates, which leads to a change in investment, which leads to a change in aggregate demand, which leads to a change in prices, and/or a change in real GDP, and employment. This is called the **keynesian transmission mechanism.**

Interest Rates

In the short run, the economy has a higher rate of unemployment and the economy is not producing at its potential. If one accepts that prices and wages are sticky and will not adjust quickly to return the economy to full employment, then one can argue that the central bank should try to stimulate the economy through monetary policy. This leads to the argument that the monetary policy should target interest rates. By using an expansionary monetary policy, the central bank will influence the interest rates downward. The lower interest rates will encourage more investment and more consumption, as it becomes less expensive to borrow money. Investment and consumption are components of aggregate demand. Thus, aggregate demand increases, and the economy moves to full employment. Of course, this works as long as investment is interest rate sensitive (in other words, if it responds to the lower interest rate). If it isn't sensitive to lower interest rates, then monetary policy will be less effective. It is possible that lower interest rates will not encourage additional investment.

The expansion of the money supply by the Fed will lower the interest rates, and if investment is interest rate sensitive, investment will increase. Aggregate demand will increase, which in turns increases real GDP and employment.

Using Monetary Policy to Counter a Recession

Monetary policy can be used to promote short-run stability. Graphically, it can be illustrated as follows:

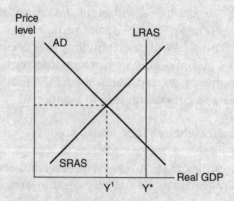

The economy here is producing at Y^1, which means that real output and employment are at less than Y^*, the full employment level. Can policymakers (the Fed) implement a policy that will correct this short-run problem? Yes, they can expand the money supply by buying bonds, lowering the discount rate, or lowering the reserve requirement. This increase in the money supply will lower the interest rates.

> The central bank's policies affect short-run, nominal interest rates. They do not impact long-run real rates. The **real rate** is the nominal rate minus the inflation rate; the long-run real rate of interest is determined by savings and investment.

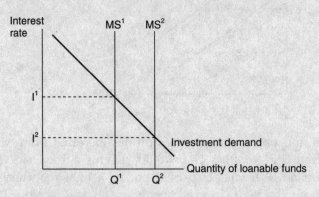

Loanable funds market

The Fed increases the money supply from MS^1 to MS^2. Interest rates fall from I^1 to I^2. At I^2, the quantity of investment demand increases. Note that the slope of the investment demand curve illustrates the investment sensitivity to interest rates. This is the elasticity of investment demand to changes in the interest rates.

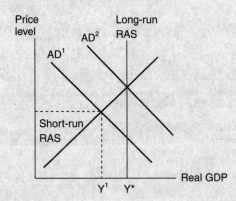

Investment increases aggregate demand, so the AD curve shifts right, from AD^1 to AD^2. Real output is increased and unemployment drops.

Using Monetary Policy to Counter Demand-Pull Inflation

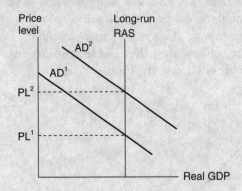

Here, we see demand-pull inflation. Aggregate demand has increased from AD^1 to AD^2, pulling the price level from PL^1 to PL^2. This would call for a monetary policy that discouraged aggregate demand. Policymakers would pursue a tight monetary policy: By contracting the money supply, interest rates would be driven up, and investment and some consumer demand would be discouraged.

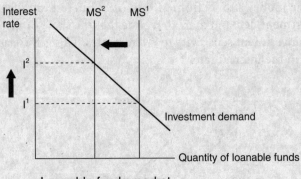

Loanable funds market

The money supply shifts from MS^1 to MS^2, increasing the interest rate from I^1 to I^2.

The effect of a contractionary monetary policy on aggregate demand and the price level would be as follows:

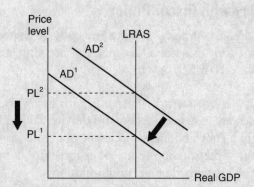

The higher interest rates shift the AD curve from AD^2 to AD^1. This reduces the price level from PL^2 to PL^1.

Stagflation

Stagflation is when there is low or negative real GDP growth, and high rates of inflation. In this situation, resolving the cost-push inflation is more difficult for monetary policymakers. Contractionary monetary policy will fight the upward pressures on price level, but will also increase unemployment. Expansionary monetary policy will increase employment, but will also increase inflationary pressures. Monetary policy is not effective at dealing with stagflation. To combat stagflation, it is necessary to have policies that will shift the AS curve to the right, because that increases employment and decreases the price level. This is what is needed to offset the dual problems of stagflation.

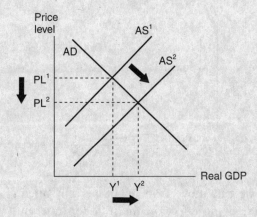

Government policies that reduce the cost of business—such as lowering corporate taxes or reducing costly regulations imposed on business by the government—can help to eliminate stagflation.

So far, we have looked at monetary policy and its impact on interest rates, real output, and prices. In open economies, the monetary policy can also affect the currency exchange rate. We'll look at that in the next unit.

Using Monetary Policy with Fiscal Policy

In the last chapter we looked at fiscal policy. You will be expected to understand the implications when *both* fiscal and monetary policies are implemented. They can work together or they can offset each other.

What if the central bank were concerned that an expansionary fiscal policy would lead to inflation? To offset the increase in aggregate demand that would result from this type of fiscal policy, it could implement a contractionary monetary policy. In doing this, the central bank would be discouraging some components of aggregate demand (investment and consumption), thus minimizing any demand-pull inflation.

If the **monetary policymakers** wanted to support the expansionary fiscal policy, they could pursue an expansionary monetary policy. This would also prevent the crowding-out effect. As the government borrows money to finance the expansionary fiscal policy, the central bank increases the money supply to offset the increased demand in the loanable funds market, keeping the interest rates from rising too much.

The Phillips Curve

The Phillips Curve is a model used to illustrate the trade-off between inflation and unemployment. The Phillips Curve illustrates that, as fiscal policies are used to eliminate unemployment, there comes a point where additional reductions in unemployment create more and more inflation.

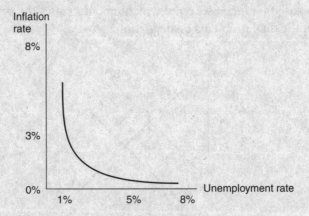

In the example above, we can move from eight percent unemployment to five percent unemployment, with little or no effect on the inflation rate. But as we try to reduce the unemployment rate beyond this point, we encounter significant increases in the inflation rate. You'll see here that there's a short-run trade off between unemployment and inflation. In the long run, there is no trade off, because in the long run, the economy is at full employment. So any policy that would increase aggregate demand would not create more employment—only a greater inflation rate.

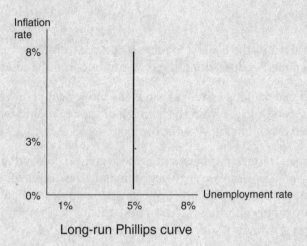

Long-run Phillips curve

The Phillips Curve model is controversial. Not all economists accept this trade-off. Nonetheless, it is a model that you will be expected to know for the AP exam.

There are two other theories on the effectiveness of fiscal and monetary policies: the *Rational Expectations Theory* and the *Adaptive Expectations Theory*. These theories are consistent with the flexible prices and wages model, stating that since the economy self-corrects, fiscal and monetary policies are somewhat futile.

The **Rational Expectations Theory** is based on the belief that people have access to information and so can predict—and respond to—monetary and fiscal policies, before they have an effect. As a result, the macroeconomic effects of these policies are negated. In other words, if people expect that expansionary policies will affect the price level, workers will demand higher wages and businesses will increase prices. Therefore, employment will not be affected—only the price level.

The **Adaptive Expectations Theory** argues that people base their expectations on past experience. If they have experienced inflation in the recent past, they'll expect it to continue, and base price and wage demands accordingly. This leads people to overestimate inflation if it is decreasing, and underestimate inflation if it is increasing. The result is that policies will affect price level, but not unemployment.

Monetary policy affects aggregate demand in the short run. But if the increase in money supply leads to increased investment which includes an increase in the capital stock, then the long-run aggregate supply curve will also shift to the right. This is economic growth.

KEY POINTS

- The central bank (the Federal Reserve Bank) controls the money supply with three tools: open market operations, the discount rate, and the reserve requirement.

- The fractional banking system expands the money supply. The banking multiplier is 1/RR. The two leakages from the banking or money multiplier are: Banks keeping excess reserves and borrowers not redepositing all the money borrowed.

- Expansionary monetary policies increase aggregate demand and contractionary monetary policies decrease aggregate demand. Classical theory had changes in money supply directly affecting aggregate demand. Keynesian theory has changes in the money supply affecting interest rates, which affect investment (depending on investment sensitivity), which affects aggregate demand.

- The quantity of money demand is determined by the interest rate. Money demand is influenced by the transaction demand, precautionary demand, and speculative demand.

- The central bank can target money aggregates in terms of a steady growth or it can target interest rates. Targeting interest rates is still part of the Fed strategy.

- The equation of exchange is : $M \times V = P \times Q$. The problem with the Quantity Theory of Money is its dependence on velocity being stable. In the short run, velocity is not stable. Velocity is equal to the nominal GDP divided by the money supply.

- Monetarists believe that the central bank should pursue a steady increase in the money supply that is commensurate with the potential growth of real GDP. That way, the central bank will avoid creating problems and the self-correcting mechanism will function better. Do not confuse monetarists with people who make monetary policy.

- Monetary policy can be used to offset fiscal policy, or, in coordination with fiscal policy, can eliminate the crowding-out affect.

- Expansionary monetary policies can be used to fight unemployment. Contractionary monetary policies can be used to fight inflation.

REVIEW QUESTIONS

1. Which of the following is not one of the tools of monetary policy?

   (A) The required reserve ratio
   (B) Government spending
   (C) The discount rate
   (D) Open market operations
   (E) All of the above are tools of monetary policy.

2. According to the quantity theory of money,

   (A) the Fed must be very careful when using monetary policy to determine the level of production.
   (B) the Fed has absolute control over the level of production.
   (C) the Fed has no control over the level of production.
   (D) the Fed has no control over the price level.
   (E) prices and output are determined by the Fed.

3. The Fed could implement a contractionary monetary policy by

   (A) Increasing the money supply
   (B) Lowering the required reserve ratio
   (C) Buying T-bonds
   (D) Increasing the discount rate
   (E) None of the above

4. If Maria takes money from her savings account to buy a T-bond from Jody, that is

   (A) an example of expansionary monetary policy.
   (B) an example of contractionary monetary policy.
   (C) an example of neutral (neither expansionary nor contractionary) policy.
   (D) the same as the Fed buying bonds.
   (E) an expansionary fiscal policy.

5. Of the three tools of monetary policy, which one is preferred for changing the money supply?

   (A) Required reserve ratio
   (B) Discount rate
   (C) Open market operations
   (D) Each of the tools is used equally.
   (E) There are no tools that can affect the money supply.

6. If the Fed wanted to increase the money supply, it can

   (A) Sell T-bonds
   (B) Increase the discount rate
   (C) Increase the required reserve ratio
   (D) All of the above will increase the amount of money in the economy.
   (E) None of the above will increase the amount of money in the economy.

7. If the nominal interest rate is eight percent and the inflation rate is five percent, then the real interest rate is:

(A) 8 percent
(B) 5 percent
(C) 13 percent
(D) 3 percent
(E) −3 percent

8. If the economy begins at long-run equilibrium, which of the following graphs depicts the effects of contractionary monetary policy using Keynesian analysis?

(A)

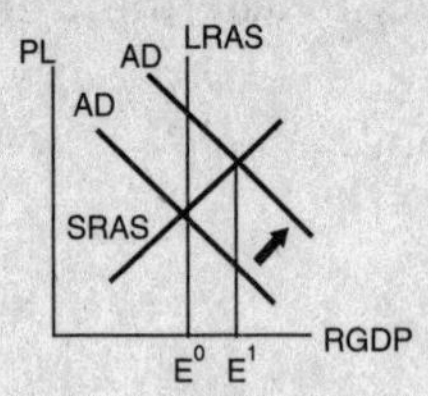

(B)

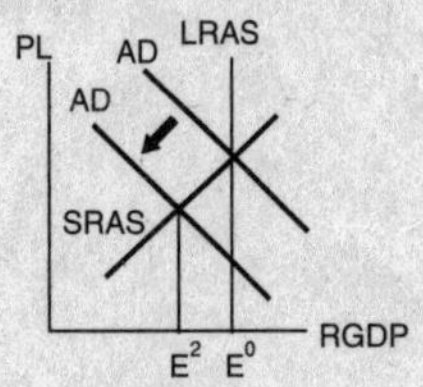

(C)

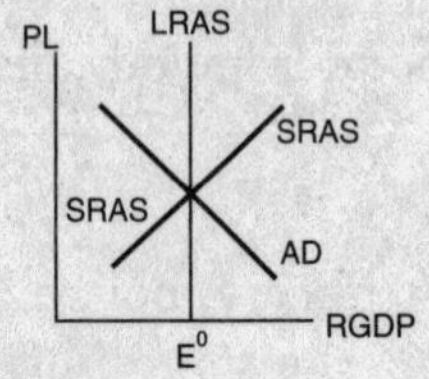

(D)

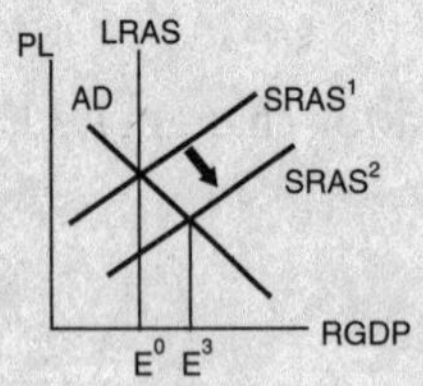

(E)

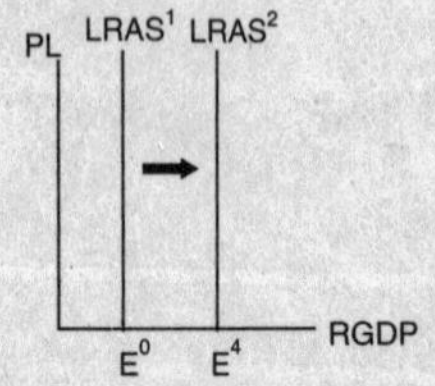

9. To induce a three percent growth rate in the economy, monetarists believe that the money supply should be

    (A) decreased by three percent per year.
    (B) kept constant.
    (C) increased by less than three percent per year.
    (D) increased by three percent per year.
    (E) increased by more than three percent per year.

10. Suppose last year's inflation rate was five percent, but Wall Street analysts expect this year's interest rate to be four percent. Which of the following correctly describes people's beliefs according to rational or adaptive expectations theories?

    (A) According to rational expectations, people will anticipate five percent inflation this year.
    (B) According to adaptive expectations, people will anticipate four percent inflation this year.
    (C) According to rational expectations, people will anticipate one percent inflation this year.
    (D) According to adaptive expectations, people will anticipate one percent inflation this year.
    (E) According to rational expectations, people will anticipate four percent inflation.

11. Monetary policy is least effective in dealing with the problems of

    (A) Inflation
    (B) Unemployment
    (C) Hyperinflation
    (D) Stagflation
    (E) Deflation

12. Assume that the reserve requirement is 20 percent and banks have no excess reserves. The Fed wants to increase the money and buys $100 million in bonds from bondholders. If, as the bondholders deposit this money into banks, the banks decide to keep excess reserves, the money supply will increase by

    (A) Less than $100 million
    (B) $500 million
    (C) More than $500 million
    (D) Less than $500 million
    (E) $600 million

Free-Response Questions

1. Suppose that the real GDP has remained constant and the unemployment rate is eight percent.

    (a) Draw a graph illustrating the economy.
    (b) What central bank policy would address this problem.
    (c) Show on your graph how this policy would affect the economy.
    (d) Explain the effect that this policy would have on the price level.
    (e) Explain two tools that the Fed could use to implement this policy.

2. Suppose that the economy is at full employment but is experiencing nine percent inflation.

    (a) Draw a graph illustrating the economy.
    (b) What central bank policy would address this problem?
    (c) Show on your graph how this policy would affect the economy.
    (d) Explain the effect that this policy would have on the unemployment rate.
    (e) Explain two tools that the Fed could use to implement this policy.

3. Let's say the government decides to pursue an expansionary fiscal policy that would threaten private investment.

    (a) Using a graph of the loanable funds market, explain why this might happen.
    (b) Explain what the central bank could do to support the fiscal policy and minimize the negative effect on private investment.
    (c) Illustrate your answer to (b) on the graph you did for part (a).

ANSWERS TO REVIEW QUESTIONS

1. (B)

Government spending is an aspect of fiscal policy. The three tools of monetary policy are: the required reserve ratio, the discount rate, and open market operations.

2. (C)

According to the quantity theory of money, there is a natural rate of production. Monetary policy has no effect on this level and only affects the price level. Therefore, quantity theorists don't support the use of monetary policy. The theory suggests that the Fed has no control over the level of production, only the price level, so (A) and (B) are wrong. (D) is the opposite of what is true: Quantity theorists believe the level of output is determined by forces beyond the control of the Fed.

3. (D)

The discount rate acts as a penalty to banks for falling below their required reserves, since it's the interest they must pay to bring their reserves back up to the legal minimum. If banks face a harsher penalty for going below their required reserves, in other words a higher discount rate, then they are less likely to go below the required reserve level. This means banks make fewer loans, and the money supply contracts.

4. (C)

Since the money used to purchase the bond was already in circulation, it doesn't affect the money supply. Think of it this way—if the bond was purchased in the secondary (resale) market, the person who sold the bond had two choices about what to do with the money: spend it or save it. Either way, the money ends up in a bank (if the money is spent, someone else has the same choice, and eventually the money is put into a bank). (A) and (B) are incorrect because the money supply wouldn't be affected (the money was already in circulation).(D) is incorrect because the Fed uses new money to buy bonds: Mary's money was already in the economy.

5. (C)

Of the three tools, open market operations are used most often. In fact, open market operations are used almost constantly. The Fed buys and sells a large amount of government bonds every day. Over time, the general trend of these transactions (more buying than selling, for example) defines what policy the Fed is implementing. (A) is wrong since the Fed rarely changes the required reserve ratio: It is fundamental to the stability of the banking system. (B) is incorrect since banks don't borrow from the discount window very often.

6. (E)

None of the answer choices will have the desired result. To increase the money supply, the Fed should *buy* bonds using open market operations, *decrease* the discount rate, or *decrease* the required reserve ratio. Selling T-bonds, (A), would remove money from the economy. (B) would make banks tighter with their loans, keeping some funds from being released into the economy. (C) would force banks to keep a larger share of their deposits as reserves, decreasing the amount of money available for loans.

7. (D)

The real interest rate is computed by subtracting the inflation rate from the nominal rate. Eight percent minus five percent is three percent.

8. (B)

Contractionary monetary policy decreases investment, which decreases aggregate expenditures, which shifts the aggregate demand curve to the left, changes the equilibrium and lowers the equilibrium RGDP.

9. (D)

Monetarists believe that to induce growth, the Fed should stick to a steady money growth rule. If the goal is three percent growth per year, monetarists believe the Fed should increase the money supply by three percent each year. The economy has shown a growth rate averaging around three percent since WWII, so (E) can be eliminated. Increasing the money supply by more than three percent would lead to inflation.

10. (E)

According to rational expectations, people base their expectations about the future of the economy on a wealth of information, so their expectations are likely to match those of the Wall Street analysts, 4 percent. According to adaptive expectations, people base their expectations on what happened in the recent past, so their expectations are likely to match last year's inflation, or five percent. (C) and (D) are traps if you thought you needed to subtract four percent from five percent; there's no valid reason to do that here.

11. (D)

Stagflation is a simultaneous decline in real GDP and increase in inflation. It represents a problem for monetary policy. To stimulate GDP, expansionary monetary policy is called for. To combat inflation, contractionary monetary policy is needed. These contradict each other, so when faced with stagflation it's not clear what a central bank should do.

12. (D)

$100 million is added to the money supply in the Fed's initial purchase. The banking multiplier is five (1/RR), but because the banks opt to keep excess reserves, there will be leakage from the full multiplier effect. So the money supply has to increase by at least $100 million, and at most less than $500 million.

Free-Response Questions

1. **(a)** The following two graphs represent an economy with eight percent unemployment. Either one is good to use.

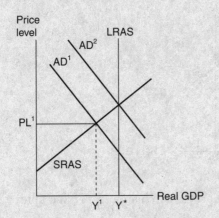 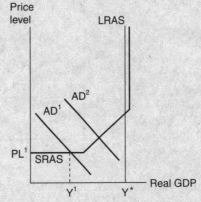

The economy is currently at real gross domestic product Y^1. With an unemployment rate of eight percent, the economy is not at full employment (Y^*).

(b) The Central Bank would initiate an expansionary monetary policy to address this problem.

(c) The expansionary policy would shift the demand curve from AD^1 to AD^2 as shown on the graph. It doesn't matter whether the new equilibrium reaches Y^* as long as it is to the right of Y^1, indicating more output and less unemployment.

(d) The effect on the price level must be consistent with your graph. In both graphs, an increase in the price level is indicated. If, however, on the graph to the right, the AD^2 curve shifted right but remained on the horizontal portion of the short run aggregate supply curve, then one would argue that the price level had not changed.

(e) Tools that the Fed could use are (i) open market operations—buy bonds expanding the money supply; (ii) Lower the discount rate and expand the money supply; or (iii) reduce the reserve requirement, expanding the money supply

2. **(a)** The following graph illustrates the economy at full employment, but with nine percent inflation:

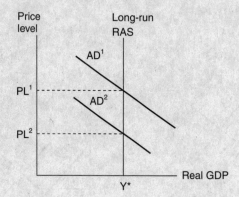

The economy is currently at AD^1, and previously, had been at full employment with a lower price level.

(b) The central bank can use a contractionary monetary policy to fight inflation. This type of policy would decrease demand from AD^1 to AD^2, and lower the price level from PL^1 to PL^2.

(c) The shift from AD^1 to AD^2 is illustrated above.

(d) The contractionary monetary policy illustrated above would have no impact on unemployment. It's possible to show an upward sloping supply curve where the contractionary monetary policy would shift the real GDP equilibrium to the left. In this case, one would argue that the unemployment rate would increase.

(e) The Fed could use any *two* of the following: Sell bonds (OMO); raise the discount rate; or increase the reserve requirement.

3. (a)

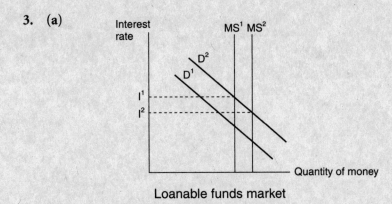

Loanable funds market

If the government pursues an expansionary fiscal policy that creates deficit spending, then the demand for loanable funds will increase from D^1 to D^2, causing higher interest rates. The higher interest rates could discourage private investment. This is the "crowding out effect."

(b) To minimize this problem, the central bank could increase the money supply, which would lower the interest rates.

(c) In the given graph, an increase in the money supply shifts MS^1 to MS^2, and lowers the interest rate to I^2.

MICROECONOMICS

Costs, Revenues, and Profits

It's time to take a closer look at firms tackling the "How to make it" question discussed in the last chapter. But first, we need to understand how economists define economic costs, economic profit, and economic loss.

Let's start with a simplified accounting approach to profit. We begin with the revenues generated by a business. To keep things simple, we'll assume that there are no business taxes in this economy.

Sales revenue: $100

Deduct:

Labor cost:	60
Material cost:	20
Overhead cost:	10
	$10

The accounting profit is $10. The accountant will deduct all of the explicit costs (the actual dollar costs to be paid out) from the total revenues. The economist, however, will be sure to deduct implicit costs as well; that is, opportunity costs.

- First, there's the opportunity cost of the forgone income that could be earned from the capital tied up in this business (rather than in the next best use of this capital).
- Second, there's the value of the owner's time, as measured by the next best alternative income that could have been generated.

Let's say that the owner has capital valued at $20 committed to the business. And suppose that his next best business opportunity would have been to convert the capital to $20 cash, and invest it in bonds paying 5 percent. Five percent of $20 is $1. By choosing to run this business instead, the owner is forgoing $1 of interest that would have been earned in that alternative investment. This forgone interest of $1 represents a normal profit for the $20.

If the owner were not running this business, he would be earning $5 in wages at a job for which he is qualified. This $5 will also be treated as a normal profit. So, the **total implicit cost** will be $1 forgone interest plus $5 forgone wages, so $6.

Now let's determine the **economic profit**:

Revenues:	$100
Explicit costs:	90
Accounting profit:	$10

Minus:

Implicit costs:	6 (Normal profits)
Economic profit:	$4

> In economics, you should assume that both explicit and implicit costs are included in given costs, unless otherwise stated.

We have calculated the implicit cost by determining the opportunity cost of the assets, and, if applicable, the owner's labor. Notice we do not include the total value of the assets invested in the business, though we do include the income (fair market return) that the assets would have generated—had they been put to work in the next best alternative.

We now know that *accounting profit minus implicit costs (normal profits) equals economic profit*. So if there is no economic profit, then there's normal profit. And if there is economic profit, then there's higher than normal profit. If there's an economic loss, then there's lower than normal profit.

Note that the *implicit costs are equal to normal profits*. Normal profits are the **fair market** return (opportunity cost) for the resources invested in the business (capital and labor).

FIXED AND VARIABLE COSTS

When analyzing production and cost behavior, costs must be classified as either fixed or variable. We will assume that fixed and variable costs include all economic costs.

Fixed costs are costs that a firm is committed to in the short run, even if it produces no product at all. In fact, as the firm produces output, the total fixed costs remain the same, at least for a period of time and a range of production activity.

One example of a fixed cost would be a lease. If a firm leases factory space for six months, it must pay the rent regardless of whether it produces any product. Other fixed costs could be contractual obligations to certain employees, insurance coverage for some assets, or the opportunity costs of assets invested in the business.

Variable costs are costs that increase when output increases, and decrease when output is reduced. Labor costs (or those that are not restricted by contract) are variable because the more a firm produces, the more labor it needs to hire. If the firm decreases output, it can reduce its labor. Raw materials are also variable costs: The more a firm produces, the more materials it will use. Conversely, the less the firm produces, the less material it needs.

> Firms (also referred to as businesses, enterprises, or companies) can be organized as proprietorships (one owner); partnerships (more than one owner); or corporations (legal entity separated from the people who own it).

Short-run status in microeconomics is dependent on a firm recognizing at least *one fixed cost*. Over time, a firm may eliminate certain fixed costs, but as long as one fixed cost remains, the firm is considered to be "in the short run." The **long run** is the period of time in which *all costs are variable*. If a firm is committed to a lease or an employee contract, or has assets committed to the possible production of goods, it's in the short run. Regardless of the length of time it takes to eliminate the lease and employee contract, and to reallocate assets elsewhere, the firm is in the short run. Once the firm eliminates all the fixed costs, it is considered to be in the long run.

For example, let's assume that a firm is limited by the amount of factory space available. In the short run, it cannot increase—or eliminate—its factory space. As long as the space cannot be changed, the firm is considered to be in the short run.

Eventually, the firm will be able to increase or decrease the factory space, and at that time, it will be in the long run. In the long run, the factory space is a variable resource. Remember, all resources are variable in the long run.

Whenever there's a reference to a fixed cost or fixed resource, it means that you're dealing with short-run analysis. Let's look at a sample cost schedule for a firm:

Output	Fixed Costs	Total Variable Costs
0	$100	0
1		$400
2		$900
3		$1,500
4		$2,200

We know that this is a short-run cost schedule because it includes fixed costs. The fixed costs remain $100, whether the firm produces zero units or four units. On the other hand, the total variable cost increases as the level of production increases.

In the short run, the total costs include the total fixed cost and the total variable cost at each level of production (0–4 here). We can compute this by adding the variable costs to the fixed costs, which you'll notice remains $100 even with the increase in volume.

Output	Fixed Costs	Total Variable Costs	Total Costs
0	$100	0	$100
1	$100	$400	500
2	$100	$900	1,000
3	$100	$1,500	1,600
4	$100	$2,200	2,300

Now, if the cost schedule were given in the following format, the fixed costs could still be determined. If the output is zero, there are no variable costs. So the total cost of $100 has to be the fixed cost.

Output	Variable Costs	Total Costs
0	0	$100
1	$400	500
2	$900	1,000
3	$1,500	1,600
4	$2,200	2,300

Now let's look at how to compute average fixed cost, average variable cost, and average total cost. The only computation needed is to divide the total fixed cost, total variable cost, and total cost *by the level of output*.

A	B	C	D	B/A	C/A	D/A
Output	Fixed Costs	Variable Costs	Total Costs	Average Fixed	Average Variable	Average Total
0	$100	0	$100	—	—	—
1		$400	500	100	400	500
2		900	1,000	50	450	500
3		1,500	1,600	33 1/3	500	533 1/3
4		2,200	2,300	25	550	575

The **average fixed cost** is the total fixed cost divided by the output. Here, that's column B divided by column A. The **average variable cost** is the total variable divided by output: column C divided by column A. The **average total cost** is the total cost divided by output: column D divided by column A.

Note that just as total cost is the sum of total fixed costs and total variable costs, average total cost is the sum of average fixed and average variable costs.

MARGINAL COST

The marginal cost of something is the change in total cost as one additional unit is produced. It is the change in total cost divided by the change in output.

A	B	C	D	B/A	C/A	D/A	ΔD/ΔA
	Fixed	Variable	Total	Average	Average	Average	Marginal
Output	Costs	Costs	Costs	Fixed	Variable	Total	Cost
0	$100		$100	—	—	—	—
1		$400	500	$100	400	500	400
2		900	1,000	50	450	500	500
3		1,500	1,600	$33\frac{1}{3}$	500	$533\frac{1}{3}$	600
4		2,200	2,300	25	550	575	700

(Δ = change)

Computing the marginal cost here is fairly simple, as the output increases one unit at a time. As a result, we divide the change in total cost by one. But let's look at a slightly different output schedule—one that increases by 10 units at a time.

Output	Total Cost	Marginal Cost				
0	$100					
10	500	$40	=	ΔTC/ΔOutput	=	400/10
20	1,000	50	=	"	=	500/10
30	1,600	60	=	"	=	600/10
40	2,300	70	=	"	=	700/10

To find the marginal cost, divide the change in total cost by the change in output. For the first 10 units, that's 400 by 10, equalling $40.

Now we turn to analyzing the *short-run behavior* of marginal cost. In the short run (when one production input is fixed), as production increases, the marginal cost will increase. This occurs because in the short-run production process, the law of diminishing marginal returns will be experienced.

When inputs are added to production, the total product will increase. That is, the number of items produced will increase. In the early stages of production, the change in total output may increase at an increasing rate: Initially the firm may take advantage of assembly line technology and job specialization. But eventually, as long as one input is held constant (fixed input), the increase in total output will advance at a diminishing rate. Output is still increasing, but the additional output produced by adding one more input—labor for example—is not as great as the previous increase. Eventually, if we keep adding units of labor we may actually experience a decrease in total output (negative returns).

If our fixed resource is factory space, it's easy to understand that initially, as we go from one unit of labor to two, there will be an increase in marginal product (**increasing returns**).

That's because the manufacturing process improves. As we add units in a fixed space, we increase total output. But with every additional unit of labor, the *gains* are less and less (**diminishing returns**), so that, eventually, if we continue to increase units of labor without additional space, the crowding that occurs in the manufacturing process becomes so detrimental that our total output decreases. At that point, we're experiencing **negative returns**.

Let's say we want to produce widgets. We rent factory space for $10,000 a month, and sign a six-month lease. We'll have to pay $10,000 a month for six months regardless how many units we produce. Let us also assume that we cannot afford to rent any additional space for at least six months. Consequently, our short run will be at least six months. It could be longer, if, at the end of six months, we sign another lease, but we can't yet afford to rent additional space.

Now let's suppose that the cost of a unit of labor is $1,000 a month, and the cost of materials used in producing one widget is $1. These are the only costs that our firm will have.

Fixed cost: Factory Space ($10,000 per month)
Variable costs: Materials ($1 per unit)
                 Labor ($1,000 per month)

Next, we'll compute our production cost on a monthly basis. (We could also do it daily, weekly, etc.)

Units Labor	Total Output	Labor Cost	Material Cost	Total Variable	Fixed Cost	Total Cost	Marginal Cost
0	0	0	0	0	$10,000	$10,000	
1	200	$1,000	$200	$1,200	10,000	11,200	$6
2	500	2,000	500	2,500	10,000	12,500	4.33
3	900	3,000	900	3,900	10,000	13,900	3.50
4	1,200	4,000	1,200	5,200	10,000	15,200	4.33
5	1,400	5,000	1,400	6,400	10,000	16,400	6
6	1,300	6,000	1,300	7,300	10,000	17,300	

When there is no production, total cost and fixed cost are the same: $10,000. And there are no variable costs (labor and material). When production begins, the variable costs are recognized. As production increases, the second and third units of labor are added, and total output is increasing at an increasing rate. The second unit of labor adds 300 units of marginal product, while the third adds 400 units.

We can now identify the point where diminishing productivity sets in: at the level of production beyond an output of 900. When we add one unit of labor beyond the level at three units of labor, marginal productivity is 300. Total output is increasing, but at a diminishing rate: An increase of 300 is less than an increase of 400.

Output continues to increase at a diminishing rate through the output of 1,400. Then, as the sixth unit of labor is added, the firm experiences negative returns. At this point, total output has decreased. (Note: At the level of production that is consistent with the onset of diminishing returns, marginal cost begins to increase.)

At the production level 900, the marginal physical product is 400 units. The variable cost has increased by $1,400 (labor plus materials, $1,000 plus $400).

$$\frac{\$1,400}{400} = \$3.50$$

At the production level of 1,200, the marginal physical product is 300 units. The variable cost has increased by $1,300 (labor plus materials, $1,000 plus $300).

$$\frac{\$1,300}{300} = \$4.33$$

COMPUTING COSTS

Let's compute the marginal cost, average variable cost, and average total cost from the previous table of production data.

Output Level	Marginal Cost	Average Variable Cost	Average Total Cost
0			
200	$6.00	$6.00	$56.00
500	4.33	5.00	25.00
900	3.50	4.33	15.44
1,200	4.33	4.33	12.67
1,400	6.00	4.57	11.71
1,300			

Firms will not operate at a level that produces negative returns.

Others things to note here are:

- The marginal cost increases before the average variable cost increases.
- The average variable cost increases before the average total cost increases.
- As long as the marginal cost is less than the average variable cost, the average variable cost is decreasing.
- As long as the marginal cost is less than the average total cost, the average total cost is decreasing.
- The marginal cost can be increasing and still below the average variable and average total cost.

Graphing Short-Run Cost Curves

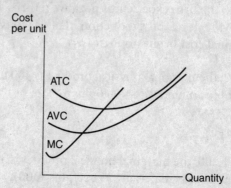

The graph above represents a firm's short-run cost curves. The MC curve, AVC curve, and ATC curve are u-shaped: That's because of the increasing cost per unit that sets in at the production level, where diminishing marginal productivity starts.

The marginal cost increases before average variable cost and average total cost. The marginal cost intersects both the AVC and ATC curves at their respective minimums. The ATC curve is above the AVC curve because it includes the average fixed cost.

As production increases, the ATC curve and AVC curve get closer to each level, because the average fixed cost decreases with the increasing level of production.

Graphing Long-Run Cost Curves

Short-run cost curves are u-shaped because of diminishing marginal productivity. Diminishing marginal productivity is a short-run occurrence, as it is caused by the existence of a fixed resource.

Long-run cost curves are also u-shaped, but not because of a fixed input. (In the long-run, there are no fixed inputs.) Long-run cost curves are u-shaped because of economies of scale, returns to scale, and diseconomies of scale. **Scale** refers to the relationship of inputs used. In the short run, we had the problem of a fixed input. The fixed input affected the relationship of inputs, and eventually led to diminishing marginal productivity and to an increasing cost per unit.

1. **Economies of scale** means that higher production results in lower average production costs. In other words, the more a firm produces, the lower its per-unit costs become. It is the ability of a firm to alter the quantity of all inputs; therefore it is a long-run condition. No input is fixed. The firm can continue to decrease its per unit cost for a greater range of output in the long run because it isn't hampered by a fixed resource. In the graph below, the long-run AC curve is decreasing for an increasing level of production, as the firm experiences economies of scale.

2. **Constant returns to scale** is the range of production where all inputs are increased by the same percentage, in order to maintain to lowest per unit cost. It is the bottom of the long-run ATC curve that depicts a range of lowest cost per unit.

3. **Diseconomies of scale** means that increased production brings about a higher average costs of production. It refers to the range of production where the average cost per unit increases in the long run, despite the fact that inputs are not fixed. This occurs when a firm becomes so large that problems of efficiency occur: bureaucracy, decision-making problems, input quality, or rising input prices, for example.

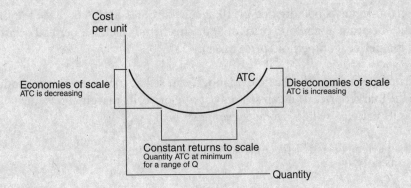

REVENUES

Revenues are the gross receipts that a firm gets for selling its products. If a firm were to sell 1,000 units of a good for $5 a unit, its revenues would be $5,000. This is *not* profit.

Now, let's look at a revenue schedule. Assume that the given product sells for $60.

Output	Total Revenue
0	$0
10	600
20	1,200
30	1,800
40	2,400

To get the total revenue, we multiply the selling price by the output. That means 10 times $60 is $600, 20 times $60 is $1,200, etc. To get marginal revenue, we take the change in total revenue and divide by the change in output.

Output	Total Revenue	Change (Δ) in Revenue	Change in Output	Marginal Revenue
0	$0			
10	600	$600	10	$60
20	1,200	600	10	60
30	1,800	600	10	60
40	2,400	600	10	60

The marginal revenue is 600 divided by 10: a constant $60. That's because the firm can sell any amount of output at a selling price of $60. This firm is facing a perfectly elastic demand curve and is a perfect competitor (price taker).

When a firm faces a perfectly elastic demand, it can sell as many units as it produces, but it must take the market price. If it can sell only at one price, its marginal revenue will always be the same as its price, as will its average revenue.

A graph of a perfectly elastic MR curve would look like this:

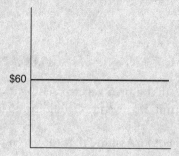

What if this firm faced a downward sloping demand curve instead? That would mean the company would have to lower the good's price if it wanted to sell more products.

Output Level	Selling Price	Total Revenue
0	$0	$0
10	$80	800
20	$70	1,400
30	$60	1,800
40	$50	2,000

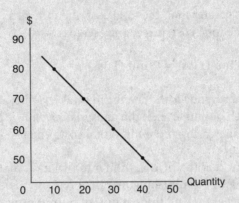

To compute the marginal revenue, we divide the change in total revenue by the change in output.

Output Level	Selling Price	Total Revenue	Marginal Revenue ΔTotal Revenue/ΔOutput	
$0	$0	$0		
10	$80	800	800/10	= 80
20	$70	1,400	600/10	= 60
30	$60	1,800	400/10	= 40
40	$50	2,000	200/10	= 20

When faced with a downward sloping demand curve, the marginal revenue changes at each output level. This firm is a price seeker.

We should also note that the marginal revenue will also be less than the price. That's because the firm has to charge the same price to all customers. When output increases and price is lowered to increase the quantity demanded, the firm has to charge the lower price to all customers—even those that *would have* paid a higher price at a lower level of output. (They have now gained or increased consumer surplus). There are situations where a firm may charge different prices to different customers (price discriminate), but unless stated, we should assume that it does not.

> Average revenue will equal price if the firm is:
> - A perfect competitor;
> - A price taker that faces a perfectly elastic demand curve; or
> - An imperfect competitor that faces a downward sloping demand curve but that cannot charge different prices to different customers.

PROFIT

To determine profit, we subtract the total cost (including all explicit and implicit costs) from the total revenue (payments for goods and services).

Profit = Total Revenue – Total Cost

If the total revenue is greater than the total cost, then the firm recognizes a profit. If the total revenue is less that the total cost, it recognizes a loss.

Total Revenue – Total Cost = Profit (Loss)

As we know, marginal revenue is the change in total revenue, and marginal cost is the change in total cost. So at each output level, if the marginal revenue is greater than the marginal cost, total revenue will be increasing more than total cost. The result is greater profit or less loss.

In the range of output that the firm is willing to produce, marginal cost increases as output increases (as per the law of diminishing marginal returns). The firm will maximize profit (or minimize loss), as long as each additional unit of output provides a greater marginal revenue than it does a marginal cost.

Economists like to make decisions at the margin. The **profit maximizing rule** (or **loss minimizing rule**) is:

Marginal Revenue = Marginal Cost

Firms will continue to increase production until the marginal revenue of the last unit produced is equal to the marginal cost of that unit. Since marginal costs are increasing, to produce more would mean that the marginal cost would be greater than the marginal revenue. This would lead to less total profit or more total loss, whichever applies. We can illustrate the profit maximizing rule:

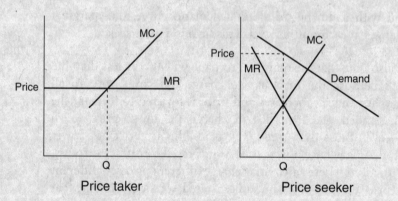

This graph for a price taker (perfectly elastic demand) and a price seeker (downward sloping demand) shows how firms determine the profit maximizing quantity to produce. The price taker determines profit maximizing quantity that is consistent with the market price. The price seeker determines profit maximizing combination of quantity and price. The MR = MC equation provides the quantity information, and at that quantity, the price is determined from the demand curve.

Firms need to understand their costs to compete successfully in the market. They should strive to produce an item in the most efficient way, i.e., using the most efficient combination of resources (land, labor, and capital). Doing this will deliver the lowest cost, and by not doing this, the firm is sure to lose customers to more efficient producers. Thus, competition in a given market will determine how the product will be made.

THE FACTOR MARKET

When firms decide what combination of resources to use to create their product, they must "hire" these resources from the factor market. The factor market is also called the resource market. Households provide firms with labor and capital in return for wages and interest.

The factor market is a **derived market**. This means that the product market determines the demand in the factor market. If consumers demand pizza, then firms will demand pizza labor and pizza ovens. But if consumers don't have much demand for pizza, firms won't need labor or ovens.

We can illustrate this dependency on the product market as follows:

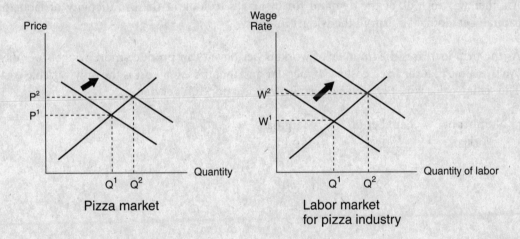

An increase in the demand for pizza will increase the price and the quantity of pizza supplied. This, in turn, will increase the demand for pizza labor, which will push up wages as well as increase the amount of labor hired.

If the demand for pizza dropped, there would be a decreased demand for pizza labor.

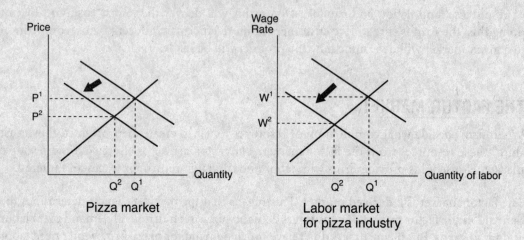

Pizza market

Labor market
for pizza industry

Reduced demand for pizza in the product market will result in fewer pizza workers hired and a lower wage rate.

Another way to look at the demand for factors is to look at the productivity of labor or capital. Let's look at a firm in the widget industry.

As the firm increases the number of workers per day, it can produce more widgets per day. We'll assume that the fixed cost is $10 per day and that the labor cost is the only variable cost. The selling price is $2 per widget. Each worker is paid $100 per day.

Number of Workers	Number of Widgets	Marginal Product
0	0	0
1	80	80
2	180	100
3	250	70
4	310	60
5	350	40

From the above schedule, we see that diminishing productivity sets in when the firm hires the third worker. The marginal output has decreased to 70 units. So how many workers should this firm hire? The rule is that a firm will hire additional workers as long as the marginal revenue product (MRP) is equal to the marginal resource cost (MRC). In other words, the firm will hire more workers as long as the additional revenue created by the additional worker (the MRP) equals the marginal wage paid (the MRC).

Marginal Revenue Product = Marginal Resource Cost

In actuality, we try to get the MRP as close to equaling the MRC—without the MRC being more. This is the **resource optimization rule**.

We can calculate the total revenue product by multiplying the total output by the price.

Number of Workers	Number of Widgets	Marginal Product	Total Revenue	Marginal Revenue Product
0	0	0	$0	$0
1	80	80	$160	$160
2	180	100	$360	$200
3	250	70	$500	$140
4	310	60	$620	$120
5	350	40	$700	$ 80

Since the marginal resource cost is $100 (the wage rate), the profit maximizing number of employees will be four. The fourth employee produces $120 of marginal revenue product while costing $100. If the firm hired the fifth worker, it would gain $80 of revenue, while paying an additional $100 in wages. This would reduce the profit (or increase the loss) of the firm.

You should be able to recognize that the above firm is a perfect competitor, because it can sell as many widgets as it produces for a price of $2. Therefore, it is a price taker.

Be careful in the example above: We could multiply the marginal product by the price (80 units x $2) to get the MRP. But if the firm were an imperfect competitor facing a downward sloping demand curve, this would not be correct. The firm would have to lower the price to sell more, and the lower price would be available to all customers. So in that case, you must calculate the MRP by first calculating the total revenue product at each price level, and then calculating the change in total revenue product.

The resource optimization rule, MRP = MRC, works well for capital as well as labor. In the example above, we could easily substitute units of capital for number of workers, and calculate the optimal units of capital to use.

Note: In the short run, MRP is decreasing as the firm hires more workers because of diminishing marginal productivity. If we were to graph the MRP at quantity of workers, we would have a downward sloping curve for the range where diminishing productivity occurs.

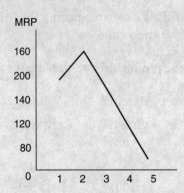

In the short run, firms will find it most profitable to produce in the range where diminishing marginal productivity occurs. Therefore, the MRP curve will be the firm's demand curve for labor (or capital). The MRP curve is also the firms demand curve for a resource.

THE LABOR MARKET

For the topic of a perfectly competitive resource market, it's important that you understand the difference between an industry graph and a firm graph.

There are two types of analysis for the resource market that you should be familiar with: a perfectly competitive resource market, and a monopsonist.

Let's analyze the resource of labor, looking at the market for unskilled labor. In this market, the supply and demand of unskilled labor will give us the equilibrium wage and the equilibrium quantity of workers that will be employed. A firm that hires workers in a **perfectly competitive labor market** is a **wage taker**.

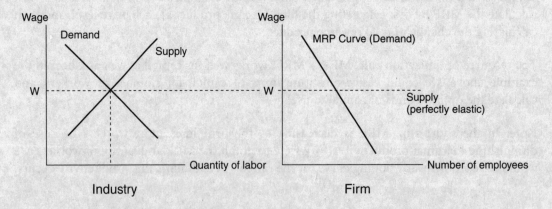

In a perfectly competitive market, the wage is determined by market equilibrium. The firm may hire as many employees as it wants, but they must all be paid the market wage. The firm is faced with a perfectly elastic supply curve of workers.

In a **monopsony**, the firm is not facing a perfectly competitive resource market. The firm has some market power over resources. Using labor as the resource, we can graph a monopsonist as follows:

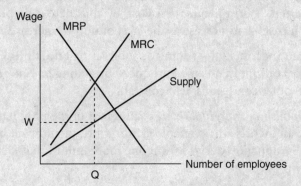

The monopsonist faces an upward sloping supply curve, and an upward sloping marginal resource cost curve. That's because the firm has to increase the wage paid to all employees if it hires more workers. Using the resource optimization rule, we determine that the firm will hire Q number of workers. At this number of workers, we go to the supply curve to determine the wage paid, W.

KEY POINTS

- Businesses can organize as proprietorships, partnerships, or corporations.

- The *production* function of a firm tells us the maximum quantity the firm can produce with a given combination of resources. The *cost* function of a firm tells us the relationship between output and the cost of producing that output.

- In economics, all costs are included, whether or not they correspond to money payments. *Explicit costs* are the opportunity costs of the resources that the firm pays for with cash. *Implicit costs* are opportunity costs with no cash payment. This includes the opportunity cost of time and of capital invested in the business by the owner.

- Total revenue is the price of the product multiplied by the total quantity sold. Profit is the total revenue received by the firm minus the total cost.

- Per unit profit is the average revenue minus the average cost. Normal profit is the accounting profit earned when all resources used earn their opportunity cost. When normal profit is earned, the firm is "breaking even." Perfectly competitive firms earn a normal profit in the long run. Economic profit is the income business owners receive after explicit and implicit costs have been subtracted from the total revenue received. Perfectly competitive firms can earn an economic profit only in the short run.

- A fixed resource, such as the building a firm uses, cannot be varied in the short run. A variable resource, such as a particular material or unit of labor, can be varied in order to increase or decrease the output level in the short run.

- Short run is the period when at least one of the firm's resources is fixed. Long run is the period when all resources used by the firm can be varied.

- Fixed costs are production costs that don't change in the short run, independent of the level of output. A firm incurs these costs even if there is no output. Variable costs are production costs that increase as the level of output increases.

- Marginal means incremental—adding or subtracting one "thing." Marginal product is the additional output that can be produced by adding one more unit of a specific input, with all other conditions held constant.

- The *law of diminishing marginal returns* states that in the production process, there is a point where an increase in a variable factor of production will result in a decline in the additional production derived from one more unit of that factor, holding other inputs constant.

- Marginal cost is the additional cost when one additional unit of output is added. It is inversely related to the marginal product.

- The total cost function is a summary picture of the firm's short-run cost structure. Since it includes both fixed and variable inputs, total costs are equal to fixed costs plus the variable costs: TC = FC + VC. The FC curve is a horizontal line because the costs remain unchanged regardless of output. Since the total cost is the sum of the fixed and the variable costs, and the fixed costs don't change in the short run, the TC curve is parallel to the VC curve and starts at the FC curve.

- As output increases, the following things happen. First, the AFC curve falls because the fixed costs are being spread out among more output. Second, the AVC curve falls initially, but then rises because of diminishing marginal returns. Third, the ATC curve falls initially, but then rises because of diminishing marginal returns. And fourth, the MC curve falls initially, but then rises because of diminishing returns.

- The MC curve intersects the ATC and the AVC curves at their minimum points.

- The long-run AC curve, made up of segments of all the firm's short-run ATC curves, is called the firm's *planning curve*. The short- and long-run AC curves intersect at the point of "the least cost of production," for the specific output level represented by the short-run AC curve.

- When a firms grows and increases production while simultaneously experiencing a drop in cost per unit, it experiences *economies of scale*. In this situation, the long-run ATC curve will drop. When a firm grows and increases production yet experiences a *rise* in cost per unit, it experiences *diseconomies of scale*. In this case, the long-run ATC curve will increase.

- When the long-run cost curve is flat, the firm is experiencing *constant returns to scale*. This means the average total cost neither increases nor decreases with the change in output.

- EQUATIONS:

  Total Cost (TC) = Fixed Cost (FC) + Variable Cost (VC)

  Marginal Cost (MC) = $\Delta TC/\Delta Q$ where Q = Quantity of total output.

Average Fixed cost (AFC) =FC/Q

Average Variable cost (AVC) = VC/Q

Average Total cost (ATC) = TC/Q

Total Revenue (TR) = Price (P) × Quantity (Q)

Average Revenue = TR/Q

Total Profit = Total Revenue – Total Cost (TR – TC)

Unit Profit = Average Revenue – Average Cost (AR – AC)

Resource Utilization = MRP = MRC

REVIEW QUESTIONS

1. The economic profit of a firm includes the opportunity costs of all resources used in production. What do these opportunity costs measure?

   (A) The economic condition of the firm, by listing everything the firm owns
   (B) The growth of the firm over time
   (C) Explicit costs
   (D) The amount of profit earned
   (E) The value of resources at their next best alternative use

2. Nicole, who had been earning $30,000 in a retail department store, decided it was time to open her own clothing shop. To start up, she used $15,000 from her savings account earning five percent interest. She worked six days a week at her store.

   At the end of her first year in business, Nicole's total revenue was $300,000. Her explicit costs included $150,000 for clothing purchased wholesale, $30,000 for the lease and other fixed costs, and salary for two part-time sales clerks, at $15,000 each. How much economic profit did Nicole earn?

   (A) $300,000
   (B) $195,000
   (C) $210,000
   (D) $59,250
   (E) She did not earn an economic profit.

3. In the long run, all costs are (always)

   (A) Constantly decreasing
   (B) Constantly increasing
   (C) Fixed
   (D) Variable
   (E) Constant

4. Total profit is equal to

   (A) total revenue + total variable cost.
   (B) total revenue – total fixed cost.
   (C) total revenue – total variable cost.
   (D) total revenue – (total fixed cost + total variable cost).
   (E) total revenue – (average variable cost x quantity).

5. Total profit is equal to

    (A) total revenue – (total fixed cost × quantity).
    (B) (average revenue × quantity) – (average total cost × quantity).
    (C) average revenue – average total cost.
    (D) average revenue – (average fixed cost + average variable cost).
    (E) (total revenue × quantity) × (total cost × quantity).

6. If marginal cost is increasing,

    (A) average cost must be increasing.
    (B) average variable cost must be increasing.
    (C) average fixed cost must be increasing.
    (D) both Average total cost and average variable cost must be increasing.
    (E) average total cost and average variable cost may be decreasing or increasing.

7. Marginal cost is the change in

    (A) average cost × change in quantity
    (B) total cost ÷ change in quantity
    (C) average variable cost ÷ change in quantity
    (D) total revenue ÷ change in quantity
    (E) fixed cost ÷ change in quantity

8. Diminishing marginal returns occurs as the result of

    (A) Hiring inferior labor
    (B) Having one of the resources fixed
    (C) Paying too much for variable resources
    (D) Having diseconomies of scale
    (E) Poor management of capital

9. In the short-run production process, as long as output continues to increase,

    (A) average fixed cost will always be decreasing.
    (B) average total cost will always be decreasing.
    (C) average variable cost will always be decreasing.
    (D) average total cost will always be increasing.
    (E) average variable cost will always be increasing.

10. In the long run, diminishing marginal returns

    (A) Sometimes occurs
    (B) Always occurs at some point in production
    (C) Never occurs
    (D) Become negative returns
    (E) Change to increasing returns as output increases

Free-Response Questions

1. Sally had $100,000 in the bank earning five percent interest. She leaves a job earning $35,000 a year to open a business selling shoes. The business is organized as a sole proprietorship, and Sally uses the $100,000 that she had in the bank to buy a building for the business. At the end of one year, she has $200,000 in revenue. Her explicit expenses are:

   $100,000 for the shoes and goods she sold retail
   $40,000 to employees
   $30,000 for utilities, maintenance, taxes and other explicit costs

   (a) (i) Does Sally earn an accounting profit?
       (ii) Show how to determine the accounting profit.

   (b) (i) Does Sally earn normal profits?
       (ii) Show how to determine normal profits.

   (c) (i) Does Sally earn an economic profit?
       (ii) Show how to determine economic profit.

2. The ABC Corporation has total revenues of $500,000 at an output of 10,000 units. At this level of output, average total cost is $50, and marginal cost is $40. The ABC Corporation could sell more output if it chooses, but only if the current price stays the same.

   (a) What is the selling price per unit?

   (b) (i) Is ABC Corporation currently earning a profit, experiencing a loss, or breaking even?
       (ii) Show how you calculate your answer.

   (c) (i) Should ABC Corporation increase production?
       (ii) Explain your answer.

ANSWERS TO REVIEW QUESTIONS

1. (E)

Opportunity costs measure the value of resources at the next best alternative use. This implicit cost is important when determining the economic profit of a business. Implicit costs refer to the opportunity cost of using resources provided by the firm's owners without a cash payment. (A) is wrong because a list of a firm's assets is part of a balance sheet used in calculating accounting profits. (B) is wrong because the growth of a firm would be measured by looking at the costs and revenues of the firm during a specific period. (D) is out because economic profit is the income received after explicit and implicit costs have been subtracted from the total revenue.

2. (D)

The total revenue was $300,000. From that, one subtracts the explicit costs of $210,000, and the implicit costs, which include Nicole's lost salary of $30,000, and the lost interest of $750 on her savings. $59,250 is the economic profit earned by the store.

3. (D)

In the long run, all costs are variable. (A) and (B) are not always true in the long run: Cost could be decreasing if the firm is experiencing economies of scale, and could be increasing if it is experiencing diseconomies of scale. Fixed costs occur in the short run, not in the long run, so (C) is out. Constant costs can occur through a range of output but will not always be true, so (E) is out as well.

4. (D)

Total profit is total revenue minus total cost. Total cost is total fixed cost plus total variable cost. (A) is wrong, as one would never add cost to revenue to get profit. (B) is out because it does not subtract total variable cost. (C) is wrong because it does not subtract total fixed cost. And (E) is out because average variable cost times quantity equals total variable cost. The total fixed cost is not included.

5. (B)

Total profit is total revenue minus total cost. Total revenue equals average revenue times quantity. Total cost equals average total cost time quantity. (A) is nonsensical: Total fixed cost times quantity doesn't equal any relevant cost. (C) and (D) provide solutions to per unit or average profit. (E) does not give a relevant cost.

6. (E)

If the marginal cost is increasing but below the average variable and average total cost, then they would both be decreasing. If the marginal cost is increasing but above the variable cost and below average total cost, the average variable cost would be increasing and the average total cost would be decreasing. If the marginal cost is increasing and above both the average variable and average total cost, they would both be increasing. (A) is not true unless one knows the marginal cost is above the average cost, and (B) isn't true unless one knows that the marginal cost is above the variable cost. (C) is out because average fixed cost would be decreasing as output increases, not increasing. (D) is only true if one knows that the marginal cost is above both of these costs.

7. (B)

Choices (A), (C), and (E) do not compute marginal cost. (D) computes marginal *revenue*, not the marginal cost.

8. (B)

Diminishing returns occurs because one of the resources is fixed. Diminishing returns has nothing to do with (A) or (C), so they're clearly wrong. (D) is out because diseconomies of scale is a long-run event, while diminishing returns is a short-run event. Poor management of capital has nothing to do with diminishing returns—having fixed capital would. So (E) is wrong as well.

9. (A)

In the short run, since fixed cost is constant as output increases, the average fixed cost must be decreasing. The other answer choices are wrong because as output increases, average costs decrease for a range of output before beginning again to increase.

10. (C)

Diminishing marginal returns happens only in the short run. (A) and (B) are never true in the long run. And firms would not produce where negative returns were experienced, so (D) is out. (E) is wrong because diminishing returns do not occur in the long run and would not change to increasing returns as output increases.

Free-Response Questions

1. (a) Yes, Sally earns an accounting profit. With $200,000 in revenue, her explicit costs are:

Shoes =	$100,000
Wages =	40,000
Other =	30,000
	$30,000 Accounting profit

   (b) No, Sally earns less than normal profits. Normal profits are the fair market return for her labor and her capital.

Value of labor =	$35,000 Forgone wages
Value of capital =	$5,000 Forgone interest
Normal profits =	$40,000

(c) No, Sally has an economic loss.

Accounting profit = $30,000
Implicit cost   <u>40,000</u> Forgone normal profits
Economic profit (loss)   ($10,000)

2. **(a)** The selling price per unit is $50. Total revenue divided by quantity is the selling price. So $500,000 divided by 10,000 is $50.

(b) The Corporation is breaking even. Average revenue equals $50, and average cost equals $50, so total revenue equals total cost.

(c)

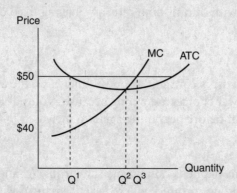

ABC should increase production. The price will remain $50. If the firm continues to produce the marginal cost (which is $40 before increasing production) will increase as output increases. It will also pull the average total cost down from $50 until the marginal cost and the average cost are equal. As the average cost decreases, total cost will be less than total revenue and the firm will experience an economic profit.

Another way to look at this—

In terms of the picture above, the firm is breaking even at a quantity of Q^1 where AR = ATC = 50. At this point, MC = 40 < MR = 50. (Note since price is fixed, AR = MR.) Hence the firm should produce more. In fact, it should continue to increase production until MC = MR at an output level of Q^3. At this point, AR > ATC, and the firm is making an economic profit.

Market Structures

CHAPTER NINE

It is time to review the different competitive environments in which firms operate. Economists look at four market structures:

1. **Perfect Competition**

and within the area of **Imperfect Competition**,

2. Monopoly
3. Monopolistic Competition
4. Oligopoly

Market structure depends on the competition a firm faces in its particular industry. In other words, it is determined by how many competitors a firm faces that produce a near substitute product. As we analyze different market structures in this chapter, we will examine the following issues:

- The number of firms in the industry, and the ease with which they can enter or exit
- The differentiation of product (Is the product produced by each firm identical, or is it slightly different but still a substitute?)
- The extent of a firm's influence over the product's price
- Whether the firm produces at the productively efficient or allocatively efficient level
- Whether the firm can earn economic profit in the short- and long-run

PERFECT COMPETITION

In a perfectly competitive industry, many firms sell one homogeneous product. Because there are few barriers in this type of industry, firms enter and exit easily, though since industry supply and demand determine what price will prevail, firms are **price takers**. That is, they have no influence on price. No one firm is able to significantly affect the industry supply. And since there is no product to differentiate, firms have no reason to advertise.

Other characteristics of a perfectly competitive industry are:

(a) Perfect competitors will not achieve long-run profits. They may experience profit (or loss) in the short run, but the industry adjusts because it is so easy to enter or exit. If there is a profit, firms will enter, shifting the industry supply curve to the right (increase); that will lower the market price so that eventually the economic profit disappears. If firms experience a loss, they'll drop out of the industry in the long run. As enough firms drop out, the industry supply curve will shift left (decrease), and the market price will go up, eliminating the loss for the remaining firms.

(b) Because perfectly competitive firms are price takers, price will always equal the marginal revenue (MR) and the average revenue (AR). In the long run, the MR curve will intersect the MC curve of the firm at the minimum of the ATC curve. Consequently, when average total cost (ATC) equals average revenue, there are no economic profits. When average total cost is at its minimum, there's productive efficiency. And when price equals marginal cost (MC), there's allocative efficiency.

Since the firms in this industry produce an identical (homogenous) product, no one firm has market power. **Market power** is the ability to influence the price of a product. Since a perfect competitor has no influence on price, it can only sell its units *at the industry price*. As a result, the industry demand will be a downward sloping demand curve, but the firm's demand is perfectly elastic.

In the following diagram, one graph represents the industry and the other represents a typical firm in the industry. The industry graph illustrates how the laws of supply and demand determine the market equilibrium price. The firm must then "take" that price.

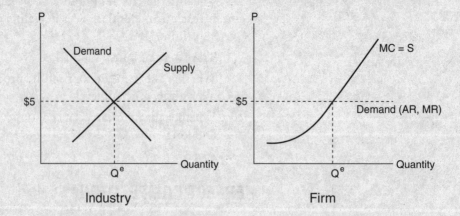

The industry determines a price, and the firm has to take that price. Any determinant of demand and/or supply can shift the industry curve, thus changing the price. The firm will then get more or less money for the product. Because there are so many other firms in the industry, the firm has no significant impact on industry supply. Its short-run supply curve is its MC curve above the average variable cost. Because the demand curve is perfect elastic (there's only one price for the price taker), it is, at the same time, the AR curve and the MR curve.

The average revenue is the total revenue divided by quantity, and the marginal revenue is the change in total revenue as one more product is sold. If there's only one possible price, average revenue and marginal revenue have to be the same. Let's look at the firm's graph with the addition of average total cost and average variable cost.

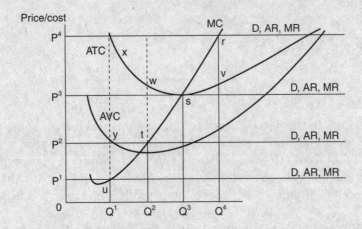

This type of graph is common in microeconomics. We know it represents a perfectly competitive firm because the price lines are horizontal, illustrating a perfectly elastic demand for the firm. In this case, there are four possible prices. This does *not* mean that the firm has a choice of prices; it merely illustrates four possible conditions created if the industry, for reasons related to the determinants of supply or demand, had price P^1, P^2, P^3, or P^4.

All firms determine the profit maximizing output at the quantity where marginal revenue is equal to marginal cost. If the industry price is P^3, the firm will produce Q^3 output. At this price and output, average revenue equals average cost, so there's no economic profit. The quantity that the firm produces at price P^3 will also be at the minimum of the ATC curve. This is productive efficiency (minimum ATC) and also allocative efficiency (P = MC), and is the long-run condition for a perfectly competitive firm.

At a price of P^4, the marginal revenue intersects the MC curve at point r (MR = MC). This equality occurs at the output level of Q^4. Since this is the profit maximizing output, it's the best production level at which the firm can operate. At this output, the AR curve is at r and the ATC curve is at v. Since r is greater than v, the firm will have an economic profit (AR > AC). The vertical distance between points r and v indicates the per unit profit. If we drew a horizontal line from point v to the vertical axis, and used the line P^4 from point r to the vertical axis, we would have the width of a rectangle. The vertical points from Pv to P^4 would describe the left vertical boundary of the rectangle, while the vertical points r and v would describe the right vertical boundary.

In the diagram below, the rectangle P^4,r,v,Pv represents the total economic profit. Remember that the per unit profit is r minus v, and the quantity is O,Q^4, represented by the width of the rectangle. Per unit profit times quantity equals total profit.

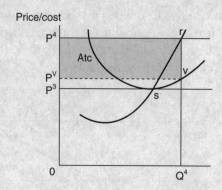

Since at a price of P^4, the firm recognizes a profit, we know that this is a short-run condition. That's because in the long run, a perfect competitor will have no economic profit. One characteristic of this market structure is ease of entry. Other firms in pursuit of the economic profit available will enter the market, shifting the market supply curve right (an increase), and bringing about a lower price, where economic profit is no longer available.

What happens to eliminate the economic profit in the long run? Other firms, attracted by the higher than normal profits, enter the industry, which shifts the industry supply curve to the right, lowering the market price.

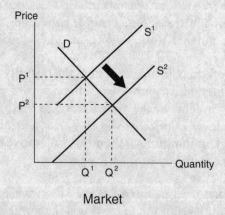

Market

Price drops from P^1 to P^2. All the firms now have to take a lower price and the economic profit is no longer available. Let's look again at our graph with four possible prices.

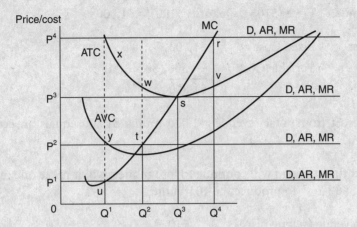

If industry conditions led to a price of P^2, this firm's profit maximizing (loss minimizing) output would be Q^2. This is where marginal revenue equals marginal cost. At a price of P^2 and an output of Q^2, the firm's *average cost* (point *w*) is greater than its *average revenue* (point *t*), so the firm is incurring a loss.

As for what would be done in this situation, as long as the price is higher than the average variable cost, the firm will continue to operate in the short run, to minimize the loss. In the long run (when all costs are variable), it will shut down if it continues to experience a loss. This is known as the **shut-down rule**: The shut-down point is the output and price at which the firm just covers its total variable cost. In the short-run, the firm is indifferent between producing the profit-maximizing output and shutting down temporarily.

> The marginal cost is not the average variable cost, but rather, the variable cost of producing one more unit of output.

Let's look at a price of P^1. At this price, marginal revenue equals marginal cost at an output of Q^1. At this profit maximizing (loss minimizing) output, the price is less than the average variable cost (point *y*), and as a result, the firm should shut down immediately. To stay in operation would only increase its loss. We should now understand why the MC curve above the AVC curve is the supply curve for the perfectly competitive firm. The firm would not produce at a quantity where the MC curve was below the AVC curve. The output that the firm will produce is determined by the **golden rule of profit maximization:** As long as average revenue is above average variable cost, marginal revenue is equal to marginal cost. That is, to maximize profits, the firm should produce where marginal revenue equals marginal cost.

Let's approach the shut-down rule another way. A firm has a fixed cost of $1,000. The firm is a price taker and can sell all of its output for $10 per unit. At its current level of output, the firm's average variable cost is $8. Is this firm achieving a profit or a loss if it produces a quantity of 100?

Total Revenue: Price ($10) × Quantity (100) = $1,000

Total Costs: Fixed Cost = $1,000
                 Variable Cost =   800 ($8 × 100)
                                   ―――――――
                                   $1,800

Subtract total cost from total revenue: $1,000 minus $1,800 equals an economic loss of ($800).

Despite the fact that the firm will continue to lose money, will it make one more unit with a variable cost of $8 ? Yes! To produce the 101st unit:

Marginal revenue (selling price) $10

Marginal cost (variable cost of
producing one more unit) $8
                                        ―――――
Contribution $2

As long as the next unit of production produces revenue that exceeds its variable cost, it will help offset the loss created by the fixed cost. At a production level of 101 units, the firm has a total revenue of $1,010 and a total cost of $1,808. The economic loss is now $1,010 − $1,808 = ($798). It is better to lose $798 than to lose $800.

What would happen if the marginal cost were $11?

Marginal revenue $10

Marginal cost $11
                           ―――――
Contribution   -$1

If the variable cost of producing one more unit exceeds the selling price, the firm recognizes a negative contribution to offset the fixed cost. This will only increase the loss. In this scenario, the total revenue will be $1,010 and the total cost will be $1,811. The loss now is $801. If we did not make the 101st unit of output, the loss would be only $800. Better to lose $800 than to lose $801!

If we could project ahead what the average variable cost would be at different levels of output, we could determine the **break-even quantity** that the firm will produce in the long run. The break-even point refers to the quantity of output that produces neither economic profit nor economic loss.

Price − Average variable cost = Contribution per unit

Fixed cost ÷ Contribution per unit = Break-even quantity

The firm would need a positive contribution per unit to break even. Remember that at break even, there are normal profits but not economic profits.

IMPERFECT COMPETITION

Firms that are not perfect competitors are classified as imperfect competitors. The imperfectly competitive markets are *monopolies*, *oligopolies*, and *monopolistic competitors*. All three of these structures include firms that face a downward sloping demand curve, with a marginal revenue curve that is inside the demand curve.

Questions about imperfect competition are very common on the AP Exam. To approach them, analyze the situation given, using a downward sloping demand curve with the MR curve set inside of it. The graph below could be used to represent any form of imperfect competition: The perfect competitor would produce quantity Q^e and price P^e.

There's a good chance you'll be asked to compare the price and production level of an imperfect competitor with that of a perfect competitor. Although this graph is for an imperfect competitor, a firm in a perfect competition industry would be producing the socially optimal amount where P = MC. So the equilibrium quantity and the equilibrium price for perfect competition would be P^{pc} and Q^{pc}. A perfect competitor will always produce more at a lower price than an imperfect competitor.

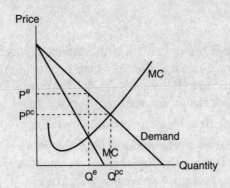

If we look at the imperfect competitor graph, recalling that a perfectly competitive industry would be producing at the socially optimal amount, we can analyze the differences in consumer surplus and the existence of deadweight loss (loss of total surplus).

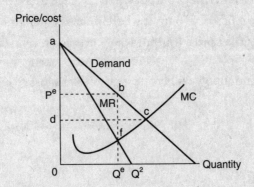

The imperfect competitor would be producing Q^e at a price of P^e. The consumer surplus is the area of the triangle P^e,a,b. Perfect competition producing the socially optimal quantity would have a consumer surplus equal to the area of triangle d,a,c. The deadweight loss that occurs for an imperfect competitor is equal to triangle b,c,f. This deadweight loss does not occur in perfect competition.

A firm's goal is to maximize *total profit—not total revenue*. The profit maximizing rule determines that the quantity Q^e will be the production level of the firm.

To determine the output level at which the total revenue would be maximized, look at where the MR curve hits the horizontal axis, point Q^2. As long as the marginal revenue is positive, total revenue is increasing. Once the marginal revenue is zero, any additional output would lead to a negative return, indicating that the total revenue would begin to drop. It also indicates that the firm would begin to produce at a level consistent with the inelastic portion of its demand curve. This is not where the firm wants to be!

Let's take a closer look at the individual markets in imperfect competition.

Monopoly

By definition, a monopoly is the only firm in the industry. It retains its "only firm" status because of barriers to entry. Since it is the only firm producing the product, it has no near substitutes, which means the firm has significant market power. With such market power, it can control its output to seek the profit-maximizing price. In addition:

(a) The monopolist can have long-run economic profits.

(b) A monopolist will always produce less—and charge more—for its product than a firm in a perfectly competitive industry producing that same product. The monopolist is able to set price above the marginal cost of production.

(c) The profit maximizing output for a monopolist is determined by the MR = MC rule.

(d) In the long run, an unregulated monopoly will not necessarily:

• Have productive efficiency (output where average total cost is at the minimum)

• Have allocative efficiency (output where price is equal to marginal cost)

• Have the fair market price (output where average revenue is equal to the average total cost)

(e) An unregulated monopoly will create a deadweight loss.

Let's look at a monopoly graph. This graph assumes no price discrimination.

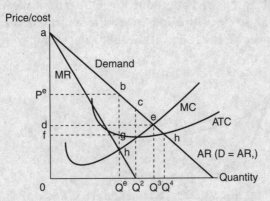

If unregulated, the firm will produce the profit maximizing quantity Q^e (MR = MC at point h). The firm's per unit economic profit will be the vertical distance b to g. At quantity Q^e, the average revenue is found at b, and the average total cost is found at g. Total profit would be the rectangle b,g,f,P^e. This describes the per unit profit times the quantity.

The total revenue would be described by rectangle O,P^e,b,Q^e, and the total cost would be described by rectangle O,f,g,Q^e. The firm is operating in the elastic portion of its demand curve. Point c represents the unitary elastic point of the demand curve, because at that quantity of output, marginal revenue is zero.

The demand curve to the left of point c is elastic because the marginal revenue is positive (greater than zero). To the right of point c, it is inelastic because the marginal revenue is negative.

The firm is underallocating resources to the production of this good because it is not producing the **socially optimal amount** (also referred to as *allocative efficiency*, where MC = price). The socially optimal amount is Q^3. At point e, the marginal cost intersects the demand curve. This is where price will equal marginal cost.

The monopoly is not producing at the minimum average total cost; therefore it is not productively efficient.

Monopoly Regulation

For the exam, you will be expected to interpret the monopoly graph in cases where the government may opt to regulate. One option would be to get the firm to produce at the fair market price (P = ATC). This would be where the ATC curve intersects the demand curve (point h). The quantity at this point would be Q^4.

Monopolies and oligopolies have barriers to entry, caused by:

- **Patents and copyrights:** Granted by the government, these restrict other firms from producing the same item or process for a number of years. If there are no similar products or processes that firms can use to compete, the competition is eliminated.

- **Other legal restrictions:** The government might want only one producer. In many communities, for instance, only one cable television firm is allowed to operate.

- **Control of a key resource:** The DeBeers Diamond Company has controlled much of the world's diamond supply for many years. Lately, reports suggest that DeBeers is starting to back away from its near total dominance because of the great expense, though it still has an enormous amount of market power.

- **High start-up costs:** In some industries, the initial cost of entering as a competitor may be so high that it discourages competition.

Another option would be to try to get the firm to produce the socially optimal amount, Q^3. On this graph, the socially optimal quantity is where average revenue is higher than average cost, so there's an economic profit at this level of production. One cannot always assume that this is the case. A graph could illustrate a situation where the socially optimal quantity is where average revenue is below average cost. Look at the following example:

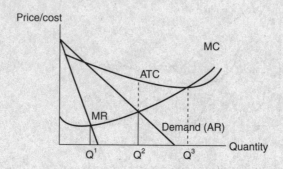

Here the socially optimal quantity is Q^2, where P = MC. At this quantity ATC is more than AR, so there is an economic loss at this level of production.

Natural Monopoly

You might be confused about the definition of a natural monopoly. It has nothing to do with natural resources. A **natural monopoly** refers to an industry where there's not enough demand for a product for even one firm to produce and reach the lowest average cost. Therefore, it is economically impractical to have competitors in the given industry. In the graph above, the demand curve is to the left of the minimum point on the ATC curve. This is a monopoly, so the demand curve also represents the industry demand. If this firm produced Q^3, it would be producing units that it could not possibly sell. If the regulators tried to enforce competition, each firm would be unable to sell as much as the monopoly. Consequently, no firm could produce at as low a cost as the single firm. In this case, a monopoly can produce at the lowest possible cost. So, it makes sense to allow the monopoly to exist.

Price Discrimination

When a firm charges different prices for a product to different consumers, even though the production and transaction costs are the same, it's called **price discrimination**. If a firm were able to perfectly price discriminate, it could charge each customer a different price. In that scenario, the MR curve and the demand curve would be the same. The firm would not have to lower the price for consumers who were willing to pay more. Perfect price discrimination is an extreme scenario, but you should be prepared to analyze more realistic situations where firms find ways to price discriminate among consumer groups. A firm may want to price differently for business and tourist travelers, for instance, or for working and retired consumers.

A firm must have market power if it intends to price discriminate. In addition:

(a) It must be able to identify two or more groups of consumers with different demand curves (the elasticity of demand differs for each group).

(b) It must be able to prevent one group from being able to resell the product to the other group. (The group paying less cannot resell to the group that would otherwise agree to pay more).

Let's look at price discrimination of two consumer groups.

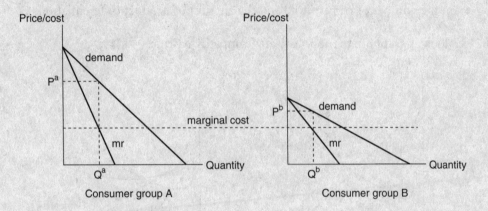

From the figures above, we can determine the following:

- Consumer group B has a more elastic demand curve.
- Consumer group A will pay the higher price, P^a.
- Consumer group B will pay the lower price, P^b.
- The marginal cost is illustrated as a straight line, intersecting the MR curves of both at the same cost. This is not because of constant cost, but because of the firm's marginal cost when its production level is equal to Q^a plus Q^b.

> If a firm charges different prices at two locations because of different transportation, safety, or property costs, this is not price discrimination. Price discrimination refers to different prices—when costs are the same.

Monopolistic Competition

In monopolistic competition, many competing firms deal with a somewhat differentiated product. This somewhat differentiated product can be of benefit to consumers because it provides them with a greater selection. Monopolistically competitive firms engage in advertising as a form of nonprice competition. There is ease of entry or exit in the market. In addition,

(a) Firms have some leeway with regard to pricing. As price searchers, firms can differentiate their product's results in a price that is higher than the marginal cost.

(b) Monopolistic competitors will have long-run profits. This is the only type of imperfect competitor that cannot sustain economic profits in the long run.

(c) In the long run, a firm's ATC curve will be tangent to the demand curve at the profit maximizing level of output. Therefore, average revenue will equal average cost and there will be no economic profit.

(d) Output level will not reach the minimum average cost level, so firms will not be productively efficient (minimum ATC).

(e) Price is higher than marginal cost, so firms are not allocatively efficient (they're not producing the socially optimal amount where price equals marginal cost).

(f) The demand facing a monopolistic competitor is very elastic because there are many competitors with close substitute products. The degree of elasticity depends on the number of competitors and the amount of product differentiation.

Now let's look at graphing monopolistically competitive firms.

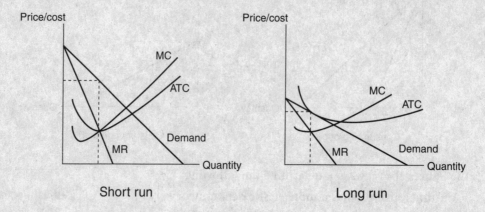

Short run   Long run

The term *monopolistic* in the term "monopolistic competition" is confusing. In fact, this industry is a lot more like a perfectly competitive industry because of the many firms and the ease of entry and exit.

The graph on the left represents a monopolistically competitive firm in the short run. We would not be able to distinguish this graph from another type of imperfect competitor market unless told. Once we have identified this as a monopolistic competitor graph, we can conclude that it's a short-run graph. It illustrates a price higher than the ATC curve, meaning that there's an economic profit. As such, more firms will enter the industry (ease of entry), and as a result, this firm's demand will decrease and become more elastic. As the demand decreases (shifts to the left), it reaches a point where in the long run it is tangent to the ATC curve. The economic profit has disappeared.

A monopolistically competitive firm does not achieve productive efficiency because it will have excess capacity. The competitive nature of the industry will not allow it to produce at a level that is efficient. The firm will need to advertise in order to differentiate its product. It will not be able to achieve the production level necessary to minimize these costs on a per unit basis.

Oligopoly

In an oligopolistic industry, there are a few dominant firms dealing with a product that is either homogenous (steel, for example) or differentiated (automobiles). Interdependence is the key to understanding oligopolies. They have competitors but only a few. As such, each firm can have a significant impact on the industry as a whole. Consequently, the firms are much more concerned with each other's cost structures, advertising to gain market share, pricing, etc. Other characteristics of an oligopoly are:

(a) There are barriers to entry.

(b) An oligopoly does have pricing power but it must be conscious of the effects on competitors.

(c) An oligopoly can achieve long-run economic profit.

(d) An oligopolistic firm will usually not produce at the productively efficient level of output.

(e) Price will be greater than marginal cost. The firm will not be allocatively efficient.

For the purposes of a microeconomic basics course, the most common way to determine whether an industry is oligopolistic is the **concentration ratio**. To get this, one measures the total market share of the largest companies. If the four largest companies have a significant market share, let us say 75 percent or more, one can conclude that the firms have oligopolistic power. (There is nothing that says we must use the *four* largest companies and not the *five* largest. Nor is there any reason we can't use 65 percent as opposed to 75 percent of the market share as our benchmark.)

One problem with the concentration ratio approach is that it usually refers to national market share and it doesn't account for localized markets that may have firms with local oligopolistic power. Perhaps there are many sand and gravel businesses throughout the country, so that no four firms have an exceptionally large percentage of the total national business. But because of the high transportation costs and relatively low price, a firm in Denver will not deliver a truck of gravel to Boston. It's possible that within a smaller geographical region where transportation costs have less of an impact, a few firms may dominate the sand and gravel business.

As economists analyze the behavior of firms that are mutually interdependent, a number of models are developed. An older model that is becoming less popular is the **kinked demand model**. Following is one type of graph that can be used to analyze the behavior of an oligopoly.

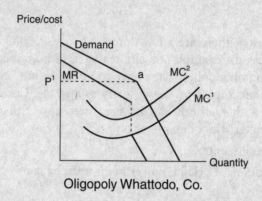

Oligopoly Whattodo, Co.

This graph represents the behavior of the Whattodo Company. At point *a*, the demand is kinked. To the left of *a*, the demand curve is more elastic; to the right, it is more inelastic. Firms must deal with the mutual interdependence that exists when a few firms dominate market supply. The Whattodo Company faces the problem that, if it were to increase its price, its competitors would not do the same. And with that increased price, its demand would become more elastic because some customers would buy from competitors. If Whattodo lowered its price to gain market share, its competitors would respond by lowering their prices. The result is that a lowering of price would put the company into the inelastic portion of its demand curve.

> The kinked demand curve is only one of the models used to describe a type of oligopoly. Not every oligopoly faces a kinked demand curve.

Even if the firm's marginal cost increased from MC^1 to MC^2, it would not be able to pass on the increase to the consumer by charging a higher price.

Game Theory

Game theory is a more popular model for explaining the predicament of decision-making for an oligopoly. Game theory analyzes the strategic moves firms make in their decisions about pricing, output levels, advertising, etc.

One popular example of game theory is the "prisoners dilemma." Most of us have seen enough crime dramas to have some idea how this works. The police capture two suspects and separate them from each other. Interrogators then try to get each suspect to confess or turn in evidence against the other. If neither one gives evidence or confesses, they both face a three-year sentence. If one gives evidence against the other, he will receive a suspended sentence, while the other will receive a 10-year sentence. If both give evidence, they both face a five-year sentence. Look at the **payoff matrix** below:

		Prisoner 2	
		Give evidence	Do not give evidence
Prisoner 1	**Give evidence**	box a 5 years	box b Prisoner 1 suspended Prisoner 2 10 years
	Do not give evidence	box c Prisoner 1 10 years Prisoner 2 suspended	box d 3 years for both

Box A represents both prisoners' decisions to give evidence. In this case, each would receive a five-year sentence. **Box B** represents prisoner 1's decision to give evidence, and prisoner 2's decision to not give evidence. Here, prisoner 1 would receive a suspended sentence, and prisoner 2, a 10-year sentence. Similarly, **Box C** reflects prisoner 2's decision to give evidence, and prisoner 1's decision to not give. **Box D** represents the decision by neither prisoner to give evidence, resulting in a three-year sentence for both.

The problem comes about because they cannot collude: They don't know what the other one will do. What strategy should each one take? Give evidence or not give evidence?

The solution will be represented by box A. If the prisoners could collude (talk to each other), they would both *not* give evidence and get a 3-year sentence each. However, each prisoner has an incentive to "cheat," since if he gives evidence while the other does not, he will get a suspended sentence and the other prisoner will get a 10-year sentence. So they both "cheat" and give evidence: They get a 5-year sentence each and the solution is box A.

Now let's use the analogy in the situation of two competitors trying to decide between a high- or a low-price policy. Neither firm knows what the other will do.

		Company A	
		High price	Low price
Company B	**High price**	A $100,000 $100,000	B $25,000 $150,000
	Low price	C $150,000 $25,000	D $50,000 $50,000

Here, the matrix illustrates the profit that each company will receive depending on the mutual pricing decisions. Box A represents the profit if both companies charge a high price. Box D is the profit if both charge a low price. Box B shows that if company 1 prices high, and company 2 prices low, then company 1 will have a profit of $25,000, and company 2 will have a profit of $150,000. In box C, if company 1 prices low, and company 2 prices high, then profits for company 1 will be $150,000 and for company 2, $25,000. Remember that if one company prices low while the other company prices high, the low-priced one will gain market share.

What does each company do? If they could collude, they could both charge high prices and obtain $100,000 profit each. But since they cannot, if one company picks a high price policy and the other a low price one, the high price firm will lose profits.

This game has a similar solution to the Prisoners' Dilemma above. If the two firms could collude, they would both charge high prices and get profits of $100,000 each. But again, each has an incentive to lower its price (provided it believes that the other firm will continue to price high) and gain a profit of $150,000. So each will "cheat" and price low. The solution will be box D, where each gets a profit of only $50,000.

> Firms in oligopolies are mutually interdependent. This interdependence leads them to make decisions that can fall under the category of *game theory*. Make sure you understand how to read a payoff matrix.

As you can see, the strategies are complicated. For now, you should understand that oligopolistic firms are mutually interdependent.

Price leadership is another model you should understand. Here, an industry has a few firms dominating the market, but one firm in particular is most dominant. That firm is allowed to establish a pricing policy, and the other firms establish pricing policies near that. There's no explicit communication between them (in other words, this is tacit collusion), but the smaller firms within the industry are savvy enough to understand the implications of "taking on the big guy."

Cartels

A **cartel** is an organization of different companies working together in order to maximize profit for each. This is collusion and is illegal in the United States. Classic examples are the Standard Oil cartel and OPEC.

If a few firms have a large market share and are permitted to collude, they can begin to act like a monopoly. In order to get a higher price, they agree to control the industry supply. Remember the industry is facing a downward sloping demand curve. By controlling supply, they shift the industry supply curve to the left (decrease), and obtain higher prices.

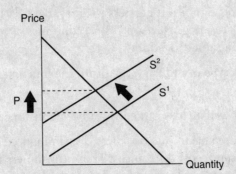

Each company agrees to limit the quantity of product it will supply, with the net result being a drop in industry supply and a rise in price. The problem facing a cartel is *maintaining discipline*. When the price increases, the individual members are tempted to increase their supply to take advantage of the higher price. But if they were to do this, the industry supply curve would shift back to the right and lower prices.

When comparing market structures, it can be difficult to decide where an industry fits. The four market structures are models meant to simplify the study of markets. Markets do not always fit neatly into a category. In addition, keep in mind that markets change. New technology can change a market's structure, and mergers can increase a firm's market power.

KEY POINTS

- A perfectly competitive firm faces a perfectly elastic demand curve. Its long-run break-even point is where marginal revenue equals marginal cost equals average total cost, occurring at the minimum average total cost. A firm's MC curve above its AVC curve is its short-run supply curve.

- If a firm has an economic loss but the price of its good is greater than the average variable cost, it will continue to operate in the short run. If the price is less than the average variable cost, the firm will shut down immediately.

- Perfectly competitive markets are both productively efficient and allocatively efficient. Productive efficiency occurs when a firm is producing at the lowest average total cost. Allocative efficiency occurs when price equals marginal cost.

- Since there's only one firm in a monopoly, the demand curve faced by the firm is also the market demand curve. The monopolist faces a downward sloping demand curve; therefore, it must lower the price if it wants to sell additional units of product. This leads to the price always being greater than the marginal revenue.

- There is no supply curve in a monopoly because the price the firm charges for a given level of output depends on the demand curve. Since the quantity offered for sale depends on demand, there is no supply curve. A monopoly is neither allocatively efficient nor productively efficient.

- A monopoly requires significant barriers to entry. Barriers to entry include control of important resources, large start-up costs, economies of scale, government granted exclusive rights, geographic location.

- For all firms in any type of industry, the profit maximizing level of output is the MR = MC rule.

- Deadweight loss or welfare loss is the loss of both consumer and producer surplus.

- Some monopolies are able to practice price discrimination. The prices are based on demand differences, not cost differences. Those consumers who are less sensitive to price increases will be charged more for the good. The more inelastic the demand, the higher the price.

- Price discrimination, can result in greater profit for the firm and more output sold to consumers. It eliminates some, if not all, consumer surplus.

- A natural monopoly is a firm that experiences decreasing average total cost over the whole range of production demanded in the market. When a firm experiences decreasing average total costs over the whole range of production, it experience economies of scale.

- A government may grant a natural monopoly an exclusive right to operate. In exchange for the exclusive right, the government regulates the firm.

- If the government sets the monopoly's price equal to its marginal cost of production, this price may be below the average total cost, and the firm may experience economic loss. In this case, the government may help the firm by subsidizing some costs of production.

- Monopolistically competitive firms cannot have long run economic profit. They can earn economic profit in the short run but this attracts more competitors shifting the firms demand curve to the left and eliminating the profit.

- An imperfect competitor faces a downward-sloping demand curve. The more inelastic the demand curve is, the more the firm can increase its price over its marginal cost.

- The degree of price elasticity of demand depends on the exact number of competitors in the industry and the degree of product differentiation. More competitors or less product differentiation means greater elasticity of demand.

- In long-run competitive equilibrium, a monopolistically competitive firm's ATC curve is tangent to the demand curve at the quantity where MR equals MC. Since the demand curve is downward sloping, the point of tangency is above the minimum of ATC, so the firm is not productively efficient.

- An oligopolist's marginal revenue and marginal cost are influenced by the actions of the other firms in the industry, so calculating the profit-maximizing level of output is not straightforward. Instead, there are many different models of oligopoly interaction.

- Collusion occurs when firms jointly determine price or output to increase their profits. A cartel is a formal collusion agreement. Unspoken or unwritten collusion agreements are called tacit collusion.

- Game theory tracks strategic moves by a firm and countermoves by rival firms. Decisions regarding pricing and output levels can depend on rival's choices. "The Prisoner's Dilemma" is a classic example.

- Price leadership is a model in which a dominant firm sets a price and other firms in the industry take that price as the market price and sell whatever quantity maximizes their profit at that market price.

- The "kinked" demand curve model assumes firms think their rivals will follow their lead if they cut prices, and will not follow their lead if they raise prices. Firms have little to gain if they lower their price and expect their rivals to do the same, but they have a lot to lose if they raise prices and their rivals don't. As a result, if costs increase, a firm may not increase its price.

- Mutual interdependence is key to understanding the behavior of firms in oligopoly. Price wars can occur in this type of industry since competitors may be able to undercut each other and earn big profits in the short run. Undercutting may drive the price down to marginal cost.

REVIEW QUESTIONS

1. Monopolistic competitors make products that are

   (A) used in conjunction with one another.
   (B) perfect substitutes.
   (C) perfect complements.
   (D) close but not perfect complements.
   (E) close but not perfect substitutes.

2. In the long run, a competitive firm

   (A) earns an economic profit, and so does a monopoly.
   (B) earns no economic profit, and neither does a monopoly.
   (C) earns an economic profit, but a monopoly does not.
   (D) earns no economic profit, but a monopoly might.
   (E) may or may not earn an economic profit, just like a monopoly.

3. Unlike a perfectly competitive industry, a monopoly

   (A) generates more consumer surplus than does a perfectly competitive market.
   (B) generates more producer surplus than does a perfectly competitive market.
   (C) reduces the effect of deadweight loss on producers.
   (D) reduces the effect of deadweight loss on consumers.
   (E) reduces the effect of deadweight loss on both consumers and producers.

4. Monopolies can earn positive economic profits because

   (A) the government subsidizes them.
   (B) barriers to entry prevent competition.
   (C) monopoly risks are high.
   (D) they face higher costs than other firms.
   (E) price floors prevent their prices from falling.

5. Compared to a single-price monopoly (no price discrimination), an industry that is perfectly competitive produces

   (A) less output at a higher price.
   (B) more output at a lower price.
   (C) more output at a higher price.
   (D) less output at a lower price.
   (E) the same output at the same price.

KAPLAN

6. In the short run, the lowest quantity at which a firm will produce is the minimum of

   (A) Marginal Cost
   (B) Total Cost
   (C) Average Fixed Cost
   (D) Average Variable Cost
   (E) Marginal Product

7. The price elasticity of demand for the output of a price-taking firm is

   (A) Equal to the price
   (B) Less than one
   (C) Infinite
   (D) One
   (E) Zero

8. Firms are mutually interdependent in which of the following market structures?

   (A) Perfect Competition
   (B) Monopolistic Competition
   (C) Oligopoly
   (D) Monopoly
   (E) None of the above

9. In a perfectly price-discriminating monopoly, there is no

   (A) Consumer surplus
   (B) Transfer of consumer surplus to the producer
   (C) Short-run economic profit
   (D) Long-run economic profit
   (E) Producer surplus

10. In a monopolistically competitive industry, when economic profit is positive, firms will

    (A) leave the industry, and demand will increase for the remaining firms.
    (B) enter the industry, and demand will decrease for the original firms.
    (C) leave the industry, and demand will decrease for the remaining firms.
    (D) enter the industry, and demand will increase for the original firms.
    (E) enter the industry, but this has no effect on demand for the original firms.

11. In perfect competition, the marginal revenue of a firm is equal to

    (A) its average revenue, but not its price.
    (B) neither its price nor its average revenue.
    (C) both its price and its average revenue.
    (D) its price, but not its average revenue.
    (E) None of the above

Questions 12-15

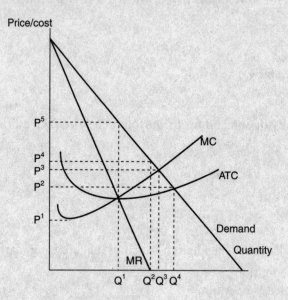

12. In the graph above, a profit maximizing firm is in imperfect competition. The firm will charge a price of and produce a quantity of

    (A) P^3, Q^3

    (B) P^5, Q^1

    (C) P^4, Q^2

    (D) P^2, Q^4

    (E) P^1, Q^1

13. If the firm above were a perfect competitor, it would charge a price of and produce a quantity of

    (A) P^3, Q^3

    (B) P^4, Q^4

    (C) P^4, Q^2

    (D) P^2, Q^4

    (E) P^1, Q^1

14. If the imperfectly competitive firm above were to produce at a price and quantity that would produce the greatest total revenue, it would produce at

    (A) P^3, Q^3

    (B) P^5, Q^1

    (C) P^4, Q^2

    (D) P^2, Q^4

    (E) P^1, Q^1

15. The fair market price for the imperfect competitor above would be

(A) P^1

(B) P^2

(C) P^3

(D) P^4

(E) P^5

Free-Response Questions

1. The Powermarket Company is an imperfect competitor that cannot price discriminate and that earns economic profit in the long run.

(a) (i) Draw a correctly labeled graph of Powermarket's long-run equilibrium.
   (ii) How does Powermarket determine output level?
   (iii) Illustrate on the graph the equilibrium price and quantity.
   (iv) Identify and illustrate on the graph Powermarket's economic profit.

(b) From the given information, how do we know that Powermarket is not a monopolistic competitor?

(c) Explain the relationship between Powermarket's demand curve and its marginal revenue curve.

(d) Identify and illustrate on the graph what the equilibrium price and quantity would be were Powermarket a perfect competitor.

2. (a) What are three characteristics that perfect competitors have in common with monopolistic competitors?

(b) What are three differences between perfect competitors and monopolistic competitors?

ANSWERS TO REVIEW QUESTIONS

1. (E)

Choice (A) may be true in some cases, but it's not one of the key characteristics of a monopolistically competitive market. (B) is close, but it's not correct. If the products were perfect substitutes, it would be a perfectly competitive market. (C) is wrong because complements are goods that are used together, something not characteristic of this market. Similarly, (D) is out, because firms in a monopolistically competitive market do not necessarily make goods that are used together.

2. (D)

A competitive firm does not earn economic profit in the long run, so (A) is out. A monopoly may indeed earn economic profit in the long run, so (B) and (C) are wrong (additionally for (C), competitive firms do not earn long run economic profit). And for this same reason, (E) is wrong.

3. (B)

The fact that the price is higher in a monopoly than it is in a perfectly competitive market means that some of the consumer surplus will instead go to the producer. (A) is incorrect since prices are higher and quantity is smaller than under perfect competition. And while it is true that a monopoly results in some deadweight loss, it is not really transferred to the producer or to the consumer, so (C), (D), and (E) can be eliminated.

4. (B)

Subsidies are not always necessary for monopolies to earn economic profit, so (A) is wrong. (C) is wrong as well since high profits would compensate investors for any high risks taken. In fact, many monopolies are in very safe lines of business. (D) and (E) are just not accurate, so they can be ruled out as well.

5. (B)

Compared to a monopoly, a perfectly competitive industry in the long-run will produce at a price equal to marginal cost = minimum average cost, so the firms will have no economic profits and will sell at the lowest possible price that allows them to stay in business. At this low price, many people will want to purchase the output, and a lot of it will be sold. So a perfectly competitive industry will supply a larger quantity at a lower price than will a monopoly. (A) is incorrect, because a perfectly competitive industry will have many firms producing and competing with each other. In long-run equilibrium, the price will be equal to the minimum average cost, and all consumers will be able to purchase at that price. (C) is partially true, in that a perfectly competitive industry will sell more, but to sell more it must sell at a lower price. (D) is wrong as well, since yes, it will sell at a lower price, but it will sell more. And (E) is clearly wrong: Output and price are very dependent on market structure. Monopolies will produce dramatically different quantities and sell at very different prices than will perfectly competitive industries. A monopolist prices above marginal cost and above minimum average cost in the long-run and short-run.

6. (D)

A firm will keep producing additional output until the marginal cost rises to the price. If marginal cost is rising, it will intersect the average variable cost at the quantity that minimizes average variable cost. If the price is lower than this, the firm will simply shut down because it won't be able to cover variable costs and will incur a greater loss. (A) is wrong because while a firm will produce where its marginal cost is equal to marginal revenue, the quantity at which marginal cost is minimized isn't necessarily the lowest quantity the firm will produce. (B) is incorrect because in the long run, firms must worry about covering their total cost, so the minimum quantity a firm will produce in the long run is the quantity that will minimize its total cost. In the short run, however, a firm only needs to cover its variable costs. And (C) can be eliminated because average fixed costs are just fixed costs (which don't change as output increases). The level of output that minimizes average fixed cost would be infinitely large. And (E) is wrong because the minimum of marginal product would be the quantity at which the additional output from one more worker is at its smallest.

7. (C)

A price taking firm is a perfect competitor and faces a horizontal demand curve. That is, price-taking firms face an infinitely elastic, or horizontal, demand curve. This means that if a firm raises its price even the slightest bit, the firm's share of the market will go to zero. (A) does not deal with price elasticity. (B) would represent an inelastic demand. (D) describes unitary elasticity.

8. (C)

Firms in an oligopoly are mutually interdependent because of the market power of the few dominant firms. Perfectly competitive firms are all price takers and can sell all that they produce at the market price, so (A) is out. (B) is incorrect since monopolistically competitive firms face competition from many different firms. (D) is clearly wrong because a monopoly has no competition.

9. (A)

Price discrimination seeks to capture consumer surplus. If a firm can perfectly price discriminate, every consumer will pay a price equal to her marginal utility and will have no consumer surplus. (B) is incorrect because consumer surplus is eliminated, not transferred. And monopolies can have economic profit in the short run and in the long run, so (C) and (D) are out.

10. (B)

When economic profit is positive in a monopolistically competitive industry, firms will enter the industry, and demand will decrease for the original firms. Profits act as signals. Positive economic profit means more resources should be allocated to that industry. Losses indicate that firms are allocating too many resources to the industry. Profits encourage entry, so (A) and (C) are wrong. (D) and (E) are out as well, since as firms enter the industry, the demand for the original firms will decrease.

11. (C)

Since perfectly competitive firms charge the same price for each unit, the marginal revenue will be constant. Additionally, average revenue is the total revenue (P * Q) divided by the quantity sold, which will be a constant equal to the price.

12. (B)

A profit maximizing firm will produce where the marginal revenue is equal to the marginal cost. This is at the output level Q^1. At this level, the price is taken off the demand curve, P^5. No other answer choice meets the MR = MC rule.

13. (A)

A perfect competitor would be producing at a level of output where the Price is equal to the marginal cost, Q^3. At this quantity, the price is P^3. This is the socially optimal amount, and also allocatively efficient. No other answer choice meets the criteria for the socially optimal amount.

14. (C)

The maximum total revenue quantity is where the marginal revenue would be zero. This is at Q^2. At Q^2, the price would be P^4.

15. (B)

The fair market price is found at the quantity where the price is equal to the ATC (This is where the ATC intersects the demand curve). At the quantity Q^4, the price would be P^2.

Free-Response Questions

1. (a) (i)

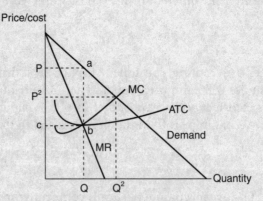

   (ii) The equilibrium is determined by the marginal revenue equals marginal cost rule.

   (iii) P and Q indicate equilibrium price and quantity.

   (iv) Economic profit is the rectangle P, a, b, c.

(b) (i) This company is not a monopolistic competitor because it has long-run economic profit. Monopolistic competitors are the only imperfect competitors that do not have long-run economic profit.

(c) The MR curve is inside the demand curve because this company cannot price discriminate. Therefore, to increase quantity sold, it must lower price. When it lowers price, it must do so for all customers. The marginal revenue will be less than the price as a result.

(d) If this were a perfect competitor, it would be operating where marginal cost is equal to price (allocative efficiency). The price would be P^2, and the quantity Q^2.

2. (a) Your answer could include any three of the following. Both market structures: have many competitors; have ease of entry; do not have long-run economic profit; and can have only short-run economic profits.

(b) Your answer could include any three of the following. Perfect competitors have undifferentiated products, while monopolistic competitors have differentiated products. Perfect competitors do not advertise, while monopolistic competitors do. In the long run, perfect competitors have price equal to marginal cost, but monopolistic competitors have price greater than marginal cost. Perfect competitors face a perfectly elastic demand curve (horizontal curve), but monopolistic competitors face a downward sloping demand curve. Perfect competitors are price takers, but monopolistic competitors have some control over price.

Efficiency, Equity, and the Role of Government

CHAPTER TEN

Markets work best when:

(a) Producers are responsible for all costs, and these costs are reflected in the price at which the good or service is supplied.

(b) Paying consumers are the only beneficiaries of the goods and services produced.

When condition (a) is met, the supply curve represents the marginal cost of producing additional units of the good or service. The marginal cost that the firm considers includes all of the marginal social cost. Therefore,

SUPPLY =

MARGINAL PRIVATE COST =

MARGINAL SOCIAL COST (MSC)
(AT VARIOUS PRODUCTION LEVELS)

The **marginal social cost** is the cost to society (the cost of all the resources used) to produce an additional unit of a good or service. The **marginal private cost** is the cost incurred by the producer of the good for producing an additional unit. When a producing firm recognizes all of the cost, the supply side of a market will produce most efficiently.

When condition (b) is met, the demand curve represents the marginal benefit received by all paying consumers, and no one benefits without paying the equilibrium price.

DEMAND =

MARGINAL PRIVATE BENEFIT =

MARGINAL SOCIAL BENEFIT (MSB)
(AT VARIOUS PRODUCTION LEVELS)

Social benefit is the utility received by all consumers in the consumption of the good or service. The **marginal private benefit**

is the utility value that consumers (who are willing to pay for the good) have, and is reflected in the demand curve. When the demand curve recognizes all of the marginal utility of consumers, it is most efficient.

When conditions (a) and (b) are present, the market produces an equilibrium quantity that is the **socially optimal amount**. Total surplus is maximized, and all consumers pay a price that includes the value of all resources used in the production process. In this case, the supply and demand graph can be illustrated as follows:

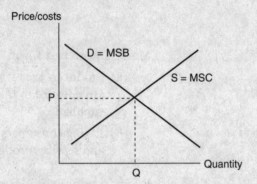

Equilibrium is at the level of production where MSB equals MSC. This is the socially optimal quantity. When the market doesn't produce the socially optimal amount, then the market is not efficient (**market failure**).

THE ROLE OF GOVERNMENT

Government has certain responsibilities in conjunction with a market economy. Not all economists would agree with the extent of government's role in each area, but most would agree that there is some role to be played.

1. Protect private property rights

When the market system is working its best, the supply and demand captures all social benefits and social costs. The government can provide a legal system that supports private property rights. Would people invest in businesses if the claims they had on those businesses were not enforced by law? Would consumers buy products, particularly products not immediately consumable, if they had no legal rights to exclude others from using their property? When property rights are not clearly defined, the market has problems efficiently allocating resources.

2. Provide public goods and addressing externalities

Public goods are goods that are not handled well by private markets. National defense is a good example: The government is responsible for national defense because of its desire to protect every citizen—and not just those that can afford to pay for it. Externalities are costs or benefits not captured by the supply and demand of private markets.

3. Insure competition

We have seen that perfectly competitive markets will produce the socially optimal amount because price is equal to marginal cost. We have also seen that in imperfect competition, the condition of P = MC does not usually exist, and the socially optimal amount of output is not encouraged. The question is, Should government encourage competition by using anti-trust regulations? When and to what extent may be argued, but many people agree that there are indeed times when it's necessary for the government to promote competition, thereby protecting consumers.

4. Provide for equity in the distribution of income

That there will be disparity of income in our society is a fact, and this serves as incentive to be productive. At the same time, there is concern over the existence of poverty and a widening gap in income levels. The government has taken steps to provide for more equity in the distribution of income by financing public education and by providing safety nets for the unemployed, ill, and elderly. With higher marginal income taxed at a higher rate, some tax revenue is used to finance these "safety net" programs. The extent to which the government redistributes income in this way can again be argued, but there is common support that the government has the moral obligation to provide some relief to needy individuals.

5. Stabilize the economy

Though there's great disagreement over the government's role in minimizing the ups and downs of the business cycle, many still look to the government to "stimulate" the economy during recessions, and to encourage economic growth. This is a topic that is fundamental to the study of macroeconomics.

NEGATIVE EXTERNALITIES

What happens if the private cost recognized by producers does not include all the costs of resources used in the production of the good or service? A **negative externality** is created; that is, a cost imposed on a third party that the producer didn't take into account. Pollution is a good example: If a firm is polluting the water in its vicinity and ignoring the costs, then a negative externality exists. The firm is passing this cost on to society and is not including the cost in its **private cost**. The **social cost** includes the private cost plus the **externalized** cost of the pollution. The private cost does not include the externalized cost.

In the following graph, the marginal social cost curve is above the supply curve. That's because the supply curve includes only the private cost and not the externalized cost. As a result, the firm recognizes less cost and can supply more at each price level.

The marginal social cost curve includes the private cost plus the externalized cost. As a result of recognizing all costs, this curve indicates that the quantity produced would be less at each price level. P and Q represent the equilibrium price and quantity when only the private cost is recognized. P^{so} and Q^{so} represent the socially optimal price and quantity when all costs are included in the supply curve.

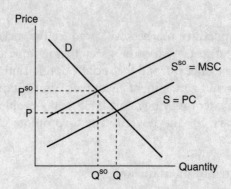

We can now conclude that when a negative externality exists, the market price (P) will be too low and the market quantity (Q) will be too great. The firm is allocating too many resources to the production of this good. This type of market failure can justify government intervention. The government could impose a tax on the firm that would drive up cost and drive the supply curve to S^{so}. Implied is that the tax would cover the externalized cost.

Another option would be government regulation that would force the firm to recognize the cost. This, too, would result in a shift of the supply curve to S^{so}. The shift can also be illustrated as a shift to S^{tax} or S^{reg} (supply with tax or supply with regulation).

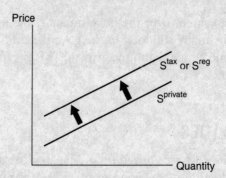

The negative externality is also referred to as a *third party cost* or *spillover cost*. The firm and the consumer are the two parties in the transaction, and they externalize the cost passed on to a third party.

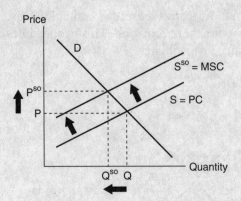

After the tax or the regulation forces the firm to decrease supply, the price will be higher and the quantity supplied will be less.

POSITIVE EXTERNALITIES

In situations where there's a benefit to those who are not paying the market price, there's a **positive externality**. This is also called a *third party benefit* or *spillover benefit*. In this case, the marginal social benefit is greater than the demand curve. The demand curve captures the marginal utilities of all the consumers willing to pay various prices, but it doesn't capture the marginal utilities of those who benefit without having to pay. Education, immunization, and beautiful parks are positive externalities.

When graphing a positive externality, the demand curve is inside the marginal benefit curve. The market will not supply the socially optimal quantity, and it would charge too low of a price. Private markets will always "underallocate" resources to production if there are beneficiaries who will not pay.

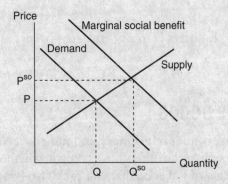

The socially optimal amount that should be produced is Q^{so}; however, the firm will only produce Q. It will underallocate resources to produce this good because it cannot get all beneficiaries to pay for the benefit they receive. The equilibrium price will also be less (P) than the price at the socially optimal amount (P^{so}). Because society is underallocating resources, the government can encourage the greater production level by regulation or a subsidy.

If we were dealing with a vaccination against a dreaded contagious disease, the government could mandate that everyone pay for the vaccination. This would shift the demand curve to the right toward the marginal social benefit curve.

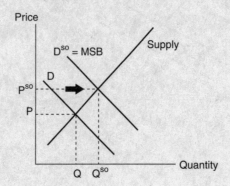

The government could also give consumers a subsidy for the purchase of the vaccination, shifting the demand from D to D^{so}, and raising the price to P^{so}. Or, it could give producers a subsidy.

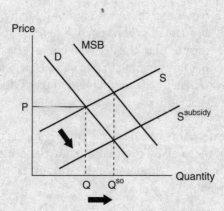

The effect of a subsidy to producers is to shift the supply curve to the right increasing the quantity from Q to Q^{so}.

PUBLIC AND PRIVATE GOODS

A public good is a good that is **nonexclusionary** and **nonrival**. *Nonexclusionary* means that the owner of the good cannot exclude others from using it, whether or not they pay for it. An exclusionary good would be a can of soda that you purchase—you can prevent others from consuming it, just like the producer can prevent anyone from consuming that can of soda until it is paid for. Obviously, the existence and enforcement of laws to guarantee "property rights" is essential. By *nonrival* we mean that one person's use does not diminish other people's ability to consume the same good; many people can enjoy and consume it at the same time. (A *rival* good, on the other hand, would be a can of soda, for example. Consuming a can of soda prevents others from consuming that same can.)

EFFICIENCY, EQUITY, AND THE ROLE OF GOVERNMENT

Products that are nonexclusionary and nonrival present a problem for the marketplace. Some people can benefit from a public good without paying for it. These people are **free riders**. It is difficult for private firms to operate successfully when some consumers are benefiting from their product without paying for it. Firms will underallocate resources to the production of these goods. Since public goods are nonexclusionary, they have a type of positive externality; that is, the marginal social benefit (even including free riders) is greater than the demand (consumers' willingness to pay) at every level of production.

A lighthouse is a classic example of a nonexclusionary good. Its purpose is to protect ships from navigational hazards. It would be difficult to operate the lighthouse solely for paying customers.

When a product is exclusionary and rival, it is a **private good**. That is, the owner of the good can exclude those who don't pay. The market does a very good job of allocating resources and products of private goods. There are no free riders. If one benefits from the product, he must pay for it. such as with a can of soda.

Public goods that are thought to be important require some government involvement. The government can provide for the country's defense by paying for it with tax dollars. People must pay their taxes or suffer the consequences. It is more difficult to be a free rider in this type of situation, and the government can provide the amount of defense that it deems necessary.

Some good or services may have only one of the two characteristics that differentiate public and private goods. Take the fish in the ocean: To the fisherman in New England, fishing is certainly a rival activity. What one fisherman catches, another one cannot. If one fisherman decides not to catch fish so that breeders will survive, other fishermen cannot be excluded and will probably catch those fish anyway. This is a case of nonexclusionary but rival consumption, and it will result in a case of overfishing. Clearly, there are no property rights that would allow for more future-oriented business decisions.

INCOME EQUITY

Income distribution illustrates how much of the economy's total income is earned by different segments of the population. The segments can be described in a variety of ways:

- By income
- By gender
- By race
- By education
- By geographic region

One popular way to look at income distribution is to compare what each quintile of households claim in terms of total income generated in the economy. The following is data gathered by the U.S. Census Bureau for 2000–2001:

Quintile	2000 Share of Income
Lowest	3.6%
Second	8.9%
Third	14.9%
Fourth	23.0%
Highest	49.7%

Each quintile represents 20 percent of the households. Here, the lowest 20 percent of households had 3.6 percent of the total income available. The highest 20 percent had 49.7 percent of the income available.

A second way to measure income distribution is to look at average or median income of various groups. The following represents the median income and poverty rate by race and Hispanic origin over a three-year average. The following information is from the U.S. Census Bureau and represents the averages for years 1999, 2000, and 2001.

	Income	Poverty rate
United States	$41,800	11.9%
White	$43,800	9.9%
White non-Hispanic	$45,500	7.8%
Black	$28,700	23.9%
American Indian and Alaskan Native	$31,800	25.9%
Asian and Pacific Islander	$52,600	11.3%
Hispanic (of any race)	$31,700	23.1%

In the United States, half the households had incomes above $41,800, and half had incomes below $41,800. The poverty rate data also indicates that 11.9 percent of the households lived below the poverty line. The **poverty line** is the level of income established by the government, below which households are said to be in poverty. As for the data for different ethnic groups, there seem to be some differences in income, although one must be careful to not draw too many conclusions from this data. The median income has been rising steadily, and the poverty rate has been declining (this is not shown in the data above). Of course, the data here does not take into consideration the consequences of the recent sluggish economy.

A third way to look at income distribution is the **Lorenz Curve**. This curve, frequently used to compare the income distribution patterns of various economies, measures how equally distributed income is.

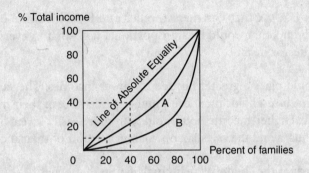

The Lorenz curve is a way of graphically illustrating the disparity in income distribution within a country and between countries. The diagonal line is the line of absolute equality. On this line, we see that 40 percent of families have 40 percent of the income in a country. Curve A indicates that 20 percent of the families in country A have about 10 percent of the income. And curve B shows that country B has even more inequality in the distribution of income than country A. The greater the distance from the line of absolute equality, the greater the disparity in income distribution.

Naturally, government has some sort of role in addressing income inequality. Several factors frequently determine low income and poverty:

1. Unemployment caused by changes in the economy

2. Poor job skills

3. Lack of education

4. Social inequities

One function of government is to redistribute income from higher income households to lower income households. Government does this through transfers. Some of the transfer programs are Social Security, food stamps, unemployment compensation, and Medicaid. In order to pay for these programs, the government must tax the incomes of those people who are employed.

TAXES

The tax that raises the largest amount of money for the federal government is the **income tax**. In the United States, the income tax is a **progressive tax**. There are three types of taxes:

- Proportional
- Progressive
- Regressive

The Federal income tax is progressive because the marginal tax rates are higher for higher income levels. The philosophy is that those that earn more money can more afford to pay higher taxes.

A **proportional tax** is a tax that has the same tax rate for all income levels. Some people advocate having a **flat tax** that would be a proportional tax—that is, everyone should pay 20 percent of his income, for instance.

A **regressive tax** would place a greater burden on lower incomes. The **sales tax** is regressive because lower-income households must use a higher percentage of their incomes to consume the necessities of life. Higher-income households can more easily save a larger percentage of their income, and thus, avoid the sales tax on a larger portion of their income.

Some taxes are levied on the "**benefit**" **principal**: Those that benefit should pay the tax. The gas tax, for example, is levied on the consumption of gasoline. The revenue that is raised is used for road construction and repair. Therefore, car owners should pay the tax.

Students are expected to determine "incidence of tax," and to graph the effects of a per unit tax. **Tax incidence** is who bears the burden of the tax. This term is usually used in conjunction with an excise tax (per unit tax). The question is, Will the supplier be able to pass the tax, or at least most of it, on to the consumer. The tax incidence is dependent on the price elasticity of supply and demand. The more elastic the demand, the less the supplier can pass the tax on to the consumer.

Let's say the government imposes a $.50 tax on every gallon of milk. The price before the tax was $2.00 per gallon.

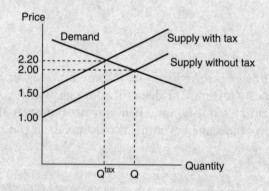

We have here a relatively elastic demand curve; a $.50 tax decreases demand, but the price rises by $.20. The incidence of tax falling to the consumer is 40 percent (.20/.50). The supplier must bear a 60 percent tax incidence.

Let's look at the same problem with a more inelastic demand.

EFFICIENCY, EQUITY, AND THE ROLE OF GOVERNMENT

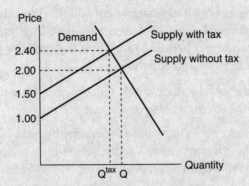

With a more elastic demand curve, $.40 of the tax (80 percent) is passed on to the consumer. The quantity supplied is reduced significantly less than with the more elastic demand curve.

If the government's main goal for the per unit tax (excise tax) is to raise tax revenue, then a more inelastic demand would be better. The total tax revenue raised would be the tax (.50) times the quantity. Since the quantity reduction is less with a more inelastic demand curve, more tax revenue will be raised. Conversely, if government's goal is to place a per unit tax to discourage consumption, then it would be more effective if the demand were more elastic.

KEY IDEAS

- The supply side of a market economy works most efficiently when producers are responsible for all the costs, and these costs are reflected in the costs of supplying the good or service.

- The demand side of a market economy works most efficiently when the paying consumers are the only beneficiaries of the goods and services produced.

- An externality occurs when a decision-maker takes an action that imposes on a third party a cost or benefit that had not been accounted for.

- A third party benefit is a positive externality (also called a *spillover benefit*). When there is a positive externality, the marginal social benefit curve is to the right of the demand curve. The "private" demand curve is less than the socially optimal demand. A third party cost is a negative externality (also called a *spillover cost*). When there is a negative externality, the marginal social cost curve is the left of the "private" supply curve.

- Externalities are a type of market failure. The government can try to rectify a negative externality by taxing or regulating the output. Either action would decrease the output, shifting the supply curve to the left. This would encourage the social optimal output.

- A private good is rival and excludable: The market has no problem dealing with private goods, as an efficient allocation of resources will occur in the marketplace. A public good is not rival and excludable, and the market will always underallocate resources to its production. The government will need to subsidize the production of a public good to obtain the socially optimal amount. The quantity of public goods that creates the greatest net benefit to society is the quantity where society's marginal cost is equal to society's marginal benefit.

- A market failure is a socially undesirable outcome resulting from markets not recognizing all of the social benefits and social costs.

- Government plays a key role in a market economy by establishing and enforcing property rights. The government also redistributes income from higher to lower income households through transfers and taxes.

REVIEW QUESTIONS

1. If a positive externality exists, a private firm will

    (A) overallocate resources to the production.
    (B) charge too high a price.
    (C) hire more workers.
    (D) underallocate resources to the production.
    (E) produce only the socially optimal quantity.

2. Which of the following is most likely to be a positive externality?

    (A) Water pollution
    (B) A soda vending machine
    (C) A purchase of a used car
    (D) The rehabilitation of a house that was in serious disrepair
    (E) The smell from a paper manufacturing plant

3. Who benefits from a negative externality?

    (A) All of society
    (B) Only the firm that creates the negative externality
    (C) The consumers who buy the product of the polluting firm
    (D) A and B
    (E) B and C

4. The reason why some ocean fish are endangered and farm-raised catfish are not is that

    (A) fishing in the ocean is not a rival activity.
    (B) catfish farms cannot exclude other fishermen.
    (C) there are no property rights to the fish in the ocean.
    (D) catfish are not edible.
    (E) there is no demand for catfish.

5. In economics, the term "free rider" refers to

    (A) the public transit system.
    (B) an addition to a contract.
    (C) a person who benefits from a good without paying.
    (D) a person who provides free transportation to others.
    (E) a person who creates a negative externality.

6. Which of the following would be consistent with market failure?

    (A) Price will be below average total cost.
    (B) Price will be greater than the total marginal cost.
    (C) Price will be equal to the minimum average total cost
    (D) Price includes all social cost of production
    (E) Price rises when the socially optimal quantity is produced

7. A sales tax on all goods and services is which of the following?

   (A) A regressive tax
   (B) A progressive tax
   (C) A proportional tax
   (D) A protective tax
   (E) An "ability to pay" tax

8. Currently the largest percent of total income is attributed to the

   (A) lowest quintile of household incomes.
   (B) second quintile of household incomes.
   (C) third quintile of household incomes.
   (D) fourth quintile of household incomes.
   (E) highest quintile of household incomes.

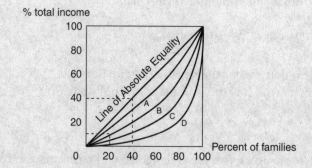

9. In the Lorenz Curve of income distribution above, curves A, B, C, and D represent various countries. Which country has the most even distribution of income?

   (A) A
   (B) B
   (C) C
   (D) D
   (E) They all have equal distribution of income.

10. Which of the following would be considered a transfer payment?

    (A) Payment by the U.S. military to Boeing Aircraft for the purchase of new jets
    (B) Payment to a federal employee
    (C) Payment by the federal government for new roads
    (D) Payment by the federal government for unemployment compensation
    (E) Payment by the federal government for the cost of the federal court system

11. Given a new excise tax, the more the price elasticity of demand,

   (A) the greater the incidence of tax falls on the consumer.
   (B) the less quantity supplied will be reduced.
   (C) the greater the tax revenue will be.
   (D) the less tax revenue will be.
   (E) the greater the consumer surplus.

12. If the U.S. government decided to regulate a firm that was ignoring a negative externality,

   (A) the market price would decrease and the firm would allocate more resources to production.
   (B) the market price would decrease and the firm would allocate fewer resources to production.
   (C) the market price would increase and the firm would allocate more resources to production.
   (D) the market price would increase and the firm would allocate fewer resources to production.
   (E) more consumers would buy the product.

Free-Response Questions

1. Assume that the soybean industry is a perfectly competitive industry with no long-run economic profit. Every firm in this industry uses pesticides that create a negative externality. The pesticides increase the productivity of every farmer. Using a correctly labeled graph, illustrate and explain how the soybean industry is misallocating resources.

   (a) Give an example of how the government might effectively eliminate the negative externality.
   (b) Explain what will happen to price and output as a result of the government action you recommend above.
   (c) Using a correctly labeled graph, illustrate and explain what will happen to a typical firm in this industry after the government takes the action recommend above.
   (d) Explain the long-run consequence to some of the firms in this industry.

2. The allergy medication industry faces a very inelastic demand. The government decides to impose a per unit excise tax of $2 on every bottle of 30 pills (assume that all sales are of 30 count bottles).

   (a) Using a correctly labeled graph, illustrate and explain the incidence of tax that will occur. Make sure that your graph clearly indicates the $2 tax and the change in price and quantity that will occur.
   (a) On your graph, illustrate and explain the tax revenues that will be collected by the government.

ANSWERS TO REVIEW QUESTIONS

1. (D)

When there is a positive externality, the marginal social benefit (MSB) is greater than the private demand. The firm produces at Q^1, P^1. If the firm produced the socially optimal amount, it would produce at Q^2, P^2. It is not producing enough output; therefore, it is underallocating resources to the production.

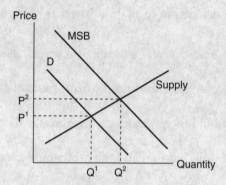

2. (D)

Cleaning up a house in disrepair adds benefit to the neighbors and improves the market value of their own homes, yet they do not pay for any of the repair work itself. (A) and (E) are negative externalities. (B) and (C) are market transactions that would not necessarily create externalities.

3. (E)

The firm benefits because it avoids costs that it should recognize. The consumers benefit because they pay a lower price than they should. (A) and (D) are wrong, as members of society who do not consume the good still bear the burden of the negative externality. (B) is wrong because it does not recognize the benefit to consumers.

4. (C)

The lack of property rights leads to overfishing.

5. (C)

A free rider is a person who benefits from a good or service without paying for it.

6. (B)

When price is greater than marginal cost, the socially optimal amount of production is not obtained. (A) describes an economic loss which may be a problem for a firm, but is not market failure. (C) is productive efficiency. (D) and (E) are necessary conditions for *no* market failure.

7. (A)

Poorer households must spend a greater portion of their incomes purchasing necessities. This means that more of their income is subject to the tax.

8. (E)

The highest 20 percent of income earners garner the largest percentage of total income available

9. (A)

The less variance from the line of absolute equality indicates that there is less disparity in income distribution.

10. (D)

Unemployment compensation is a transfer payment from the government to the households. All the other answer choices are government purchases.

11. (D)

The greater the price elasticity of demand, the more the quantity sold will be reduced. Tax revenue is calculated by taking the tax per unit and multiplying by the quantity sold. (A) is out because with more elasticity of demand, less of the tax incidence falls on the consumer. (B) is wrong because quantity supplied will be reduced more. (C) is the opposite of the correct answer. And consumer surplus will be decreased, so (E) is wrong.

12. (D)

Government regulation forces the firm to recognize the added cost of the negative externality. The firm's supply will decrease, moving toward the socially optimal supply. Consequently, price increases and quantity decreases. The decrease in quantity supplied indicates that fewer resources will be used.

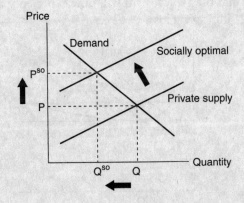

Free-Response Questions

1.

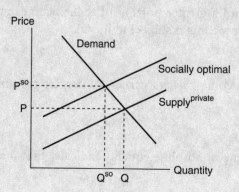

The negative externality means that the industry is not capturing all of the cost of production. The supply curve of the industry includes only the private costs that are captured. If the firm captured all of the externalized costs, the supply curve would decrease to the socially optimal level. Without recognizing the externality, the industry produces Q, not Q^{so}. The industry is overallocating resources because it is producing more than it should.

(a) The government can impose a per unit tax. This will increase the cost of producing and decrease the supply.

(b) Decreasing the private supply will increase price and decrease output.

(c) The typical firm will experience an increase in cost, shifting the ATC curve up to ATC^2 and the MC curve up. In part (a), we have identified an increase in price resulting from the tax. The firm is a price taker and therefore price will increase to P^2. However, we know that the equilibrium quantity for the industry will be less, so we can conclude that the typical firm will now experience an economic loss. P^2 will be below the ATC, indicating loss.

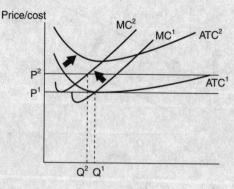

(d) In the long run, firms will drop out of the industry shifting the supply curve to the left. The remaining firms will take a higher price and have no economic profit or economic loss.

2. **(a)** Because of the inelastic demand, the burden of the tax will fall mostly on the consumer. As we increase the cost by \$2, supply will decrease from Supply to Supply^{tax}. The price increases from P1 to P2, and the quantity decreases from Q1 to Q2. Since most of the \$2 translates into a price increase rather than a decrease in quantity, we can conclude that the consumers will bear most of the incidence of tax.

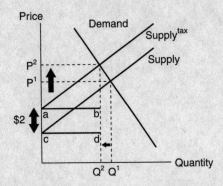

(b) The tax revenues collected by the government will be \$2 × Q^2. On the graph, total revenues are equal to the area of the rectangle a, b, c, and d.

INTERNATIONAL ECONOMICS

Section V

International Economics

We now turn to the macroeconomic implications of an economy as part of the global economy. More and more countries are engaging in trade across their borders. Financial capital is available for governments to pursue returns wherever they are profitable and secure. Although there is still some opposition to trade, as well as valid concerns that need to be addressed, there is no stopping the trend to a more and more "open economy."

An **open economy** is one that imports and exports significant amounts of goods and services. It also allows financial capital to flow into and out of its capital markets. In addition to the technology that allows for the flow of information and the improvement in transportation, the global economy is encouraged as a way to improve the standard of living for those who participate.

When dealing with an open economy, the macroeconomic model for GDP and expenditures is:

$$GDP = C + I + G + X$$

In contrast, when dealing with a **closed economy**, that is, a country that has little economic interaction with other countries, the macroeconomic model for GDP and expenditures would be:

$$GDP = C + I + G$$

Of course it is possible for a country to have a foreign sector that is not a significant part of total expenditures. The term *open economy* is a relative term; some countries are more open than others. Examining the value of an economy's export as a percent of total GDP provides a good

Examining the value of an economy's export as a percent of total GDP provides a good measure of how open an economy is. That is, it gives us the value of aggregate demand that is dependent on foreign markets.

measure of how open an economy is. That is, it gives us the value of aggregate demand that is dependent on foreign markets. Let's look at some data for the United States:

Year	1997	1998	1999	2000	2001
GDP (Billions)	8,318	8,782	9,269	9,873	10,208
Exports (Billions)	966	965	990	786	736
%	12	11	11	8	7

During the given time period, the United States exported at most 12 percent of the goods and services it produced. This is a significant amount, although other countries are even more dependent on international markets: Canada's exports are around 40 percent of its total GDP, while Mexico's are around 30 percent.

FREE TRADE

At the heart of the argument for free trade is the **Ricardian Model of Comparative Advantage**. (You'll remember that comparative advantage measures the relative opportunity cost of producing a good.) The Model advocates trade based on comparative advantage and **specialization**: If countries specialize in the products in which they have the comparative advantage, and they trade with each other, then all participating countries should attain a higher standard of living. That is, if one country produces a good at a lower opportunity cost than another country, then it should specialize—and trade—in that good. In this scenario, all parties will be better off. To review the basics of calculating comparative advantage, see chapter 2.

> Knowing how to compute absolute advantage, comparative advantage, and terms of trade is crucial when dealing with international economic analysis.

Let's take a simplified case. If country Alpha can produce 10 million computers or one million cars, and country Beta can produce 20 million computers or four million cars, what is the absolute advantage and comparative advantage?

	Cars (Millions)	Computers (Millions)	Opportunity Cost of Cars	Opportunity Cost of Computers
Alpha	1	10	$\frac{10}{1} = 10$	$\frac{1}{10} = .10$
Beta	4	20	$\frac{20}{4} = 5$	$\frac{4}{20} = .20$

Beta has the absolute advantage in producing both cars and computers. But when it comes to comparative advantage, Alpha's opportunity cost for computers is less than Beta's, so it has the advantage: It forgoes 1/10 of a car for every computer made, while Beta forgoes 2/10 of a car. Beta, however, has the comparative advantage in car production.

If Alpha remained a closed economy and used half its resources to produce cars and half to produce computers, it would have 500,000 cars and 5,000,000 computers. If it decided instead to specialize where it has a comparative advantage, it would produce 10,000,000 computers. As long as the terms of trade were agreeable, and long as it got more than its opportunity cost when trading, Alpha would be better off by doing this.

In other words, as long as Alpha does not give up more than 10 computers for every car, it will be better off. Of course, if it didn't get *at least* one car for every 10 computers, it would not trade. It would produce fewer computers and use its own resources to produce cars. If the terms of trade were one car for every eight computers, it could trade 500,000 computers for 625,000 cars. Then it would have 500,000 computers and 625,000 cars.

	Cars	Computers
Before Trade	5,000,000	500,000
After Trade	5,000,000	625,000

Now let's use this data in a production possibilities curve (PPC):

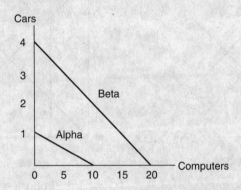

For the AP exam, you'll be expected to determine absolute advantage, comparative advantage, opportunity cost, and acceptable terms of trade from data in a constant cost production possibilities curve. Though the model above is highly simplified, it demonstrates countries with constant costs in the production of cars and computers.

An increasing cost (bowed out) PPC presents the problem of changing opportunity cost, which is dealt with at a more advanced level of economic study.

In order for countries to benefit from trade based on our understanding of comparative advantage, it is important to eliminate barriers to trade. Barriers to trade add cost and distort trade potential.

Free trade means eliminating tariffs, quotas, and other trade restrictions. The use of tariffs, quotas, and other trade restrictions is protectionism.

QUOTAS AND TARIFFS

Quotas limit the number of goods that may be imported. **Tariffs** are taxes placed on imported goods. These taxes must be paid for by the foreign producer. As a result, it increases the cost of supplying the good. The increased cost shifts the supply curve to the left (decrease).

Both quotas and tariffs lead to higher prices and less consumption by domestic consumers. Both create higher prices. With a tariff the government gets some of the value of higher prices. With a quota the foreign producer gets a higher per unit profit.

Quotas and tariffs help the domestic producer to the extent that it sells more cars at a higher price. Quotas and tariffs lead to reciprocal quotas and tariffs. The result is that domestic producers that export will be hurt.

A quota would have the following graph structure:

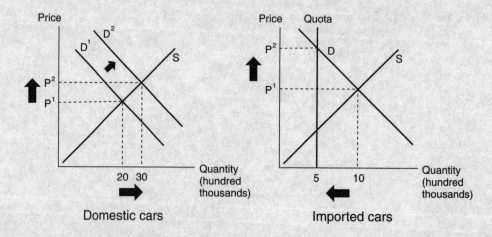

These graphs present data of the car market in the country of Omega. The graph on the left represents the domestic car market, while the one on the right represents the imported car market. Without any restrictions, the consumers of Omega will purchase 2,000,000 domestic cars at a price of P^1, and 1,000,000 imported cars at a price of p^1. The government places a quota on car imports, limiting the number to 500,000. The vertical line on the imported market at 500,000 illustrates the quota. The result is that the price of imported cars will rise

KAPLAN

to p^2. Since Omegans pay more for the foreign car, the quantity demanded of foreign cars will drop. Because some consumers of imported cars will now buy domestic cars, the demand for domestic cars will increase from D^1 to D^2, and the price of domestic cars rises to P^2.

The net result is that consumers pay more for domestic cars and imported cars. There are more domestic cars purchased but fewer cars purchased in total. Domestic producers sell more cars at higher prices.

Now let's look at a tariff graph.

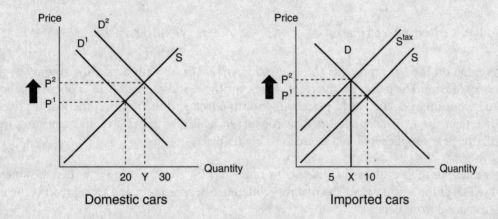

Here, the tariff shifts the supply of imported cars to the left. The price of imported cars increases to p^2, and the quantity demanded decreases to X. The drop in demand for imported cars will shift the demand for domestic cars to the right. The price of domestic cars increases to P^2, and the quantity increases to Y.

The net result is that consumers pay more for both domestic and imported cars. The total cars purchased drops because of the new prices. Domestic producers sell more cars at a higher price.

WORLD PRICES

A country that has an open economy will have markets that move to the world price of perfect substitute goods. Let's look at world prices in the oil market. Oil is a **perfect substitute**: There is no difference in oil from one country to another.

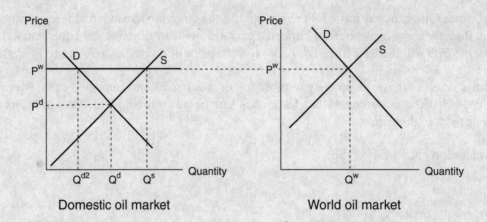

Domestic oil market   World oil market

The graph on the left represents the domestic market for oil with a closed economy in the country of Beta. The graph on the right represents the world market. If Beta opens its doors to the world market, the world price will go into effect. In this instance, the world price is higher than the original price, so Beta consumers will now pay more and consume less. Similarly, Beta suppliers will sell more for a higher price.

After entering the world market, Beta consumers pay P^w and consume Q^{d2}. Beta producers will sell Q^s at the world price. The quantity difference between Q^{d2} and Q^s represents the net exports of oil from Beta.

What about when world prices are *lower* than domestic prices? What happens then? The following graphs illustrate the effect if Beta went from a closed economy to an open economy in the oil market.

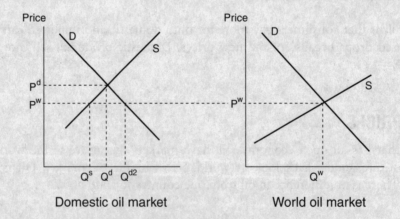

Domestic oil market   World oil market

With a lower price, Beta consumers would buy more and pay a lower price (the world price). Producers in Beta will sell fewer units of oil at the lower world price. The quantity difference between Q^s and Q^{d2} would be the net imported oil.

As economies become more global, will everyone eventually pay the same price for goods? The **law of one price** claims that everyone will pay the same price for all goods. The reasoning is that if a good costs more in one country than in another, arbitrage will occur. **Arbitrage** is the process of buying when prices are low, and reselling when prices are higher. Buying in the low-price market increases the demand in that market, pushing up prices. Selling the good in the higher price market increases the supply in that market, and will push prices down. Eventually the prices become one.

Purchasing-power parity is a theory based on the law of one price. The idea is that one nation's currency should have the same purchasing power in another country, after the currency has been exchanged for the local currency. If a shirt costs $40 in the United States, and one converts $40 to 4,000 yen and can buy the same shirt in Japan for 4,000 yen, then purchasing-power parity exists. This theory depends on the fact that the exchange rates correctly reflect the price levels in each country.

Purchasing-power parity is a model that works well in understanding a great deal in international economics. However, it has some limitations: Some goods and services may not move easily from one country to another, making arbitrage less likely. The price to have your bicycle repaired in the United States may not be the same as it is in Japan. If the price in Japan is relatively cheaper, it's unlikely that an arbitrageur will be able to gain from it. Another problem is that a similar good in one country may not be a perfect substitute. If goods are not perfect substitutes, then one can expect price differences.

How does a country account for the global economic activity? When a country imports goods and services from other countries, money flows out of that country. When a country exports goods and services to other countries, money flows in. The balance of payment accounts measures a country's international transactions.

The current account of a country measures the value of goods and services that are imported and exported, the value of income earned from assets abroad, the value of income sent to another country, and the flow of gifts and aid. The capital account measures all the international sales and purchases of assets.

The current account must equal the capital account. The equality is established in the currency market. Credits on both accounts represent demand for currency in the international currency market, while debits on both accounts represent supply of currency. In this market, the quantity of currency supplied will equal the quantity of currency demanded. So if one account has an imbalance of credit or debit, it must be offset by a debit or credit balance in the other account.

If there's a negative balance in the current account, it must be offset by an equal positive balance in the capital account.

EXCHANGE RATES

Exchange rates determine how much of currency B we get when we exchange it for currency A. It's important that you know how to analyze the currencies market using supply and demand graphs.

Fixed exchange rates are backed by gold or some other currency. If the U.S. dollar were pegged (fixed) to an ounce of gold at 36 dollars an ounce, and the British pound were pegged to an ounce of gold at 12 pounds an ounce, then the exchange rate would be three dollars equals one pound. Many developing countries use this system of pegging their currency to the U.S. dollar or some other currency. Fixed exchange rates create some problems that may require devaluation or revaluation, changing the par value of the currency.

Free-floating exchange rates: Countries with free-floating exchange rates allow their currencies to change (to float) with the supply and demand of the foreign exchange market.

If the exchange rate were one pound equals 1.5 dollars, then one dollar equals .67 pounds (1/1.5 =.67 rounded). A change in this exchange rate will be brought about by fluctuations in the supply and demand of each currency in the international currency market. Whenever Great Britain wants more goods from the United States, the demand for dollars increases. Moreover, the supply of pounds also increases—as pounds are used to buy dollars.

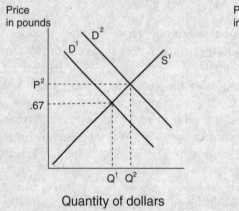

Quantity of dollars

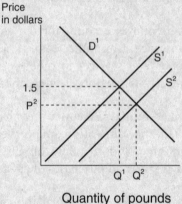

Quantity of pounds

The graph on the left represents the market for dollars, with the price in pounds. The graph on the right is the market for pounds, with the price in dollars. If there's an increase in the demand for dollars by consumers or investors in Great Britain, then the demand for dollars will shift to the right. The new demand is D^2. The new equilibrium price will be P^2. This means that it now costs more pounds than before to buy dollars. In other words, the dollar has *appreciated* against the pound.

We can illustrate the same event in the pound market. When the demand for dollars increases in Great Britain, consumers must purchase the dollars with pounds, so the supply of pounds increases. That shifts the supply from S^1 to S^2, and the price to P^2. It now takes fewer dollars to buy pounds. Both markets indicate the same event and the same result.

Dollar appreciates	Pound depreciates
Takes more pounds to buy dollars	Takes fewer dollars to buy pounds
Takes fewer dollars to buy pounds	Takes more pounds to buy dollars

What about when Americans want to buy more pounds? The demand for pounds increases from D^1 to D^2, and the supply of dollars increases from S^1 to S^2.

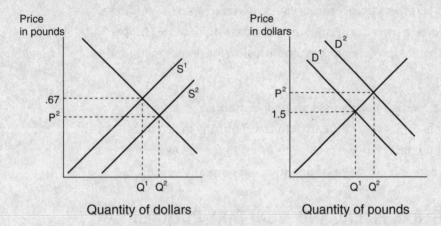

Quantity of dollars   Quantity of pounds

The price of pounds in dollars has increased to P^2. It now takes more dollars to buy pounds. And the price of dollars in pounds has decreased; it now takes fewer pounds to buy dollars.

Dollar depreciates	Pound appreciates
Takes fewer pounds to buy dollars	Takes more dollars to buy pounds
Takes more dollars to buy pounds	Takes fewer pounds to buy dollars

Currency Appreciation and Depreciation

Students should understand who is helped and who is harmed by the appreciation and depreciation of currency.

Currency Appreciation (stronger currency)

The advantages of a stronger currency are:

- Consumer can buy imports at a lower price
- Travelers abroad can get more foreign currency
- Investors can buy more foreign assets
- The competition from foreign suppliers keeps domestic prices down

The disadvantages are:

- Producers will sell fewer exports
- Foreigners traveling into the country will find it more expensive
- Foreign investment of domestic assets will be more expensive
- Domestic suppliers will have more price competition

Currency depreciation (weaker currency)

The advantages of a weaker currency are:

- Producers will sell more exports
- It becomes cheaper for foreigners to travel into the country
- Foreign investment in domestic assets will become cheaper
- There is less foreign price competition for domestic producers

The disadvantages are:

- Domestic consumer pay more for imports
- It becomes more expensive to travel outside the country
- It becomes more expensive to invest in foreign assets
- There is less foreign competition for domestic pricing

CHANGES IN FISCAL AND MONETARY POLICIES

As a country becomes more open, it must consider how unexpected changes of fiscal and monetary policies will affect the foreign sector of its economy. We can assume that expected changes have already been calculated into the international markets. The following looks at the short-run effects of policy changes in countries with a free-floating exchange rate and a free flow of financial capital.

Expansionary Policies

An **unexpected expansionary fiscal policy** will increase aggregate demand and money demand. The money demand increase pulls the interest rates higher. If the higher interest rates are not experienced in other countries, financial capital will flow into this country in pursuit of a higher return on investment. This increases the demand for the currency—and the currency appreciates. The stronger currency encourages more imports and fewer exports. The decreasing exports offset at least some of the aggregate demand stimulated by the initial fiscal expansionary policy. If the exports are a large percentage of GDP, then this offsetting effect is more important.

An **unexpected expansionary monetary policy** will lower the interest rates. The increase in the money supply and the lower interest rates will increase aggregate demand. With lower interest rates, financial capital will flow out of the country. This means a lower demand for the currency and a weaker currency. The weaker currency leads to more exports and fewer imports, which increases aggregate demand. We now have an internal and external increase in aggregate demand.

Contractionary Policies

An **unexpected contractionary fiscal policy** decreases aggregate demand and money demand. The decrease in money demand pulls interest rates lower. If the lower interest rates are not experienced in other countries, financial capital will flow out of this country in pursuit of a higher return on investment. This decreases the demand for the currency—and the currency depreciates. The weaker currency encourages more exports and fewer imports. This increases aggregate demand and offsets some of the aggregate demand lost from the decreasing government spending. Again, a lot depends on how large a part of aggregate demand is exports.

An **unexpected contractionary monetary policy** will raise the interest rates. The decrease in money supply and the increase in interest rates will decrease aggregate demand. The higher interest rates will attract foreign capital, which leads to an increase in demand for the currency and a stronger currency. The stronger currency leads to more imports and fewer exports, which in turn decreases aggregate demand. We now have an internal and external decrease in aggregate demand.

The more "open" an economy becomes, the more the macroeconomic implications of policies can affect exports and capital flows. We stated earlier that the export demand for the U.S. GDP was around 10 percent, while the export demand for the Canadian GDP was around 40 percent. Consequently the Canadian economy must concern itself with the impact of interest rates and Canadian dollar value to an even greater extent. In the United States, the short-run possible solution of a lower interest rate is seen as primarily encouraging more investment. In a country with a greater dependence on exports, the consideration of the central bank influencing short term interest rates downward is that it will depreciate the currency and increase exports. However, a country with a greater dependence of exports as a major component of aggregate demand must be more concerned with the impact on currency value, and the consequent effect that interest rate changes will have on exports.

As all industrialized economies become more global, analysis of the short-run effects of fiscal and monetary policies includes not only the impact on the variables of price level and unemployment, but also the variable of the value of the currency with its impact on aggregate demand.

KEY POINTS

- In the analysis of comparative advantage, opportunity cost and terms of trade play significant roles. The Ricardian Model states that countries should specialize in products for which they have comparative advantage. Comparative advantage can be computed from a table of information or from production possibility graphs.

- Free trade is necessary to maximize the benefits of comparative advantage. Obstacles to free trade are quotas, tariffs, and regulations. The use of these barriers is called protectionism. Protectionism appears to help producers but hurts consumers.

- In a closed economy GDP = C + I + G. In an open economy GDP = C + I + G + X. The greater the export demand for GDP, the more open the economy.

- The law of one price is dependent on arbitrage. Purchasing power parity is based on the law of one price. The law of one price does not work for every product.

- The balance of payment accounts measure the current account and the capital account. If there is a negative balance in the current account it must be offset by an equal positive balance in the capital account.

- Fixed exchange rates are pegged to gold or other countries' currencies. Free-floating exchange rates are subject to the laws of supply and demand in the foreign exchange market.

- If currency A appreciates against currency B, then currency B depreciates against currency A.

- Some economic participants are helped by a stronger currency and some are hurt by a stronger currency. Likewise, some economic participants are helped by a weaker currency and some are hurt by a weaker currency. Know who is helped and who is hurt in each situation.

- As a country becomes more "open," unexpected fiscal and monetary policies can have a significant effect on exports and imports.

REVIEW QUESTIONS

1. The law of comparative advantage implies that a country will

   (A) tend to export those goods in which it has a comparative advantage.
   (B) tend to import those goods in which it has an absolute advantage.
   (C) never export those goods in which it has an absolute advantage.
   (D) never import those goods in which it has an absolute advantage.
   (E) tend to import those goods in which it has a comparative advantage.

2. Which of the following is not a goal of protectionism?

   (A) To protect an "infant" industry
   (B) To protect domestic jobs
   (C) To preserve national security
   (D) To protect against "unfair" competition because of cheap foreign labor
   (E) To reduce prices paid by domestic consumers

3. Suppose a U.S. worker can produce 12 bushels of wheat or four brooms in a day, while an Irish worker can produce two bushels of wheat or two brooms in a day. When the United States and Ireland trade,

   (A) the United States will import wheat, and Ireland will import brooms.
   (B) the United States will export wheat, and Ireland will export brooms.
   (C) the United States will export brooms, and Ireland will export wheat.
   (D) Ireland will import both wheat and brooms.
   (E) Trade would not occur, since the United States has an absolute advantage in both wheat and broom production.

4. A quota imposed on foreign cars imported into the United States will

   (A) increase the prices of domestic cars.
   (B) increase the production of foreign cars.
   (C) decrease total employment in domestic car production.
   (D) decrease the price of domestic cars.
   (E) decrease the prices of foreign cars.

5. In country Epsilon, a worker can produce two units of food or four units of clothing in one day. In country Gamma, a worker can produce 10 units of food or five units of clothing in one day. Before trade takes place, the opportunity cost of producing

   (A) clothing in Epsilon is two units of food.
   (B) food in Epsilon is 0.5 unit of clothing.
   (C) clothing in Gamma is 0.5 unit of food.
   (D) food in Gamma is 0.5 unit of clothing.
   (E) food in Gamma is two units of clothing.

6. One effect of higher import tariffs is to

   (A) hurt everybody.
   (B) increase the number of imports.
   (C) lower exports in the long run.
   (D) increase unemployment in domestic, import-competing industries.
   (E) lower domestic employment in import competing industries

7. When a government decides to increase spending by issuing more bonds, it causes

   (A) the nation's currency to appreciate (increase in value).
   (B) demand for loanable funds to decrease.
   (C) exports to increase.
   (D) decreases merchandise trade deficit.
   (E) interest rates to decrease.

8. The balance of payments is

   (A) negative when the nation runs a trade deficit.
   (B) positive when the nation runs a trade surplus.
   (C) negative when the country is a borrower in the international capital market.
   (D) positive when the country is a lender in the international capital market.
   (E) always equal to zero.

9. Which of the following defines the concept of purchasing power parity?

   (A) A managed floating exchange rate
   (B) A gold-standard international monetary system
   (C) A balance of payment surplus maintained by capital exports
   (D) The Bretton Woods international monetary system
   (E) Goods and services cost the same in different countries (after currency is exchanged).

10. If the U.S. dollar increases in value relative to the British pound,

   (A) U.S. wheat will become cheaper in England.
   (B) British bicycles will become cheaper in the United States.
   (C) British bicycles will become more expensive in the United States.
   (D) German cars will become cheaper in the United States.
   (E) there is no change in prices.

Free-Response Questions

1. Loon and Toon are two countries with comparable resources. Both countries produce widgets and gadgets. Following is their production possibilities curve.

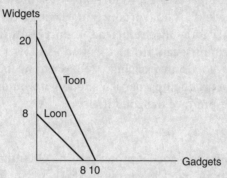

   (a) (i) Which country has the absolute advantage in the production of widgets?
        (ii) Which country has the absolute advantage in the production of gadgets?

   (b) Which country has the comparative advantage in the production of widgets? Why?

   (c) Which country has the comparative advantage in the production of gadgets? Why?

   (d) If the two countries decide to specialize and trade, which country should export gadgets? Why?

   (e) If the terms of trade are three widgets for two gadgets, will both countries trade? Why?

   (f) Which country gains from trade?

2. Assume that Openland is a country that exports 50 percent of its gross domestic product, and allows for free flow of financial capital into and out of its borders. Also assume that its currency is free-floating in the foreign exchange market. Foreign investors have no problems investing in Openland. Because of an unexpected high rate of unemployment, the government runs a large, unexpected deficit.

   (a) (i) What impact will the deficit have on its international transactions?
        (ii) Explain.

   (b) What can Openland's central bank do to improve the situation?

   (c) Draw a graph of the foreign exchange market for Openland currency and illustrate the effect of a successful policy as described in (b).

ANSWERS TO REVIEW QUESTIONS

1. (A)

Comparative advantage compares the production given up, or the opportunity cost of production, rather than the level of total production. Having a comparative advantage in one good means that the country is the more efficient producer of this particular good relative to some other goods. If the country can produce a good at a lower cost, it will tend to export that good and buy other goods in exchange. (E) is wrong because if a country has a comparative advantage in a producing a particular good, it wouldn't import the good from a "worse" producer. It would produce the good itself.

2. (E)

Reducing consumer prices is not a goal of protectionism. Oftentimes prices paid by domestic consumers increase when trade barriers are imposed. These barriers may provide benefits to individuals or groups, but these benefits come at a cost—the protection results in higher costs for consumers of the goods.

3. (B)

The United States has a comparative advantage in wheat since the opportunity cost of producing wheat there is lower. In the United States, it costs 1/3 broom to produce one bushel of wheat; in Ireland it costs one broom to produce one bushel of wheat. Ireland, however, has a comparative advantage in broom production, since it's the producer that faces a lower cost for producing brooms. In Ireland, producing a broom costs one bushel of wheat; in the United States, producing a broom costs three bushels of wheat. So when the two countries trade, the United States will export wheat, and Ireland will export brooms.

4. (A)

When the government imposes a quota on foreign car producers, the supply of cars available to U.S. consumers will decline. This is because the car market in the United States is made up of both domestic and foreign cars, and the quota will limit the supply of foreign cars coming into this car market. When the supply of cars decreases, the price of both domestic and foreign cars increases. (B) is wrong because the U.S. quota would cause diminished production of foreign cars destined for the United States. This type of quota would also increase the price of both domestic and foreign cars, so (D) and (E) can be eliminated as well.

5. (D)

The opportunity cost of producing a unit of food is equal to the clothing production given up to produce one more unit of food. A worker in Gamma gives up producing half a unit of clothing to produce one unit of food. Therefore the opportunity cost of food production is half a unit (0.5) of clothing.

6. (C)

Higher import tariffs cause price increases of both domestic and foreign goods. The tariff increases the cost of producing and selling foreign goods, decreasing the supply, which causes prices to rise. In the domestic market, the decreased supply of foreign goods decreases the total supply of domestic and foreign goods, causing the price of domestic goods to rise as well. At higher prices, quantity demanded falls, consumers start to buy less of that good, and imports fall. Decreasing imports means that the foreign producers are going to earn less, and so will decrease their spending to buy goods from the nation that originally established the import tariffs. If the foreigners are buying fewer of a nation's goods, then exports will fall in the long run. (A) is clearly wrong, so it can be eliminated immediately. (E) is out, too, because in the domestic market, the decreased supply of foreign goods decreases the total supply of domestic and foreign goods, causing the price of domestic goods to increase as well. At higher prices, domestic producers would want to increase their profit by producing more of the good, since they can sell their goods at higher prices after the higher tariffs are introduced. Therefore the domestic firms hire more labor to increase production, and employment rises in domestic, import-competing industries.

7. (A)

When government increases spending by issuing more bonds, it increases the nation's interest rates. That means (E) can be eliminated right away. Higher interest rates result in more capital inflow from the rest of the world. That's because asset ownership in the nation is a better deal when interest rate rises, so foreign investors bring their money into the economy. These capital inflows drive up the price of the nation's currency, since the demand for the currency goes up. So when the government decides to increase spending by issuing more bonds, it causes the nation's currency to appreciate.

8. (E)

The balance of payments is always equal to zero, since the current account and capital account offset each other. That's why it's called the balance of payments—the current account and capital account balance each other out. If a country has a current account deficit, then the country must be a borrower in the international capital market. As a borrower, it runs a capital account surplus. The capital account surplus will be equal to the deficit in the current account. Similarly, if a country has a current account surplus, then the country must be a lender in the international capital market; in that case, the country runs a capital account deficit. The capital account deficit will be equal to the surplus in the current account. Therefore the balance of payments is always zero.

9. (E)

According to purchasing power parity, a dollar of one nation's currency should have identical purchasing power when it's converted into another nation's currency. In other words, the purchasing power of the money after it's exchanged into another currency should be identical. (A) defines a system whereby a nation's central bank lets the nation's exchange rate be determined in the international currency market (though the central bank may step in and buy or sell currency or other assets to achieve certain exchange rate targets). (B) defines an exchange rate agreement between nations that ties the nations' currency value to the price of gold. (D) was an exchange rate agreement set between certain nations at the end of World War II. It set exchange rates between countries such as the United States and Great Britain and used purchases and sales of gold to maintain the fixed exchange rates.

10. (B)

An increase in the value of the dollar decreases the relative price of the goods in England and makes British goods cheaper in the United States. If the dollar increases in value relative to the British pound, it takes fewer U.S. dollars to buy a British pound. Therefore, it takes fewer dollars to buy a bicycle sold in British pounds, so the British bicycle will be less expensive in the United States.

Free-Response Questions

1. (a) (i) Toon has the absolute advantage in the production of widgets. It can produce more with the same resources.

     (ii) Toon also has the absolute advantage in the production of gadgets.

(b)

	Widgets	Gadgets	Opportunity Cost of Widgets	Opportunity Cost of Gadgets
Toon	20	10	$\frac{1}{2}$ gadgets	2 widgets
Loon	8	8	1 gadgets	1 widget

Toon has the comparative advantage in widget production because its opportunity cost is the least (1/2 gadget forgone versus one for Loon).

(c) Loon has the comparative advantage in the production of gadgets because its opportunity cost is the least (one widget forgone versus two for Toon).

(d) Loon should export gadgets because it has the comparative advantage in gadget production.

(e) If the terms of trade are three widgets for two gadgets, both countries will trade because they receive more in trade than in their opportunity cost. Loon will trade because it receives 1.5 widgets for one gadget, and its opportunity cost is one widget. Toon will trade because it receives 2/3 gadget for one widget and its opportunity cost is 1/2 gadget.

(f) Both countries gain from trade. If they did not, they would not trade.

2. (a) Openland's unexpected deficit will drive up the interest rates. This will attract financial capital inflows, which will drive up the value of its currency. The appreciated currency will decrease its exports.

(b) The central bank can pursue an expansionary monetary policy that will drive the interest rates down. Lower interest rates will lead to financial capital outflows, increasing the supply of currency on the foreign exchange. This will depreciate the currency, and exports will increase.

(c)

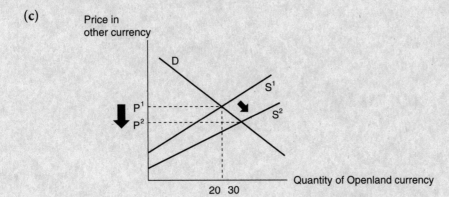

FULL-LENGTH PRACTICE TESTS

PRACTICE TEST I
ANSWER SHEET

1 Ⓐ Ⓑ Ⓒ Ⓓ Ⓔ   16 Ⓐ Ⓑ Ⓒ Ⓓ Ⓔ   31 Ⓐ Ⓑ Ⓒ Ⓓ Ⓔ   46 Ⓐ Ⓑ Ⓒ Ⓓ Ⓔ

2 Ⓐ Ⓑ Ⓒ Ⓓ Ⓔ   17 Ⓐ Ⓑ Ⓒ Ⓓ Ⓔ   32 Ⓐ Ⓑ Ⓒ Ⓓ Ⓔ   47 Ⓐ Ⓑ Ⓒ Ⓓ Ⓔ

3 Ⓐ Ⓑ Ⓒ Ⓓ Ⓔ   18 Ⓐ Ⓑ Ⓒ Ⓓ Ⓔ   33 Ⓐ Ⓑ Ⓒ Ⓓ Ⓔ   48 Ⓐ Ⓑ Ⓒ Ⓓ Ⓔ

4 Ⓐ Ⓑ Ⓒ Ⓓ Ⓔ   19 Ⓐ Ⓑ Ⓒ Ⓓ Ⓔ   34 Ⓐ Ⓑ Ⓒ Ⓓ Ⓔ   49 Ⓐ Ⓑ Ⓒ Ⓓ Ⓔ

5 Ⓐ Ⓑ Ⓒ Ⓓ Ⓔ   20 Ⓐ Ⓑ Ⓒ Ⓓ Ⓔ   35 Ⓐ Ⓑ Ⓒ Ⓓ Ⓔ   50 Ⓐ Ⓑ Ⓒ Ⓓ Ⓔ

6 Ⓐ Ⓑ Ⓒ Ⓓ Ⓔ   21 Ⓐ Ⓑ Ⓒ Ⓓ Ⓔ   36 Ⓐ Ⓑ Ⓒ Ⓓ Ⓔ   51 Ⓐ Ⓑ Ⓒ Ⓓ Ⓔ

7 Ⓐ Ⓑ Ⓒ Ⓓ Ⓔ   22 Ⓐ Ⓑ Ⓒ Ⓓ Ⓔ   37 Ⓐ Ⓑ Ⓒ Ⓓ Ⓔ   52 Ⓐ Ⓑ Ⓒ Ⓓ Ⓔ

8 Ⓐ Ⓑ Ⓒ Ⓓ Ⓔ   23 Ⓐ Ⓑ Ⓒ Ⓓ Ⓔ   38 Ⓐ Ⓑ Ⓒ Ⓓ Ⓔ   53 Ⓐ Ⓑ Ⓒ Ⓓ Ⓔ

9 Ⓐ Ⓑ Ⓒ Ⓓ Ⓔ   24 Ⓐ Ⓑ Ⓒ Ⓓ Ⓔ   39 Ⓐ Ⓑ Ⓒ Ⓓ Ⓔ   54 Ⓐ Ⓑ Ⓒ Ⓓ Ⓔ

10 Ⓐ Ⓑ Ⓒ Ⓓ Ⓔ   25 Ⓐ Ⓑ Ⓒ Ⓓ Ⓔ   40 Ⓐ Ⓑ Ⓒ Ⓓ Ⓔ   55 Ⓐ Ⓑ Ⓒ Ⓓ Ⓔ

11 Ⓐ Ⓑ Ⓒ Ⓓ Ⓔ   26 Ⓐ Ⓑ Ⓒ Ⓓ Ⓔ   41 Ⓐ Ⓑ Ⓒ Ⓓ Ⓔ   56 Ⓐ Ⓑ Ⓒ Ⓓ Ⓔ

12 Ⓐ Ⓑ Ⓒ Ⓓ Ⓔ   27 Ⓐ Ⓑ Ⓒ Ⓓ Ⓔ   42 Ⓐ Ⓑ Ⓒ Ⓓ Ⓔ   57 Ⓐ Ⓑ Ⓒ Ⓓ Ⓔ

13 Ⓐ Ⓑ Ⓒ Ⓓ Ⓔ   28 Ⓐ Ⓑ Ⓒ Ⓓ Ⓔ   43 Ⓐ Ⓑ Ⓒ Ⓓ Ⓔ   58 Ⓐ Ⓑ Ⓒ Ⓓ Ⓔ

14 Ⓐ Ⓑ Ⓒ Ⓓ Ⓔ   29 Ⓐ Ⓑ Ⓒ Ⓓ Ⓔ   44 Ⓐ Ⓑ Ⓒ Ⓓ Ⓔ   59 Ⓐ Ⓑ Ⓒ Ⓓ Ⓔ

15 Ⓐ Ⓑ Ⓒ Ⓓ Ⓔ   30 Ⓐ Ⓑ Ⓒ Ⓓ Ⓔ   45 Ⓐ Ⓑ Ⓒ Ⓓ Ⓔ   60 Ⓐ Ⓑ Ⓒ Ⓓ Ⓔ

AP MACROECONOMICS
PRACTICE TEST

Section I

Time—70 minutes

60 Questions

<u>Directions</u>: Each question below is followed by five suggested answers or completions. Select the best answer choice and fill in the corresponding oval on your answer grid.

1. Suppose country A has a production possibilities frontier (PPF) that is completely inside of country B's PPF. This means that

   (A) country A can produce more of each good than can country B.
   (B) the opportunity cost of producing each good is higher in country A.
   (C) the opportunity cost of producing each good is higher in country B.
   (D) more goods and services are being produced in country B.
   (E) country B can produce more of each good than can country A.

2. Suppose a Mexican worker can build 12 wheels or paint one frame in an hour. A Canadian worker can build eight wheels or paint two frames in an hour. Which of the following statements is true?

   (A) the Mexican worker's opportunity cost for making one wheel is painting one-sixth of a frame.
   (B) the Canadian worker's opportunity cost for making one wheel is painting four frames.
   (C) the Mexican worker has a comparative advantage in wheel production.
   (D) the Canadian worker's opportunity cost for painting one frame is making one-fourth of a wheel.
   (E) the Mexican worker has an absolute advantage in both activities.

3. Economists believe that unemployment is

   (A) All voluntary
   (B) All involuntary
   (C) All cyclical
   (D) All structural
   (E) Comprised of voluntary and involuntary elements

4. If the unemployment rate drops after the labor force has increased substantially, which of the following must be true?

   I. There are more people working in the labor force.

   II. There are fewer people unemployed.

   III. A higher percentage of the labor force is working.

   (A) I only
   (B) I and II
   (C) I and III
   (D) II and III
   (E) I, II, and III must be true.

5. The unemployment rate will increase whenever there is a(n)

   (A) increase in the number of persons classified as unemployed.
   (B) increase in the number of unemployed persons relative to the size of the labor force.
   (C) increase in the size of a nation's population with no change in the number of unemployed persons.
   (D) reduction in the size of the labor force.
   (E) reduction in the size of the labor force and a decrease in the number of unemployed.

6. Graphically, economic growth can be represented by

   I. A rightward shift of the production possibilities curve
   II. A rightward shift of the long-run AS curve
   III. A rightward shift of the AD curve

   (A) II only
   (B) III only
   (C) II and III
   (D) I and II
   (E) I, II, and III are all correct.

7. An increase in which of the following will most likely cause economic growth in the future?

   (A) Population
   (B) Level of investment
   (C) Consumption
   (D) Budget surplus
   (E) Government spending

8. In a nation, the current level of investment

   (A) shifts the production possibilities frontier inward.
   (B) is half the current level of consumption.
   (C) has no effect on economic growth.
   (D) affects future capacity to produce.
   (E) is not affected by consumption.

9. If the nominal GDP increases by 10 percent when the inflation rate is four percent, then the increase in real GDP is

   (A) 4 percent
   (B) 6 percent
   (C) 14 percent
   (D) 2.5 percent
   (E) 10 percent

10. On the following graph, moving from A to B represents

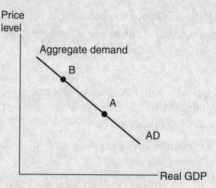

   (A) a decrease in aggregate demand.
   (B) an increase in aggregate demand.
   (C) a decrease in the aggregate quantity demanded.
   (D) an increase in the aggregate quantity demanded.
   (E) no change in the aggregate quantity demanded.

11. Changes in all of the following except one will shift aggregate demand. Which one will not cause a shift in aggregate demand?

   (A) Consumption
   (B) Investment
   (C) Imports
   (D) Exports
   (E) Prices

GO ON TO THE NEXT PAGE. ➡

12. Which of the following events would cause the AD curve to shift from AD^1 to AD^2, as illustrated in the graph below?

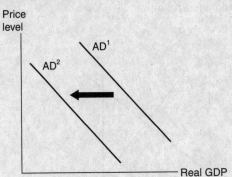

(A) The government decides to cut spending in order to decrease the national debt.

(B) Consumers increase their expenditures during the Christmas season.

(C) Businesses invest in larger inventories in preparation for potential nationwide computer-related problems.

(D) A decrease in the purchasing power of the United States dollar causes an increase in the price level.

(E) The Canadian government locates a large gold mine in Canada, and as a result, the government eliminates taxes on Canadian citizens.

13. When an economy is operating at full capacity,

(A) it could produce more if it were more efficient.

(B) it is using only some of its resources.

(C) it is producing the output with the highest value possible.

(D) there is no extra aggregate demand.

(E) All of the above

14. How could production costs change to shift the AS curve from AS^1 to AS^2 in the following graph?

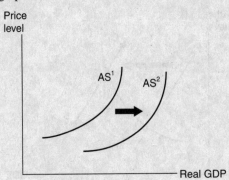

(A) Production costs increase.

(B) Production costs decrease.

(C) Production costs remain the same.

(D) Production costs cannot cause a shift of the AS curve.

(E) Any change in production costs will cause a shift from AS^1 to AS^2.

15. Let's assume that recent oil prices are higher than normal. What effect will this have on aggregate supply?

(A) The AS curve will shift to the right.

(B) The AS curve will shift to the left.

(C) The economy will move upward along the AS curve.

(D) The economy will move downward along the AS curve.

(E) Oil prices have no effect on aggregate supply.

16. In the graph below, suppose an economy begins in equilibrium on AD^1. If spending increases, driving AD from AD^1 to AD^2, then equilibrium

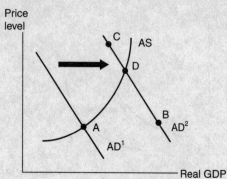

(A) shifts from point A to point C.
(B) shifts from point A to point B.
(C) shifts upward from point A to point D.
(D) remains at point A.
(E) shifts to lower prices and output.

17. A defining characteristic of long-run AD/AS equilibrium is

(A) a zero percent unemployment rate.
(B) a zero percent structural unemployment rate.
(C) the economy operates at full employment.
(D) the economy operates at full capacity.
(E) a horizontal AS curve.

18. If a person loses her job because the economy dips into a recession, this is an example of

(A) structural unemployment.
(B) frictional unemployment.
(C) seasonal unemployment.
(D) cyclical unemployment.
(E) voluntary unemployment.

19. If the economy is at the equilibrium illustrated below, which combination of actions would have the best chance of moving the economy to long-run equilibrium?

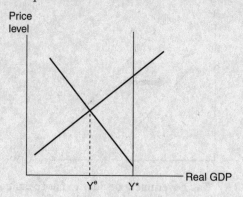

(A) An increase in the tax rate and the sale of bonds
(B) A decrease in government purchases and the sale of bonds
(C) An increase in government purchases and the purchase of bonds
(D) A decrease in the tax rate and the purchase of bonds
(E) An increase in government purchases and an increase in the reserve requirement

GO ON TO THE NEXT PAGE. ➡

20. If an economy begins in long-run equilibrium, as in the graph below, where will it end up if there's a sudden decline in consumer confidence? Select the graph that best illustrates this.

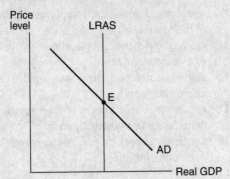

(A)

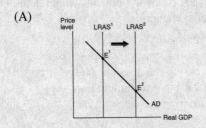

(B)

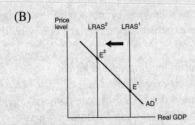

(C)

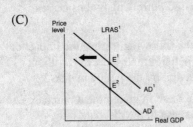

(D)

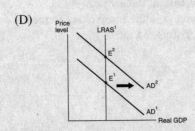

(E) The economy would remain at point E as shown in the initial graph.

21. The marginal propensity to consume (MPC) represents the

  (A) ratio of consumption to income.
  (B) difference between new consumption and total consumption.
  (C) share of any additional disposable income spent on consumption.
  (D) consumption level relative to the income level.
  (E) change in disposable income divided by the change in consumption.

22. Suppose taxes decrease by $100 billion. If everything else stays constant and the marginal propensity to consume is 0.8, the value of equilibrium output increases by

  (A) $100 billion
  (B) $80 billion
  (C) $500 billion
  (D) $320 billion
  (E) $400 billion

23. Which of the following does not characterize the classical view of the economy?

  (A) An economy automatically moves to equilibrium at the full-employment level of GDP.
  (B) Prices and wage variations are the mechanism for short-run adjustments leading to long-run equilibrium.
  (C) The economy will stay out of equilibrium only for short periods.
  (D) The level of production determines the short-run economic equilibrium.
  (E) Prices and wages do not automatically adjust in the short run.

GO ON TO THE NEXT PAGE. ➡

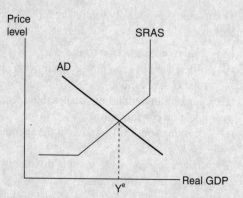

24. When the economy is in equilibrium as illustrated above, an expansionary monetary policy will

    I. Increase unemployment

    II. Increase price level

    III. Increase employment

    IV. Decrease price level

    (A) I and II
    (B) I and IV
    (C) II and IV
    (D) II and III
    (E) Only IV

25. A contractionary fiscal policy would be the one that

    (A) lowers both government spending and taxes.
    (B) raises both government spending and taxes.
    (C) lowers government spending and/or raises taxes.
    (D) lowers tax rates.
    (E) raises government spending.

26. A reduction in tax rates may not stimulate the economy if

    (A) the tax cut is permanent and raises permanent disposable income.
    (B) the tax cut is temporary and does not change permanent disposable income.
    (C) the tax cut is too large.
    (D) consumption decisions are based solely on current income as opposed to permanent income.
    (E) the tax cuts are distributed evenly throughout the population in the economy.

27. One justification for a personal income tax cut is to increase the labor supply. Given that this policy will increase aggregate demand and supply, there will be an inflationary pressure if

    (A) aggregate demand and supply grow roughly at the same rate.
    (B) aggregate demand grows more rapidly than aggregate supply.
    (C) aggregate demand grows less rapidly than aggregate supply.
    (D) aggregate supply grows, and aggregate demand remains unchanged.
    (E) aggregate supply grows, and aggregate demand is falling.

28. Which of the following policies would definitely not discourage exports?

    (A) Tariffs
    (B) Increasing government purchases
    (C) Increasing the discount rate
    (D) Purchasing government bonds
    (E) Decreasing the discount rate

29. Which of the following events would lessen the effect of an expansionary monetary policy by the Fed?

    (A) Increased lending by the banks
    (B) Increased excess reserves
    (C) Increased deposits by home owners
    (D) Increased borrowing by home owners
    (E) Increased borrowing by businesses

30. Which of the following lessens the impact of decreased output in the short run, without requiring action by the policy makers?

    (A) An increase in government purchases
    (B) A decrease in the discount rate
    (C) A decrease in the tax rate
    (D) A decrease in the reserve requirement
    (E) The existing tax rate

GO ON TO THE NEXT PAGE. ➡

31. The reserve requirement is 10 percent. Mary takes $1,000 that she has held in currency in a shoebox and deposits it in the bank. In this case, the money supply can change by as much as

(A) $1,000
(B) $4,000
(C) $5,000
(D) $9,000
(E) $10,000

32. When a firm decides to invest in new capital, it looks at

(A) the interest rate and the return on investment.
(B) the interest rate.
(C) the return on investment.
(D) inflation.
(E) inflation and the return on investment.

33. In the short run, which of the following would be the biggest problem with the monetarists' view of constant growth of the money supply?

(A) Increased excess reserves
(B) Increased borrowing by business
(C) Inconstant velocity
(D) Unplanned inventory
(E) Government spending

34. The Fed uses monetary policy to

(A) set all the interest rates in the economy.
(B) offset the effects of fiscal policy.
(C) directly manipulate consumption.
(D) guide government expenditures.
(E) alter the money supply.

35. If monetary policy is to be effective at promoting a short-run increase in aggregate demand and a long-run increase in aggregate supply, investment must be

(A) sensitive to interest rates and include increases in capital stock.
(B) insensitive to interest rates and include increases in capital stock.
(C) sensitive to interest rates and include increases to inventory.
(D) insensitive to interest rates and include increases in capital stock.
(E) sensitive to interest rates and include unplanned investment.

36. Why is the long-run Phillips curve vertical?

(A) Because any level of inflation can occur at the full-employment rate of unemployment in the long run.
(B) Because any level of unemployment can occur at the full-employment rate of inflation in the long run.
(C) Because it represents a relationship between two real variables in the long run.
(D) Because the natural rate of unemployment never changes.
(E) Because the inflation rate is always the same.

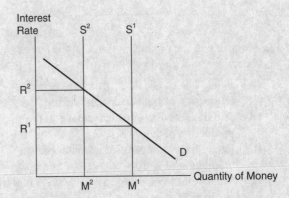

37. Referring to the money market graph above, a change of the interest rate from R^1 to R^2 will result when

(A) consumers borrow more money.
(B) businesses borrow more money.
(C) the Fed sells government bonds as part of open market operations.
(D) the Fed buys government bonds as part of open market operations.
(E) investment is not interest rate sensitive.

Questions 38–39

Fundy and Mundy are two countries with comparable resources. Both countries produce carrots and celery, using all of their resources to do so.

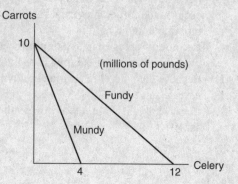

38. According to the production possibilities graph above,

(A) Fundy has an absolute advantage in the production of both celery and carrots.
(B) Mundy has an absolute advantage in the production of celery.
(C) Fundy has a comparative advantage in the production of carrots.
(D) Mundy has the comparative advantage in the production of celery.
(E) Fundy has the absolute advantage in the production of celery.

39. Given the information in the graph, we can conclude that

(A) neither country should trade for carrots.
(B) Fundy should specialize in the production of celery.
(C) Mundy should specialize in the production of celery.
(D) Fundy should specialize in the production of carrots.
(E) Mundy cannot gain from trade.

40. A tariff imposed on foreign cars imported into the United States will

(A) be a benefit to consumers.
(B) be a benefit to domestic producers.
(C) lower the price of domestic cars.
(D) lead to an increase in the total quantity of domestic and imported cars sold in the United States.
(E) be a benefit to both domestic consumers and domestic producers.

41. If the U.S. dollar decreases in value relative to the British pound,

(A) U.S. wheat will become more expensive in England.
(B) British bicycles will become cheaper in the United States.
(C) British bicycles will become more expensive in the United States.
(D) German cars will become cheaper in the United States.
(E) there will be no change in prices.

42. Relative to the price level in the United States, how will an increase in the price level in Japan affect U.S. exports to Japan and the dollar's value, compared to the yen?

	Exports	Value of the Dollar
(A)	Decrease	Increases
(B)	Increase	Increases
(C)	Decrease	Decreases
(D)	Increase	Decreases
(E)	No change	No change

43. An excess of savings over investment in a nation is necessarily reflected in

(A) an appreciation (increase) of the foreign exchange rate.
(B) more imports than exports.
(C) more exports than imports.
(D) changes in the money supply.
(E) capital inflow from other countries.

GO ON TO THE NEXT PAGE. ➡

44. All else being equal, which of the following effects is most likely in an open economy, when the government deficit spends?

	Interest rates	Investment	Exports
(A)	Decrease	Decrease	Decrease
(B)	Increase	Increase	Increase
(C)	Decrease	Increase	Decrease
(D)	Increase	Decrease	Decrease
(E)	Increase	Decrease	Increase

45. When the central bank decides to decrease the money supply to combat inflation, it

(A) Reduces the interest rates.
(B) Increases the merchandise trade deficit.
(C) Increases private spending.
(D) Causes the price of the U.S. dollar to fall.
(E) Causes capital to flow out of the United States.

46. If the economy is at full employment and the price level increases as the money supply remains constant, we can conclude that

(A) aggregate demand decreased
(B) aggregate supply increased
(C) the velocity of money increased
(D) fiscal policy was contractionary
(E) monetary policy was contractionary

47. Which of the following events will lessen the affect of the banking multiplier?

(A) Banks increase loans
(B) Households pay less taxes
(C) Banks reduce excess reserves
(D) People increase their holdings of currency
(E) Interest rates drop

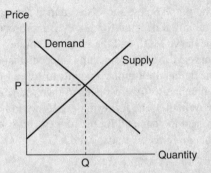

48. The above graph represents the initial equilibrium in the automobile industry. An oil crisis occurs that decreases the oil supply. Oil is both a complementary good to the demand for automobiles and a key energy cost of producing automobiles. As a result, we can state that the following will happen to the equilibrium price and quantity for automobiles:

	Price	Quantity
(A)	Increases	Increases
(B)	Increases	Decreases
(C)	Decreases	Indeterminant
(D)	Indeterminant	Increases
(E)	Indeterminant	Decreases

49. According to the law of one price, if a particular bottle of perfume costs $2 in the United States and 200 yen in Japan, and if transaction costs are zero, the exchange rate should be

(A) 10 yen per dollar
(B) 100 yen per dollar
(C) 100 dollars per Yen
(D) 10 dollars per Yen
(E) 20 yen per dollar

50. The graph below shows the market for money. The initial demand for money is represented by the curve MD^1, and the supply of money is the curve MS. Then, something happens that causes the demand for money to shift to curve MD^2, which causes interest rates to increase from I^1 to I^2. Which of the following events could have caused the demand for the money curve to change in the way that it did?

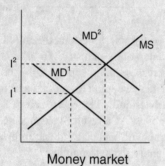

Money market

(A) The Fed sells bonds
(B) Stock and bond prices start to rise
(C) The Fed buys bonds
(D) Congress passes a budget that includes a surplus
(E) Incomes rise, which causes households to purchase more goods and services.

51. Which of the following events would be most likely to increase both aggregate demand and long run aggregate supply?

(A) The government increases unemployment benefits
(B) Businesses replace worn out equipment with comparable new equipment
(C) Government increases taxes
(D) Businesses build more factories and increase capacity
(E) Household increase consumption.

52. Which of the following graphs represent the long run Phillips curve?

(A)

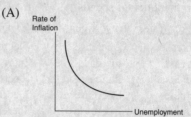

(B)

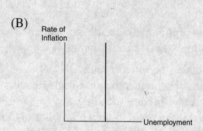

(C)

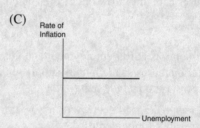

(D)

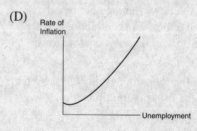

(E)

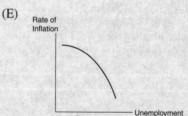

GO ON TO THE NEXT PAGE. ➡

KAPLAN

53. In the short run, which of the following will most likely lead to a decrease in aggregate demand?

    (A) A depreciation of the currency
    (B) An increase in the money supply
    (C) A decrease in the tax rate
    (D) A decrease in consumer confidence
    (E) An increase in the marginal propensity to consume

54. Which of the following combinations of actions by the Fed will have the greatest expansionary effect?

	Open Market Operations	Discount Rate	Reserve Requirement
(A)	Sell bonds	Decrease	Decrease
(B)	Buy bonds	Decrease	Increase
(C)	Sell bonds	Increase	Increase
(D)	Buy bonds	Decrease	Decrease
(E)	Buy bonds	Increase	Increase

55. Which of the following combinations of fiscal and monetary policies would have the greatest effect on inflation?

	Fiscal Policy	Monetary Policy
(A)	Decrease taxes	Buy bonds
(B)	Decrease G spending	Sell bonds
(C)	Increase taxes	Buy bonds
(D)	Increase G spending	Buy bonds
(E)	Increase G spending	Sell bonds

56. If the economy is in long-run equilibrium, there is no

    (A) Structural unemployment
    (B) Frictional unemployment
    (C) Cyclical unemployment
    (D) Unemployment
    (E) Part-time employment

57. In a small country, the GDP was $500 billion in year one, and $510 billion in year two. Inflation was one percent, and the population increased by 10 percent. We can conclude that

    (A) Real GDP decreased
    (B) Cost of living decreased
    (C) Only nominal GDP increased
    (D) Per capita nominal GDP increased
    (E) Per capita real GDP decreased

58. According to a flexible wages and prices model, an increase in the money supply in the long run will

	Price Level	Output	Nominal Wages
(A)	No change	Increase	Increase
(B)	Increase	No change	Increase
(C)	Increase	Decrease	No change
(D)	Decrease	Increase	Increase
(E)	Increase	Increase	Increase

59. If the inflation rate increased unexpectedly this year, and is expected to increase again next year, the market price of existing bonds and the interest paid by the initial borrower will

	Bond Price	Interest Paid
(A)	Increase	Increase
(B)	Increase	No change
(C)	Decrease	Increase
(D)	Decrease	No change
(E)	No change	Decrease

60. Which of the following would be inconsistent with the Phillips curve?

    (A) Stagflation
    (B) Intermediate section of the short-run supply curve
    (C) Natural rate of unemployment
    (D) Price changes
    (E) Wage changes

END OF SECTION I

Section II

Time—60 minutes

One Long Question and Two Short Questions

<u>Directions</u>: You have one hour total to answer all three of the following questions: one long question and two shorter questions. The first 10 minutes is for planning and review, and the remaining 50 minutes for answering the questions.

Although you can spend the 50 minutes any way you would like, we recommend that you spend half the time answering question 1, and divide the remaining time between questions 2 and 3.

Your answers should emphasize the line of reasoning you used to arrive at your answer; it is not enough to simply list the results of your analysis. When appropriate, include correctly labeled diagrams that have all axes and curves clearly labeled, and that show directional changes.

1. Assume that a country is in a recession and that the country exports 50 percent of its GDP.

   (a) Draw a correctly labeled graph that illustrates this condition.

   (b) (i) Let's say the government pursues an expansionary fiscal policy that requires deficit spending, and that monetary policy does not change. Using a graph of the loanable funds market, show what will happen to interest rates.

       (ii) What will happen to real GDP as a result of the change in interest rates? Explain.

   (c) If an expansionary monetary policy were used instead of an expansionary fiscal policy, what would be the effect on real GDP? Explain.

2. If productivity increases in the United States but the same increase in productivity does not occur in Great Britain,

   (a) What effect will this have on exports to Great Britain from the United States? Use an AD/AS graph to illustrate. Explain.

   (b) Draw a graph of the international currency market for U.S. dollars, and illustrate and explain what will happen to the value of the dollar.

3. (a) Assuming banks currently have no excess reserves, and Mary Quitecontrary takes the $100,000 that she has been saving in shoe boxes under her bed and deposits it into a bank, what will happen to the money supply? Explain.

   (b) What is the maximum effect that this deposit can have on the money supply, if the reserve requirement is 20 percent?

   (c) List two events that could minimize the effect of this deposit on the money supply.

END OF TEST

STOP.

Answers and Explanations to Macroeconomics Practice Test

1. (E)

A PPF represents the quantity of goods and services a country can produce if operating at full efficiency. If country A's PPF is inside that of country B's, country B can potentially produce more than A of each good. Choice (A) is the exact opposite of that. (B) and (C) are wrong because even though the slope of the PPF does indicate opportunity cost, we can make no comparison of opportunity costs based only on whether one PPF is higher or lower than another. Instead, we would have to compare the change on one axis with the change on the other axis. For (D), also incorrect, the PPF doesn't indicate anything about the quantity of goods being produced; it shows what production is possible.

2. (C)

It costs a Mexican worker only 1/12 of a frame to build a wheel, while it costs a Canadian worker 1/4 of a frame. (E) is wrong because the Canadian worker can produce two frames in an hour, as opposed to the Mexican worker's one frame in an hour.

3. (E)

There are four types of unemployment. *Structural* unemployment (involuntary) is caused by the types of production and laws of an economy that govern whose skills are valuable in the marketplace. *Frictional* unemployment (voluntary) is associated with job change, often because workers are searching for better opportunities or moving to a new location. *Cyclical* unemployment (involuntary) is caused by changes in real GDP that are associated with the business cycle. And *seasonal* unemployment (involuntary) is caused by changes in employment associated with changes in the seasons.

4. (C)

Statement II is not necessarily correct. If the unemployment rate drops once the labor force has increased significantly, it is possible to have more people unemployed. If there were 100 people in the labor force and 11 percent were unemployed, that would mean that 11 people were unemployed. If the labor force increased to 125 people and 12 were unemployed, the unemployment rate would be 12/125 or 9.6 percent. The unemployment rate has dropped from 11 percent to 9.6 percent, but more people are unemployed.

5. (B)

The unemployment rate is the ratio of the number of people unemployed to the number of people in the labor force. This is the percentage of the workforce not working but actively looking for a job. If the number of unemployed increases more than the number of people in the labor force, the unemployment rate will increase. (A) might not happen if there's an increase in the size of the labor force. (C) would most likely decrease the unemployment rate, since an increase in the labor force size with no change in the number of unemployed workers only makes the ratio of labor force to unemployed workers smaller. (We're assuming that an increase in the population will create a corresponding increase in the labor force.) (D) isn't necessarily true: If the number of unemployed is also decreasing, the unemployment rate may decrease, increase, or stay the same. (E) would be impossible to determine without more information.

6. (D)

Economic growth is the increase in potential output of an economy. A rightward shift of the demand curve can lead to an increase in output if the economy is in a recession but this is not economic growth.

7. (B)

Two of the sources of economic growth, increased capital and technological advancement, are related to the quantity of investment in the economy. Investment generates some economic growth today, but it generates significantly more economic growth in the future. That's because investment is purchases of capital goods, and more capital results in an increase in the economy's PPF. So investment in capital goods creates economic growth in the future. (A) might cause future economic growth because it might increase the number of laborers in the nation. And laborers are a resource. But that's not a given, and there's a better answer choice here. Similarly, (D) and (E) are not given facts.

8. (D)

Investment is purchases of capital goods. More capital results in an increase in production for an economy. Therefore investment in capital goods affects future capacity to produce. (A) is out because investment doesn't decrease the production possibilities frontier—it shifts it outward, which is an increase. (E) can be ruled out because consumption affects the level of savings in the economy. The total amount of investment in the economy is equal to the total amount of savings in the economy, so it also affects the level of investment.

9. (B)

The increase in nominal GDP minus the inflation rate equals the increase in real GDP.

10. (C)

Movement along an AD curve represents a change in the aggregate quantity demanded. In this case, the movement is in response to a price increase and represents a decrease in the aggregate quantity demanded. (A) and (B) are wrong because the AD curve did not shift: When aggregate demand decreases or increases, the entire curve shifts. (D) is wrong because while movement along an AD curve represents a change in the aggregate quantity demanded,

ANSWERS AND EXPLANATIONS TO MACROECONOMICS PRACTICE TEST

this isn't an increase in aggregate quantity demanded. When prices rise, aggregate quantity demanded falls; when prices fall, it rises.

11. (E)

A shift of the AD curve (also called a change in aggregate demand) is caused by changes in consumption, investment, government expenditures, exports, or imports—that have not been caused by a change in the price level. The only answer choice that doesn't cause a shift in aggregate demand is (E), prices. A change in prices causes a movement along the AD curve.

12. (A)

A decrease in government expenditures on goods and services will cause the AD curve to decrease (shift to the left). Aggregate demand is composed of the following expenditures: household consumption (C), business investment (I), government spending on goods and services (G), and net exports (NX). Changing any of these will change AD. If the net change is positive, AD will increase and the AD curve will shift right. If the net change is negative, it will decrease and the AD curve will shift left.

13. (C)

Full capacity is the level of real GDP that corresponds to the maximum value of production possible. When an economy is at full capacity, it is using all of its resources, and producing at the highest level of real GDP possible. It can't shift around its resource use to produce at a higher level of real GDP. (D) is a trap: Full capacity has to do with the aggregate *supply* of an economy, not aggregate demand.

14. (B)

A drop in production costs results in an increase in aggregate supply, shifting the AS curve to the right. At every price level, producers are willing and able to supply more goods and services. For choice (D), you may be thinking of a change in the price level, which can't cause a shift of the AS curve. Rather, a change in the price level causes movement to a different point on the same AS curve.

15. (B)

Oil is used in many production processes: to heat office buildings, to run machinery, and so on. If oil prices increase, the cost of producing many goods increases as well—everything from corn on the cob to dental floss to wood furniture. A price increase will cause many firms to decrease production. The aggregate supply for the economy will decrease, and the AS curve shifts left. When that happens, firms will produce fewer goods and services at every price level than they would have before the shift.

16. (C)

Shifts in the AD curve result in movement along the AS curve to a new equilibrium. The new AD curve intersects the original AS curve at the new equilibrium point D, resulting in a higher price level and greater output. Remember, equilibrium is where aggregate supply and aggregate demand intersect. (E) is wrong because an increase in aggregate demand results in a rightward shift of the AD curve, so equilibrium moves along the AS curve to a higher price and output.

17. (C)

Full employment is the highest level of real GDP an economy can maintain without inflationary price increases. Full employment is the level of output at which cyclical unemployment does not exist, though structural, frictional, or seasonal unemployment may indeed exist. With choice (A), you may be thinking that AD/AS equilibrium occurs at the full-employment level of output. But full employment doesn't mean zero percent unemployment. With (B), you may be remembering that long-run equilibrium occurs at full employment. But at full employment, the structural unemployment rate is greater than zero.

18. (D)

Cyclical unemployment is unemployment caused by the business cycle. All economies go through periodic expansions and contractions. During contractionary periods, some people may lose their jobs; this is cyclical unemployment. (E) is a trap: Economists don't talk of "voluntary unemployment" as a formal category, though it may be used to refer to someone who chooses to not work—perhaps to stay at home with a child. People like this aren't considered "unemployed"—they're just not counted as part of the labor force.

19. (D)

Answer choice (D) includes both an expansionary fiscal policy and an expansionary monetary policy. All other answer provide one expansionary and one contractionary policy.

20. (C)

A decline in consumer confidence causes a decrease in consumption (one of the components of aggregate demand) and, so, a decrease in aggregate demand. A decline in aggregate demand shifts the economy to a new equilibrium point on the long-run AS curve.

21. (C)

Here's a hint: In economics, you can usually substitute the word *additional* for *marginal*. So you should expect a definition of MPC to include the word *additional*. The marginal propensity to consume is the share of additional disposable income spent on consumption. In other words, it's the percentage of another dollar of income that's spent rather than saved. (E) is incorrect since MPC is change in consumption divided by the change in disposable income.

22. (E)

To figure the increase in output, you first need to calculate the tax multiplier by using the MPC. When MPC is equal to 0.8, the tax multiplier will be equal to: .8 divided by $1 - .8 = .8/.2 = 4$. The value of equilibrium output will increase by $400 billion.

23. (E)

The classical view says two things: Prices and wages automatically adjust to create equilibrium, and equilibrium is determined by the quantity of production the economy is capable of. Classical economists believe the economy automatically adjusts to full employment. Their argument depends on the flexibility of prices and wages. (E) is the only answer choice that does not characterize the classical view.

24. (D)

An expansionary monetary policy will shift the aggregate demand to the right. Since the initial equilibrium is illustrated to be on the intermediate portion of the short-run AS curve, a rightward shift of aggregate demand leads to an increase in the price level and in real GDP, which means an increase in employment.

25. (C)

Cutting government spending and/or raising taxes is contractionary.

26. (B)

If a tax cut is temporary and doesn't change permanent disposable income, a tax rate reduction may not stimulate the economy. If your taxes decrease, how much of that additional money you'll spend depends on whether you expect the tax decrease to continue forever or to be a one-time thing. If it's a one-time thing, you'll save a lot more of the money than you would if you expected the tax decrease to last. That means the size of the multiplier will be a lot smaller if you expect it to be a one-time thing. If you save more, less is put into the economy to create income for others, and there's less growth in real GDP. (A) is clearly wrong, as is (C), because a very large tax cut would definitely stimulate the economy: Individuals would have more income to spend. Similarly, (E) is wrong, because evenly distributing the tax cuts would still increase individuals' consumption, and ultimately stimulate the economy. (D) is wrong because if the consumption decisions were based solely on current income as opposed to permanent income, a tax rate reduction would definitely stimulate the economy. Since individuals would make their consumption decisions based on current income, when taxes decreased they'd spend part of this additional income. But this isn't true; economists believe consumption expenditures depend on both current and future expected income.

27. (B)

When aggregate demand grows more rapidly than aggregate supply, the economy moves to a new equilibrium. At this new equilibrium, both real GDP and the price level will be higher than they were before, but the increase in the price level will be larger than the increase in real GDP. Since the increase in prices is larger relative to the increase in real GDP, there will be inflationary pressures. This is inflationary because the new equilibrium level of real GDP can be sustained only at much higher prices. (A) is wrong because when aggregate demand and supply grow roughly at the same rate, the economy moves to a new equilibrium where real GDP will be higher, but price level will not change. As a result, there will be no inflationary pressure. Similarly, for (C), real GDP will be higher, but the price level will change only slightly. Since the increase in prices is much smaller relative to the increase in real GDP, there will be no inflationary pressure. (D) and (E) would cause the price level to be lower, and with a real GDP that's increasing, there will be no inflationary pressure.

28. (E)

Decreasing the discount rate would be an expansionary monetary policy that would lead to lower interest rates. The lower interest rates would not be likely to put upward pressure on the currency value, and thus not affect exports. Tariffs would likely lead to reciprocal tariffs, discouraging exports, so (A) is wrong. Increasing government purchases would likely lead to the crowding-out effect that would increase interest rates and attract more international financial capital. This would lead to an appreciation of the currency and to fewer exports, so (B) is incorrect. (C) and (D) are contractionary monetary policies that would cause higher interest rates and currency appreciation.

29. (B)

Increased excess reserves leads to less money being created by the banking system. All other answer choices would help to increase money creation.

30. (E)

The existing tax rate acts as an automatic stabilizer. The decrease in output leads to less income, but since some of that income is paid in taxes, the impact on disposable income and consumption is "automatically" less. Answer choices (A), (B), (C), and (D) require actions by the policymakers.

31. (D)

The money multiplier is 1/reserve requirement, or in this case, 1/.1 or 10. However, the original $1,000 that Mary deposits is already part of the money supply. Thus, $1,000 time 10 equals $10,000—less the original $1,000—is $9,000.

32. (A)

Firms are interested in one thing when deciding whether to take out a loan: They want a maximum return on their investment. If the return on investment is greater than the interest rate, then the investment is worth doing. (B) represents only the cost side, while (C) represents only the benefits side. Firms must also look at the cost of their investment, the interest rate. (D) is wrong because inflation doesn't directly affect a firm's decisions on investment. The real interest rate and the return on investment are what firms need to consider. Inflation is accounted for when the firm compares the real interest rate and the return on investment. Similarly, (E) is wrong.

33. (C)

The monetarist view of increasing the money supply is based on increases consistent with potential growth of the GDP. However, this theory depends on the velocity being constant. If velocity isn't constant in the short run, then problems occur with this policy.

34. (E)

Monetary policy is used to change the quantity of money in the economy. As the quantity of money changes, it in turn affects other things in the economy—interest rates, investment, aggregate demand, level of production, and price level. Except for the discount rate, the Fed doesn't set interest rates, so (A) is wrong. You'll sometimes hear the media speak as if the Fed does set the interest rates, but this is a simplification of the real process.

35. (A)

In order for monetary policy to effectively increase aggregate demand, investment needs to be sensitive to interest rates. Lower interest rates lead to more investment. In order for an increase in investment to have an effect on economic growth, the investment must include increases to capital stock.

36. (A)

In the long-run, unemployment always returns to its full-employment level, sometimes called the *natural* rate of unemployment. Therefore, any level of inflation can be associated with the full-employment rate of unemployment. (C) is wrong because the Phillips curve represents the relationship between a real variable, unemployment, and a nominal variable—the inflation rate. While some nominal variables can be adjusted for inflation and turned into real variables, inflation can't be. (Imagine adjusting inflation for inflation!) And (D) and (E) are clearly wrong, because the natural rate of unemployment and the inflation rate definitely change over time.

37. (C)

The increase in interest rates results from a decrease in the quantity of money from S1 to S2. This results from a contractionary money policy such as selling bonds by the Fed. Buying bonds would increase the money supply, shifting S to the right. Choices (A) and (B) would shift the demand for money, and (E) would change the slope of the demand curve.

38. (E)

Fundy has the absolute advantage in the production of celery. (A) is wrong, as neither country has the absolute advantage in carrot production. (B) is wrong because Mundy doesn't have absolute advantage in either product. (C) and (D) assign the comparative advantage to the wrong country—they should be switched around.

39. (B)

Fundy should specialize in the production of celery because it has the comparative advantage. Its opportunity cost of producing celery is less. Mundy should specialize in the production of carrots because it has the comparative advantage. Trade will be beneficial for both.

40. (B)

Only the domestic producers can benefit from the tariff. They will produce and sell more cars at a higher price. Domestic consumers are hurt by the higher price, so (A) and (E) are wrong. (C) is the opposite of what will happen: Domestic prices will be higher, not lower. (D) is out because although consumers will buy more domestic cars, the higher prices for both domestic and imported cars will cause fewer total cars to be sold.

41. (C)

A decrease in the value of the dollar increases the relative price of the goods in England, and makes British goods more expensive in the United States. If the dollar decreases in value relative to the British pound, this means it takes more U.S. dollars to buy a British pound.

Therefore it takes more U.S. dollars to buy a bicycle sold in British pounds, so the British bicycle will be more expensive in the U.S.

42. (B)

The higher price level in Japan means that U.S. goods will be less expensive, and so the United States will export more. The demand for U.S. dollars by the Japanese will increase the value of the dollar. (Of course this secondary affect will eventually slow down some of the exports but overall, the United States will export more.)

43. (C)

The excess of savings over investment in a country is necessarily reflected in an excess of exports over imports. When a country's domestic savings exceeds its investment, the country will be a lender in the international capital market and will have a capital account deficit. This means it must have a current account surplus. A surplus in current account means an excess of exports over imports.

44. (D)

Deficit spending is likely to lead to the crowding-out effect. This raises interest rates and discourages investment. The higher interest rates attract foreign financial capital, which leads to an appreciation of the currency and a decrease in exports.

45. (B)

A decrease in money supply will increase the merchandise trade deficit. When the Fed decreases the money supply, interest rates increase. The higher interest rates create more capital inflow from the rest of the world. Asset ownership in the United States is a better deal when the interest rate rises, so foreign investors bring their money here. These capital inflows drive up the price of U.S. currency, since the demand for U.S. currency goes up. The higher exchange rates increase imports and decrease exports, increasing the merchandise trade deficit. Therefore, the merchandise trade deficit increases when the money supply decreases. Decreases in the money supply aimed at combating inflation are generally intended to decrease private spending, so (C) is wrong.

46. (C)

If the money supply remains unchanged and the economy is at full employment, then velocity has to change. Use the equation of exchange: $M \times V = P \times Q$. Given, Q and M are constant. P increased, so V must have increased. Answer choices (A), (B), (D), and (E) would lead to a lower price level.

47. (D)

Two events that minimize the banking multiplier are increased holdings in currency by households and increased excess reserves by banks.

ANSWERS AND EXPLANATIONS TO MACROECONOMICS PRACTICE TEST

48. (E)

The decreased supply of oil will increase the price of oil and oil-based products. Given that oil is a complementary good, the increased prices will decrease the demand for automobiles. This decreases both price and quantity demanded. The increased cost to the production of cars decreases supply, which increases price and decreases quantity supplied. Thus, effect on price is inconclusive and the quantity will decrease.

49. (B)

According to the law of one price, the cost of the perfume should be the same in both countries. 200 yen/2 dollars = 100 yen per dollar.

50. (E)

As households buy more goods and services they need to acquire more money for transactions.

51. (D)

The increase in capital stock increases the aggregate demand in the short run and increases the long-run aggregate supply. (A), (B), and (E) increase AD but not LRAS. (C) would decrease AD if the government did not also increase spending.

52. (B)

In the long run, labor is fully employed. There can be only an increase in the price level.

53. (D)

A decrease in consumer confidence will lead to less consumption and therefore, a decrease in aggregate demand. All other alternatives would lead to an increase in demand.

54. (D)

The expansionary tools of the Fed are to buy bonds, decrease the discount rate, and decrease the reserve requirement.

55. (B)

To fight inflation, a combination of both fiscal and monetary contractionary policies would be most effective. Contractionary fiscal policies are to decrease G spending and increase taxes. Contractionary monetary policies are to sell bonds, increase the discount rate, and increase the reserve requirement.

56. (C)

Cyclical unemployment occurs when the economy is not at full employment. At full employment, there is still structural and frictional unemployment. Part-time employment can occur at any time. Part-time employees are considered employed.

57. (E)

GDP increased by $10 billion from year one to year two. This is a nominal GDP increase of two percent. Inflation increased by one percent, so real GDP increased by one percent. That means (A) and (C) are wrong. Per capita GDP is GDP divided by the population. Nominal GDP increased by two percent while population increased by 10 percent, so per capita nominal GDP decreased. That means (D) is wrong, as is (E), because real GDP increased by one percent and population increased by 10 percent, meaning per capital real GDP decreased.

58. (B)

In the long run, output cannot increase. An increase in the money supply will merely increase nominal prices and nominal wages, according to the flexible prices and wages model.

59. (D)

The interest rate paid by the initial borrower remains the same, regardless of changes in the market rate. When unexpected inflation occurs, the market interest rate will increase. Since the inflation rate was originally unexpected, the initial rate did not include a premium for this change in price level. As market rates increase, the value of existing bonds paying a lower rate will go down.

60. (A)

The Phillips curve measures the trade off between inflation and unemployment. Stagflation describes the increase in both the inflation and unemployment.

FREE-RESPONSE QUESTIONS

1. **(a)**

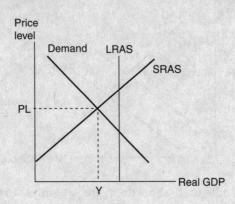

(b) **(i)**

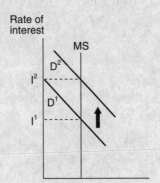

Loanable Funds Market

The additional demand for funds from the loanable funds market as a result of the deficit spending will increase the interest rates from I^1 to I^2.

(ii) The higher interest rate will discourage investment, decreasing the aggregate demand. The higher interest rates will attract foreign capital flows, which will increase the value of the dollar. In turn, the increased dollar value will discourage exports, which will decrease aggregate demand. Both of these effects will shift the AD curve to the left, decreasing real GDP.

(c) If an expansionary monetary policy were used, interest rates would drop as the money supply increases. Investment, if it is sensitive to the lower interest rates, will increase, increasing the aggregate demand. Lower interest rates would cause capital outflows that would weaken the dollar. The weaker dollar would encourage exports, increasing the aggregate demand. As the aggregate demand shifted to the right, real GDP would increase.

2. (a)

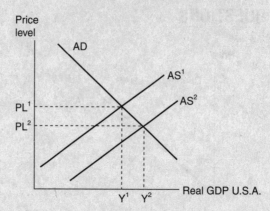

The increase in productivity shifts the aggregate supply to the right, lowering the price level. The lower price level leads to prices that are relatively lower than the prices in Great Britain. Consequently, exports from the United States to Great Britain will increase.

(b)

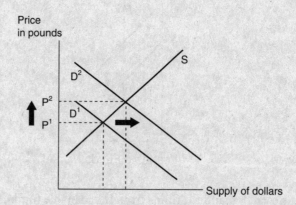

As consumers in Great Britain consume more products from the United States, demand for the dollar increases from D^1 to D^2, pulling up the price to P^2. This is an appreciation of the dollar.

3. (a) As banks proceeded to loan out portions of the given $100,000, the money supply would increase. If the bank's initial deposit was not lent out then there would be no change in the money supply.

(b) The maximum amount of the increase is $400,000. The money multiplier is 1/RR. So 1/.2 = 5. The money multiplier is five, but we must deduct the original $100,000 that was already part of the money supply as it sat in the shoe box.

(c) Two ways to minimize the money multiplier are for banks to keep excess reserves, and for borrowers to keep some of the borrowed money in the form of currency.

PRACTICE TEST II
ANSWER SHEET

1 (A)(B)(C)(D)(E)   16 (A)(B)(C)(D)(E)   31 (A)(B)(C)(D)(E)   46 (A)(B)(C)(D)(E)

2 (A)(B)(C)(D)(E)   17 (A)(B)(C)(D)(E)   32 (A)(B)(C)(D)(E)   47 (A)(B)(C)(D)(E)

3 (A)(B)(C)(D)(E)   18 (A)(B)(C)(D)(E)   33 (A)(B)(C)(D)(E)   48 (A)(B)(C)(D)(E)

4 (A)(B)(C)(D)(E)   19 (A)(B)(C)(D)(E)   34 (A)(B)(C)(D)(E)   49 (A)(B)(C)(D)(E)

5 (A)(B)(C)(D)(E)   20 (A)(B)(C)(D)(E)   35 (A)(B)(C)(D)(E)   50 (A)(B)(C)(D)(E)

6 (A)(B)(C)(D)(E)   21 (A)(B)(C)(D)(E)   36 (A)(B)(C)(D)(E)   51 (A)(B)(C)(D)(E)

7 (A)(B)(C)(D)(E)   22 (A)(B)(C)(D)(E)   37 (A)(B)(C)(D)(E)   52 (A)(B)(C)(D)(E)

8 (A)(B)(C)(D)(E)   23 (A)(B)(C)(D)(E)   38 (A)(B)(C)(D)(E)   53 (A)(B)(C)(D)(E)

9 (A)(B)(C)(D)(E)   24 (A)(B)(C)(D)(E)   39 (A)(B)(C)(D)(E)   54 (A)(B)(C)(D)(E)

10 (A)(B)(C)(D)(E)   25 (A)(B)(C)(D)(E)   40 (A)(B)(C)(D)(E)   55 (A)(B)(C)(D)(E)

11 (A)(B)(C)(D)(E)   26 (A)(B)(C)(D)(E)   41 (A)(B)(C)(D)(E)   56 (A)(B)(C)(D)(E)

12 (A)(B)(C)(D)(E)   27 (A)(B)(C)(D)(E)   42 (A)(B)(C)(D)(E)   57 (A)(B)(C)(D)(E)

13 (A)(B)(C)(D)(E)   28 (A)(B)(C)(D)(E)   43 (A)(B)(C)(D)(E)   58 (A)(B)(C)(D)(E)

14 (A)(B)(C)(D)(E)   29 (A)(B)(C)(D)(E)   44 (A)(B)(C)(D)(E)   59 (A)(B)(C)(D)(E)

15 (A)(B)(C)(D)(E)   30 (A)(B)(C)(D)(E)   45 (A)(B)(C)(D)(E)   60 (A)(B)(C)(D)(E)

AP MICROECONOMICS
PRACTICE TEST

Section I

Time—70 minutes

60 Questions

Directions: Each question below is followed by five suggested answers or completions. Select the best answer choice and fill in the corresponding oval on your answer grid.

1. The basic economic problem that every economy faces is

   (A) Not enough money
   (B) Technological change
   (C) Central planning
   (D) Scarcity of resources
   (E) Inflation

2. The demand for oranges increases in response to a report by the American Medical Association. At the same time, the supply of oranges increases. What do we know will happen to equilibrium price and equilibrium quantity?

Equilibrium Price	Equilibrium Quantity
(A) Increase	Increase
(B) Indeterminate	Increase
(C) Increase	Decrease
(D) Increase	Indeterminate
(E) Decrease	Increase

3. Assume that coffee and cream are complements, and that a frost severely harms the coffee crop. What effect will this have on the price and quantity sold of cream?

Price	Quantity Sold
(A) Decrease	Decrease
(B) Decrease	Increase
(C) Indeterminate	Decrease
(D) Increase	Indeterminate
(E) Increase	Increase

4. Betty operates a hot dog stand in a mall. Which of the following events will most likely allow her to sell more hot dogs at a higher price?

   (A) A new hot dog steamer that can cook the hot dogs faster
   (B) The opening of a hamburger stand in the mall
   (C) A drop in the cost of hot dogs
   (D) The opening of a major new store in the mall
   (E) Hiring extra help to work the hot dog stand

5. If an increase in consumer income decreases the price of sausages, which of the following must be true?

(A) The demand for sausages increased.
(B) The price of a substitute for sausages increased.
(C) The price of a complement good dropped.
(D) The supply of sausages decreased.
(E) Sausage is an inferior good.

6. Which of the following statements are true for a monopolistic competitor in the long run?

  I. There are no long-run economic profits.

  II. Price is greater than marginal cost.

  III. The firm does not achieve productive efficiency.

(A) I only
(B) I and II
(C) II only
(D) II and III
(E) I, II, and III are correct.

7. If firms in an industry always operate where P = MC, and MC is equal to the minimum ATC in the long run, then the firms in this industry must be

(A) Monopolies
(B) Perfect competitors
(C) Oligopolies
(D) Monopolistic competitors
(E) Experiencing economic loss in the long run

8. In the long run, when a monopolist profit maximizes,

(A) the quantity he produces and the price he charges will both be greater than if he were a perfect competitor.
(B) the quantity will be greater and the price lower than if he were a perfect competitor
(C) the quantity and price will be less than if he were a perfect competitor
(D) the quantity will be less and the price higher than if he were a perfect competitor
(E) the quantity and price will be the same as they would if he were a perfect competitor

9. If the government places an excise tax on each unit of production of computers, what will occur in the computer market?

(A) Price will decrease.
(B) Demand will increase.
(C) Demand will decrease.
(D) Quantity demanded will decrease.
(E) Quantity demanded will increase.

Questions 10–12

Following is a graph of a profit-maximizing perfectly competitive firm.

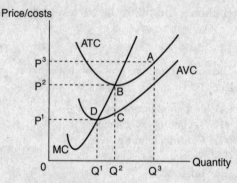

10. At a price of P^2, this firm has

(A) Economic profit
(B) Economic loss
(C) Neither economic profit nor loss
(D) Profit equal to BC
(E) No normal profit

11. If the price falls below P^1, the firm will

(A) Increase production and raise the price
(B) Shut down
(C) Eliminate some variable cost
(D) Advertise
(E) Higher more workers

12. Which vertical distance would represent average fixed cost?

(A) P^3 to P^2
(B) A to Q^3
(C) D to Q^2
(D) P^1 to 0
(E) B to C

GO ON TO THE NEXT PAGE. ➡

13. Juanita goes to the store with the intent of buying a sweater, willing to spend $50. In the end, the sweater's price was only $40. Juanita has

    (A) overestimated its value to her.
    (B) producer surplus.
    (C) consumer surplus.
    (D) purchased a product with an increasing shift in demand.
    (E) purchased a product with a decreasing shift in supply.

14. If milk sells for $2.50 a gallon, and the government set a price floor of $2.00 on it, the quantity

    (A) supplied will increase.
    (B) demanded will decrease.
    (C) supplied will decrease.
    (D) demanded will increase.
    (E) supplied and demanded will not change.

15. A monopoly that is operating at the profit maximizing level of output will always be operating where

    (A) price is equal to marginal cost.
    (B) price is equal to average cost.
    (C) price is equal to marginal revenue.
    (D) marginal revenue is equal to marginal cost.
    (E) marginal revenue is equal to average cost.

16. Which of the following statements is true of a monopolistically competitive firm but not of a perfectly competitive firm?

    (A) Long-run economic profit is possible.
    (B) Marginal revenue is equal to marginal cost in the long run.
    (C) There is ease of entry.
    (D) There are many competitors.
    (E) Price is greater than marginal cost.

Questions 17–18

Following is a production possibilities graph for the Transportation, Inc., which manufactures trucks and automobiles.

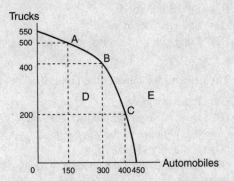

17. Assume that the firm is currently producing at point B. What would be the opportunity cost of increasing truck production by 100 units?

    (A) 150 automobiles
    (B) 100 automobiles
    (C) 300 automobiles
    (D) 50 automobiles
    (E) 0 automobiles

18. Which of the following would not allow the firm to produce at level E in the future?

    (A) An increase in labor
    (B) An increase in capital
    (C) An improvement in technology
    (D) An increase in labor and capital
    (E) An increase in management

19. Assume that a competitive industry is in long-run equilibrium. An oil crisis occurs that impacts this industry. Which of the following changes will occur to a firm that is less dependent on oil than most of its competitors?

	Short-Run Price	Short-Run Firm Output	Short-Run Economic Profits
(A)	Decrease	Decrease	Decrease
(B)	Increase	Increase	Increase
(C)	Decrease	Increase	No change
(D)	No change	Decrease	Decrease
(E)	Increase	Decrease	Decrease

GO ON TO THE NEXT PAGE. ➡

20. Which of the following is not a characteristic of an oligopolistic market?

    (A) Interdependence
    (B) Few firms
    (C) Substitute goods
    (D) Strategic behavior
    (E) Long-run profit is not possible.

21. The demand for labor in the factor market is

    (A) Perfectly elastic
    (B) Derived from the product demand
    (C) Independent of the wage
    (D) Positively sloped
    (E) Independent of the product market

22. Which of the following will increase a table manufacturer's demand for labor?

    (A) A decrease in productivity
    (B) An increase in the wage rate
    (C) An increase in the demand for tables
    (D) An increase in the price of wood
    (E) A decrease in the price of tables

23. If there is an inelastic demand for salt, and the government places a per unit tax on salt, then which of the following is true?

    (A) The producers will bear most of the burden of the tax.
    (B) The consumers will bear most of the burden of the tax.
    (C) The quantity supplied will have a greater percentage change than the percentage change in price.
    (D) The demand curve will shift to the right.
    (E) The supply curve will shift to the right.

24. If a firm is producing a product and creating a negative externality, then the firm's price and resource allocation is not at the socially optimal level. The price and resource allocation is

	Price	Resource Allocation
(A)	Too low	Overallocated
(B)	Too high	Overallocated
(C)	Too low	Underallocated
(D)	Too high	Underallocated
(E)	Just right	Overallocated

25. In order for a good to be a pure private good, it should be

    (A) Low priced and rival
    (B) Low priced and nonrival
    (C) Exclusionary and rival
    (D) Nonexclusionary and nonrival
    (E) Nonexclusionary and rival

26. If the government establishes an effective price floor, then

    (A) the regulated price will be below the equilibrium price.
    (B) the quantity demanded will be greater than the quantity supplied.
    (C) the quantity demanded will equal the quantity supplied.
    (D) the quantity demanded will be less than the quantity supplied.
    (E) there will be a shortage.

27. If the marginal social benefit exceeds the marginal private benefit, then

    (A) resources will be overallocated.
    (B) price will be too high.
    (C) resources will be underallocated.
    (D) there will be no free riders.
    (E) private business will supply too much.

28. A firm that is a monopsonist will hire the quantity of workers where

    (A) the marginal revenue product is less than the wage rate.
    (B) the marginal revenue product is equal to the wage rate.
    (C) the marginal revenue product is greater than the wage rate.
    (D) the supply of workers is perfectly elastic.
    (E) the marginal revenue product is perfectly elastic.

Questions 29–31

Following is a graph of an imperfect competitor.

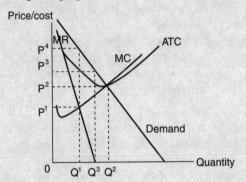

29. To profit maximize, this firm should produce at what quantity and price?

    (A) Q^1, P^1
    (B) Q^1, P^3
    (C) Q^1, P^4
    (D) Q^2, P^3
    (E) Q^3, P^2

30. This firm faces an elastic demand curve only above

    (A) P^1
    (B) P^2
    (C) P^3
    (D) P^4
    (E) There is no elastic portion of this demand curve.

31. The quantity and price that would produce the most revenue is

    (A) Q^1, P^1
    (B) Q^1, P^3
    (C) Q^1, P^4
    (D) Q^3, P^3
    (E) Q^2, P^2

Questions 32–34

Following is a chart of total output for Yellow Widget and Sons.

Number of Workers	Total Output
0	0
1	10
2	22
3	36
4	44
5	50

32. What is the marginal productivity of the third worker?

    (A) 35
    (B) 9
    (C) 14
    (D) 67
    (E) 12

33. Diminishing marginal productivity begins when how many workers are hired?

    (A) One
    (B) Two
    (C) Three
    (D) Four
    (E) Five

34. If the fixed cost is $1,000, average material cost is $1, and workers are paid $100, what is the average cost when 50 units are produced?

    (A) 11
    (B) 31
    (C) 20
    (D) 30
    (E) 1,500

GO ON TO THE NEXT PAGE. ➡

35. A firm that hires labor in a perfectly competitive labor market faces a supply curve that is

    (A) Perfectly elastic
    (B) Perfectly inelastic
    (C) Upward sloping
    (D) Downward sloping
    (E) Less elastic than the supply curve faced by a monopsonist

36. If the government wants the private sector to supply a good that the market cannot recognize all of the marginal benefit for, then the government should

    (A) Tax the private firms
    (B) Regulate the private firms
    (C) Give a subsidy to the private firms
    (D) Not interfere with the private firms
    (E) Institute a quota

37. At a price of $100 for a leather bag, a shop has total revenue of $10,000 a week, but at a bag price of $80, it has revenues of $12,000 a week. Which of the following explains this change in revenue?

    (A) The demand decreased.
    (B) The cost of producing the bags decreased.
    (C) The demand for bags is price elastic.
    (D) More bags sell at $80 because there is no consumer surplus.
    (E) The demand for bags is inelastic.

38. The Acme Company is a perfect competitor and is in long-run equilibrium. Suddenly, there's an increase in market demand. In the short-run, what happens to the quantity supplied, selling price, and economic profit of the Acme Company?

	Quantity Supplied	Selling Price	Economic Profit
(A)	Decrease	Increase	Increase
(B)	Increase	Decrease	Increase
(C)	Decrease	Increase	Decrease
(D)	Increase	Increase	Increase
(E)	Decrease	Decrease	Decrease

39. At the current level of output, the Okeedokee Company has a marginal revenue of $10, and a marginal cost is $8. This firm should

    (A) lower the price and keep its output the same, whether it is a perfect or an imperfect competitor.
    (B) increase its output if it is a perfect competitor, and increase output and price if it's an imperfect competitor.
    (C) increase price and output if it is a perfect competitor, and increase output and decrease price if it's an imperfect competitor.
    (D) increase output if it is a perfect competitor, and increase output and decrease price if it's an imperfect competitor.
    (E) decrease output if it is a perfect competitor, and increase output and decrease price if it's an imperfect competitor.

40. If labor in the construction industry works in a perfectly competitive labor market, and the demand for new building construction increases, then the effect on wages and number of laborers hired will be

	Wages	Number of Laborers Hired
(A)	Remain the same	Increase
(B)	Increase	Remain the same
(C)	Decrease	Remain the same
(D)	Increase	Decrease
(E)	Increase	Increase

GO ON TO THE NEXT PAGE. ➡

41. Two firms are operating in the same perfectly competitive industry. Both are experiencing economic loss. Firm A is operating at an output level where its average revenue is less than its average variable cost and its average total cost. Firm B is operating at an output level where its average revenue is more than its average variable cost but less than its average total cost. In the short run, what should these companies do?

	Firm A	Firm B
(A)	Continue to operate	Continue to operate
(B)	Shut down	Shut down
(C)	Shut down	Continue to operate
(D)	Continue to operate	Shut down
(E)	Increase production	Increase production

42. If steak is a normal good, what combination of events would unambiguously cause both the quantity of steak sold and the price to increase? Steak and chicken are substitute goods.

   (A) Increases in both the price of chicken and the cost of cattle feed
   (B) Decreases in both the price of chicken and the cost of cattle feed
   (C) An increase in the price of chicken and a decrease in the cost of cattle feed
   (D) Increases in both the price of chicken and average income
   (E) Decreases in both the cost of cattle feed and average income

43. Biggy Corporation is a monopoly that produces at a level where price is greater than average total cost. The government wants Biggy to produce at a level where the average total cost is equal to the average revenue. What must the government force the company to do?

	Output	Price	Profit
(A)	Increase	Increase	Increase economic profit
(B)	Increase	Decrease	Eliminate normal profits
(C)	Increase	Decrease	Eliminate economic profit
(D)	Decrease	Decrease	Increase normal profit
(E)	Decrease	Increase	Increase normal profit

44. If the total demand for an industry intersects the ATC curve at an output level that does not allow the industry to reach the minimum of the total average cost, then

   I. No company can earn a profit.

   II. The government should encourage more companies to enter the market.

   III. A monopoly could maximize the benefits of economies of scale.

   (A) II only
   (B) III only
   (C) I and II
   (D) I only
   (E) I, II, and III are correct.

45. A firm produces 10,000 units of an item that sells for $10. Its average variable cost is currently $8, and its total fixed cost is $1,000,000. In the short run, the efficient firm should

   (A) Shut down immediately
   (B) Produce less
   (C) Produce more
   (D) Raise its price
   (E) Earn a profit

46. One difference between perfect competitors and non-price-discriminating imperfect competitors is that

(A) perfect competitors cannot earn normal profits, while imperfect competitors can.
(B) there's consumer surplus in a perfectly competitive market but not in the imperfectly competitive market.
(C) there's no producer surplus in the perfectly competitive market the way there is in the imperfectly competitive market.
(D) there's deadweight loss in the perfectly competitive market, though not in the imperfectly competitive market.
(E) there's no deadweight loss in the perfectly competitive market the way there is in the imperfectly competitive market.

Questions 47–48

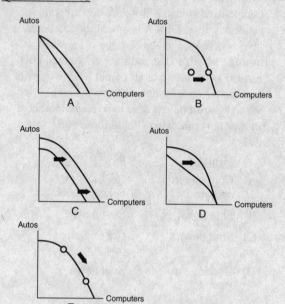

47. Which of the above events will unambiguously shift a firm's marginal revenue product for labor to the right?

(A) Increasing the number of employees the firm hires
(B) Increasing the industry demand for workers
(C) Increasing the demand for the product made by the laborers
(D) Industry-wide technology improvement
(E) Increasing the labor force

48. Which graph best illustrates the effect of technological improvement in the computer industry that does not affect the auto industry?

(A) A
(B) B
(C) C
(D) D
(E) E

GO ON TO THE NEXT PAGE. ➡

Questions 49–54

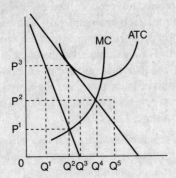

49. The above graph illustrates the long-run equilibrium of a firm in what industry?

    (A) Perfect competition
    (B) Monopolistic competition
    (C) Undifferentiated oligopoly
    (D) Differentiated oligopoly
    (E) Monopoly

50. The above firm has

    (A) an economic profit
    (B) an economic loss
    (C) a normal profit
    (D) less than normal profit
    (E) a normal loss

51. If the above firm is a profit maximizer, it will produce at what output and price level?

    (A) P^1, Q^1
    (B) P^2, Q^2
    (C) P^3, Q^3
    (D) P^3, Q^2
    (E) P^1, Q^2

52. If the firm produced the allocatively efficient quantity, it would produce

    (A) Q^1
    (B) Q^2
    (C) Q^3
    (D) Q^4
    (E) Q^5

53. If the firm produced the quantity that would maximize revenue, it would produce

    (A) Q^1
    (B) Q^2
    (C) Q^3
    (D) Q^4
    (E) Q^5

54. Which of the following is not a requirement for a price discriminator?

    (A) An ability to identify markets with different elasticities
    (B) An ability to prevent one market from reselling to the other market
    (C) Market power
    (D) Downward sloping demand curves
    (E) Different costs in different markets

Questions 55–56

Following is a table of John's total utility for pizza slices and cans of soda.

Slices of Pizza	Total Utility	Cans of Soda	Total Utility
1	12	1	4
2	21	2	7
3	27	3	9
4	30	4	10

55. If pizza costs $3 a slice, and soda costs $1 per can, John's marginal utility for a third slice of pizza is

    (A) 27
    (B) 9
    (C) 6
    (D) 60
    (E) 3

56. If John is a rational maximizer and spends $9 on pizza and soda, he will buy

    (A) three slices of pizza.
    (B) three slices of pizza and three cans of soda.
    (C) two slices of pizza and two cans of soda.
    (D) two slices of pizza and three cans of soda.
    (E) one slice of pizza and four cans of soda.

GO ON TO THE NEXT PAGE. ➡

57. A firm sells 500 baskets at $4, but sells 600 baskets when it lowers the price to $3. Which of the following would explain this result?

(A) The price of a close substitute decreased.
(B) The price of a complement increased.
(C) Demand for baskets is relatively elastic.
(D) Demand for baskets is relatively inelastic.
(E) The costs of producing baskets increased.

58. If fire protection is considered a public good, the private sector will not provide a sufficient quantity of it because

(A) the private sector could not account for all of the cost.
(B) the private sector would not be efficient at putting out a fire.
(C) the private sector could not exclude nonpayers from fire protection.
(D) the private demand would equal the marginal benefit.
(E) fire protection imposes a negative externality on the public.

59. A perfectly competitive industry in the long run will

(A) overallocate resources at the right price.
(B) allocate sufficient resources but at too low a price.
(C) underallocate resources at the right price.
(D) efficiently allocate resources at the right price.
(E) efficiently allocate resources but charge too high a price.

60. A company uses both machine and human labor in its production process, and can use any quantity of each independently. The company is currently producing as much of the product as it can sell. For a machine that costs the firm $1,000 to run, the marginal revenue product is $5,000. For a unit of labor that costs the firm $200, the marginal revenue product is $2,000. Therefore, the firm should

(A) use more machines and less labor.
(B) continue to use machines and labor in the same proportions.
(C) use more labor and less machines.
(D) hire equal amounts of machines and labor.
(E) hire more machines and more labor.

END OF SECTION I

Section II

Time—60 minutes

One Long Question and Two Short Questions

<u>Directions</u>: You have one hour total to answer all three of the following questions: one long question and two shorter questions. The first 10 minutes is for planning and review, and the remaining 50 minutes for answering the questions.

Although you can spend the 50 minutes any way you would like, we recommend that you spend *half* the time answering question 1, and divide the remaining time between questions 2 and 3.

Your answers should emphasize the line of reasoning you used to arrive at your answer; it is not enough to simply list the results of your analysis. When appropriate, include correctly labeled diagrams that have all axes and curves clearly labeled, and that show directional changes.

1. Assume that four companies, all of whom earn economic profit, produce steel, an undifferentiated product. Currently this domestic industry is protected by high tariffs.

   (a) (i) Draw a graph of a firm in this industry and illustrate how the domestic producer will determine price and quantity.

       (ii) Show the total economic profit on this graph.

   (b) (i) Now suppose the government removes all barriers to trade and that the world price for steel is lower than the domestic price. Using side by side graphs of the domestic industry and the world industry for steel, illustrate the impact of world trade on domestic producers and consumers.

       (ii) What happens to domestic price?

       (iii) What happens to the quantity consumed by domestic consumers?

       (iv) What happens to the quantity produced by domestic producers?

   (c) (i) Using a graph to illustrate your answer, explain what will happen to wages and the quantity of workers hired in a competitive labor market for the domestic steel industry.

       (ii) What will happen to wages?

       (iii) What will happen to the number of workers hired?

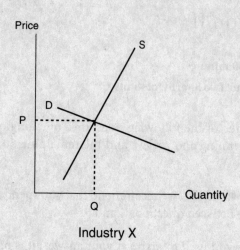

Industry X

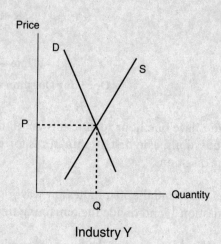

Industry Y

2. The graphs above illustrate two industries, both with the same equilibrium quantity of 1,000,000 units. The government is considering putting a $5 per unit tax on each industry.

   (a) On which industry would the tax produce the most revenues for the government? Explain.

   (b) On which industry would the tax reduce consumption the most? Explain.

3. The coal industry creates an negative externality in its production process.

   (a) Draw a graph of the private supply and demand for coal. Illustrate the effects of the negative externality.

   (b) Is the allocation of resources in the coal industry efficient? Explain.

   (c) Is price in the coal industry too high? Explain.

END OF TEST

STOP.

Answers and Explanations to Microeconomics Practice Test

1. (D)

Scarce resources is the reason why economies must make decisions regarding what to produce, how to produce, and for whom to produce. (A) is wrong because money is not a real variable: Economies could produce infinite amounts of money without solving economic problems. Nor is (B) the real problem, though it could lead to more output. (E), inflation, refers to the amount of money available to acquire the resources or products of an economy. It leads to nominal changes and not real changes.

2. (B)

We have an increase in demand that will pull up the price and increase the equilibrium quantity, and an increase in supply that will push down the price and increase the equilibrium quantity. Unambiguously, the equilibrium quantity will increase. So (C) and (D) can be eliminated right way. However, price is pulled up by one event and pushed down by the other. Net known results from the information are that price is indeterminate.

3. (A)

The frost decreases supply of coffee, resulting in a higher price and lower quantity. This will lead to decreased demand for cream, which will decrease cream's price and quantity.

4. (D)

The opening of a new store in the mall will increase the number of consumers available, which will shift the demand for Betty's hot dogs to the right. This would allow her to sell a larger quantity at a higher price. A new hot dog steamer would increase the supply, which in turn would decrease the price, so (A) is wrong. (C) would increase the hotdog supply, so it is wrong as well. (E) would shift the supply curve to the left, because costs would increase. (B) would decrease the demand for hot dogs and hence would decrease the price.

5. (E)

For a normal good, an increase in consumer income would increase the demand, which would result in a higher price. For an inferior good, an increase in income leads to a drop in demand, which leads to a decrease in price. (D) is not true, as a drop in supply would cause the price of sausages to increase, not decrease. (A), (B), and (C) would all create an increase in demand for sausages.

6. (E)

All of the statements are correct.

7. (B)

The conditions of P = MC = minimum ATC in the long run is only found in perfect competition.

8. (D)

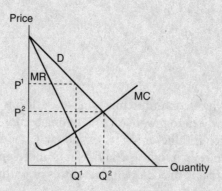

The monopolist determines profit maximization at the output where MR = MC. Price will be P^1 and quantity, Q^1. A perfectly competitive industry produces where the price is equal to marginal cost (allocative efficiency). Thus, the firm would produce at Q^2 price P^2. Since a perfectly competitive firm is a price taker, it faces a perfectly elastic demand curve; the demand curve is the marginal revenue curve.

9. (D)

An excise tax will shift the supply curve to the left, causing a decrease in the quantity demanded. Price will increase.

10. (C)

At a price of P^2, MR = MC at the minimum for the ATC. For a perfect competitor, price is also average revenue. AR = ATC = no economic profit or loss.

11. (B)

At a price below P^1, the price is below the average variable cost. To stay in business would lead to additional losses. Therefore, the firm will shut down immediately.

12. (E)

The average fixed cost is the vertical distance between the ATC and the AVC at any output level.

13. (C)

The difference between the price a consumer is willing to pay (marginal utility) and the price the item ends up being is consumer surplus—as long as the price is less. If the actual price ends up being more, the consumer will not buy.

ANSWERS AND EXPLANATIONS TO MICROECONOMICS PRACTICE TEST

14. (E)

A price floor that is below the equilibrium price is not effective, so the equilibrium price will take effect. Quantity supplied and demanded will not change.

15. (D)

Profit maximizing firms will always operate where MR = MC, regardless of market structure. Under perfect competition, P = MR, so at the profit maximizing level of output, we will have P = MR = MC. This is true only for perfect competition and not for monopoly.

16. (E)

A monopolistic competitor will operate where price is greater than marginal cost. A perfect competitor is a price taker, and price will equal marginal cost. Choice (A) is not true of either a perfect competitor or a monopolistic competitor. (B), (C), and (D) are true for both types of firms.

17. (A)

In order to increase the production of trucks from 400 to 500, you would have to reduce the production of automobiles from 300 to 150. Movement from point B to point A on the PPC illustrates this.

18. (E)

An increase in management is the only thing that would not allow the firm to produce at level E. All the other answer choices would push the production possibilities curve to the right.

19. (B)

The shortage of oil will increase the cost of production for most of the industry, shifting the industry supply curve to the right. The result will be an increase in price. This price increase will lead to more output by those firms that haven't dropped out of the industry. If a firm is less dependent on oil, it will not experience the same increase in cost, so the short run will lead to economic profit.

20. (E)

You're asked which condition is not a characteristic of an ologopoly. Long-run economic profit is indeed possible in oligopolies, so it's the correct answer choice here. All the other answer choices characterize oligopolies.

21. (B)

The demand for labor in the factor market is derived from the product demand. (A) is not correct, as the demand for labor is negatively sloped, not perfectly elastic. (C) is incorrect since the wage rate is determined in the labor market by the intersection of the demand and supply curves. Both are functions of the wage rate. (E) is the opposite of the correct answer. It is incorrect since the demand for labor is a derived demand. It depends upon the demand for the product that the labor is used to produce.

22. (C)

An increase in demand for tables will increase the price. The increase in price will shift the marginal revenue product (MRP) curve to the right. The MRP curve is the demand for labor curve.

23. (B)

The consumers will bear most of the burden of the tax. The inelastic demand for salt lets the producers pass on most of the additional cost of the tax, without a significant drop in quantity demanded.

24. (A)

A negative externality indicates that the firm is not recognizing the full costs, as indicated by the marginal social cost curve. The result is that the firm is charging too low a price and producing too great a quantity (overallocating resources).

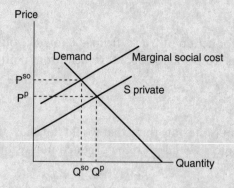

25. (C)

Exclusionary and rival are the two characteristics of a pure private good.

26. (D)

An effective price floor is above the equilibrium. The result is a surplus. The quantity supplied is greater than the quantity demanded.

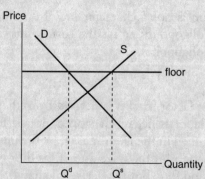

27. (C)

The socially optimal quantity is Q^2; however, Q^1 is the quantity the market will provide. Too little quantity means that resources are underallocated.

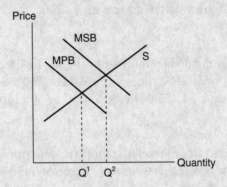

28. (C)

The monopsonist has market power in the hiring of resources in the resource market. This leads to paying a wage that is less than the marginal revenue product:

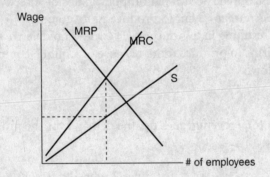

29. (C)

The profit maximizing rule is MR = MC. This leads the firm to output Q^1. At this output, price is determined from the demand curve, at P^4.

30. (C)

The point of unit elasticity is where the marginal revenue curve crosses the horizontal axis, Q3. At Q3, the price would be P3. Any point on the demand curve to the left of this point is elastic.

31. (D)

The point of unit elasticity indicates the maximum revenue possible. Output beyond this quantity leads to less total revenue (negative marginal revenue). Therefore, revenue is maximized at Q^3,P3.

32. (C)

The marginal product of the third worker is the difference is total output that results from hiring this worker. In other words, 36 minus 22. Fourteen is the answer.

33. (D)

Diminishing marginal productivity sets in when the addition to total output resulting from an additional worker is less than the addition from the previously hired worker. The third worker added 14 units, and the fourth worker adds 8 units.

34. (B)

Average cost is the total cost divided by number of units. The fixed cost is $1,000. Material is $1 times 50 units, $50. Labor is $100 times five workers, $500. So to get total cost, we add $1,000 plus 50 plus 500 to equal $1,550. Divide $1,550 by 50 units to get $31.

35. (A)

In a perfectly competitive resource market, the industry determines the wage rate. A firm can hire as many workers as it wants at this wage rate. Therefore, the supply of labor for the firm at this wage rate is perfectly elastic.

36. (C)

If the marginal benefit is greater than the quantity being supplied by the private sector, the government needs to encourage additional output. A subsidy effectively reduces the cost to the private firms and encourages them to produce more quantity. (A) and (B) would add to the cost of production resulting in less output. (D) would not change the present production level. (E), forcing the firms to produce more because of a quota, could lead to economic loss and firms could shut down.

37. (C)

If price goes down and total revenue goes up, the demand for the product must be elastic.

38. (D)

If the industry demand increases the price will go up. The firm will now recognize economic profit and produce more.

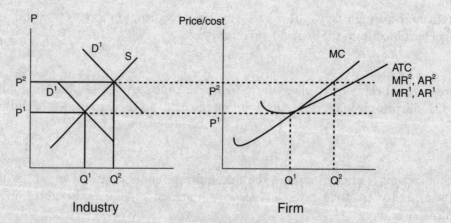

At the new price P^2, the profit maximizing rule MR = MC leads the firm to the production level Q^2. At Q^2, the firm's average revenue (AR2) is greater than the average cost. The firm has economic profit.

ANSWERS AND EXPLANATIONS TO MICROECONOMICS PRACTICE TEST

ANSWERS AND EXPLANATIONS TO MICROECONOMICS PRACTICE TEST

39. (D)

The profit maximizing rule is MR = MC. If marginal cost is less than marginal revenue, the firm should increase output. A perfect competitor is a price taker. The price will not change. An imperfect competitor faces a downward sloping demand curve. Therefore as additional units are produced, the price must be lowered.

40. (E)

The resource market is derived from the product market. Increased demand for the product (construction units) will increase quantity supplied and price. This will increase the demand for labor and the wage rate.

41. (C)

This is the shut-down rule. If a firm is experiencing economic loss but the price is greater than the average variable cost at the profit maximizing (loss minimizing) level of production, the firm should continue to produce in the short run. If not, the firm should shut down immediately. Remember price is average revenue.

42. (D)

If the price of chicken were to rise and average income increased, the demand for steak would increase. That would result in an increase in quantity sold and in the price. All other answer choices lead to a change in supply and a change in demand. This means that either price or quantity change will be indeterminate.

43. (C)

The current situation for Biggie is represented in the following graph. Q^1 is the current level of production. Q^2 is the level of production necessary to reach fair market price (AR = ATC). The firm must increase output from Q^1 to Q^2, and decrease price from P^1 to P^2. Where AR = ATC, there is no economic profit.

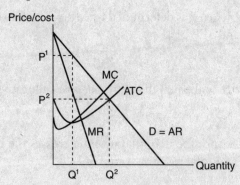

44. (B)

The question defines a natural monopoly situation. If the total quantity demanded is less than the quantity of output necessary for the minimum average total cost, then having only one producer allows the firm to produce at the output that comes closest to the minimum average total cost.

45. (C)

The firm is currently losing money; however the price is greater than the variable cost. The firm should continue to produce in the short run.

46. (E)

Answer choice (E) is the only correct statement.

47. (C)

An increase in demand for the product will increase price. The marginal revenue product is affected by price and productivity. (D) is a possible answer because it would affect productivity. However, since the technology is industry wide it will also lead to an increase in the industry supply curve. This will lower the price. Thus, the lower price shifts the marginal revenue product curve to the left and the increase in productivity shifts the marginal revenue product curve to the right. The result is ambiguous.

48. (A)

The production possibilities curve shifts out only on the axis that represents computers.

49. (B)

In the long run, a monopolistic competitor has no economic profit. MR =MC at output Q^2. At this output, the demand curve is tangent to the ATC curve: average revenue = average cost = zero economic profit.

50. (C)

The firm has no economic profit, nor an economic loss. Therefore, the firm has only normal profits.

51. (D)

This firm will produce at P^3, Q^2. It is determined by MR = MC for output. At this output, the corresponding price is found at P^3.

52. (D)

Q4 is the output where price will equal the marginal cost (allocative efficiency).

53. (C)

Output Q3 is the level of output the marginal revenue crosses the horizontal axis; therefore, marginal revenue is zero, and total revenue is maximized.

54. (E)

If firms have different costs in different markets, then different prices are not considered examples of price discrimination. All the other answer choices are requirements for price discrimination.

55. (C)

The marginal utility of the third slice is the change in total utility: 27 − 21 = 6

56. (D)

We must first determine the marginal utility per dollar.

Slices of Pizza	Total Utility	Marginal Utility	MU/P $3	Cans of Soda	Total Utility	Marginal Utility	MU/P $1
1	12	12	4	1	4	4	4
2	21	9	3	2	7	3	3
3	27	6	2	3	9	2	2
4	30	3	1	4	10	1	1

Buy the item that gives the most utility per dollar first. Then, buy the one that has the next highest marginal utility per dollar, and so on, until the $9 is exhausted. As seen here, the first purchase can be either the first slice or the first can—both have an MU/P of four. The second purchase is whichever is not purchased first. Total spent is $4. The third and fourth purchases can be either the second slice or the second can, as both have an MU/P of three. The total spent now is $8. The fifth purchase, with only $1 remaining, would be to buy the third can of soda.

57. (D)

The original total revenue is 500 times $4, or $2,000. When the price is lowered to $3, the firm sells 600. Total revenue is now $1,800. Price drops and total revenue drops. Therefore, the demand for baskets is relatively inelastic. In other words, consumers are insensitive to a change in price, so the percentage change in quantity demanded is less than the percentage change in price.

58. (C)

The marginal benefit exceeds the private demand. Firms cannot exclude nonpayers from receiving the benefit. By definition, a public good has nonexcludability.

59. (D)

Perfect competitors in the long run will always produce at an output where price is equal to marginal cost. This is allocative efficiency. Price will also equal average total cost at its minimum.

60. (C)

Whether to use more capital or more labor can be determined by the marginal revenue product per dollar spent. The machine gives $5,000/1,000 or $5 per dollar spent. The labor gives $2,000/$200 or $10 per dollar spent. There's a greater return from labor, so the firm should use more labor and fewer machines.

FREE-RESPONSE QUESTIONS

1. **(a)** The graph below represents an imperfect competitor. MR = MC determines profit maximizing quantity, Q. At that quantity, price is taken of the demand curve for a price of P. Total economic profit is the rectangle P, a, b, c.

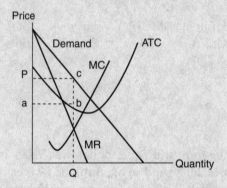

(b) Assuming all barriers to trade have been removed, and that the world price for steel is lower than the domestic price, the following graphs indicate the effect of world trade.

(i)

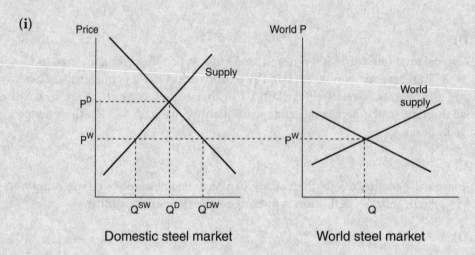

Domestic steel market   World steel market

(ii) Domestic price drops to the lower world price P^W.

(iii) Domestic consumption increases from Q^D to Q^{DW}.

(iv) Domestic producers produce less from Q^D to Q^{SW}.

(c)

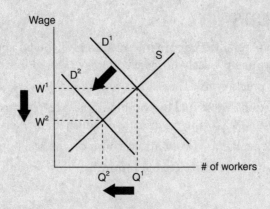

The quantity supplied by domestic producers decreases. Therefore, the demand for steelworkers drops from D^1 to D^2. Wages fall from W^1 to W^2. The number of workers employed decreases from Q^1 to Q^2.

2. **(a)** A tax on industry Y produces the most tax revenue. Inelastic demand means fewer quantities lost. Total tax revenue equals tax times quantity.

    (b) A tax on industry X produces the greatest loss of consumption because of the more elastic demand curve.

3. **(a)**

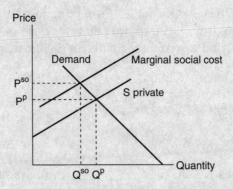

    (b) The resources in the coal industry are overallocated. The industry is producing Qp, and it should be producing Q^{so}.

    (c) The price is not too high; in fact, it is too low at P^p. It should be P^{so}.

SCORING YOUR PRACTICE TESTS

Don't take your practice test scores too literally. They are intended to give you an approximate idea of your performance. There is no way to determine precisely how well you have scored for the following reasons.

* Practice test conditions do not precisely mirror real test conditions.
* While the multiple-choice questions are scored by computer, the free-response questions are graded manually by faculty consultants. New scoring criteria are established for every test administration.
* Various statistical factors and formulas are taken into account on the real test.
* For each AP grade, the composite score range changes from year to year (and from subject to subject).

Section I: Multiple-Choice

This section accounts for two-thirds of the test. Keep in mind that the total number of points possible on the test is *90*, not 100.

_____ – (¼ × _____) × 1 = _____ (maximum of 60 points)

Number correct   Number wrong   Multiple-choice score
(out of 60)   (Round to the nearest
whole number.)

Section II: Free-Response

This section accounts for one-third of the test. Of course, it will be almost impossible for you to accurately score your own essays. In general, assign yourself one to two points for every component of the question you got right, i.e., a correctly labeled graph, and two to three points for a difficult graph.

Question 1 _____ (maximum of 15 points))

Question 2 _____ (maximum of 7.5 points)

Question 3 _____ (maximum of 7.5 points)

Free-Response Score (Add questions 1, 2, and 3) = _____ (maximum of 30 points)

Composite Score

Multiple-Choice Score _____ + Free-Response Score _____ = _____

Conversion Chart (approximate)	
Composite Score Range	**AP Grade**
71–90	5
54–70	4
42–53	3
28–41	2
0–27	1

GLOSSARIES

Potential GDP depends on quantity of labor and capital.

Glossary of Macroeconomic Terms

45-degree line

In Keynesian theory, a line on which aggregate expenditures equal income; the 45-degree line is used to determine economic equilibrium.

A

AD/AS equilibrium in the long run

Economic equilibrium characterized by the full-employment level of real GDP; the price level in long-run equilibrium is determined by aggregate demand.

absolute advantage

The ability to produce a good or service using fewer resources than other producers.

adaptive expectations theory

The idea that people make their decisions based on information from the recent past.

aggregate demand (AD)

The relationship between the price level and the total quantity of goods and services demanded by all sectors of the economy.

aggregate expenditures (AE)

The total spending of the household, business, government, and foreign sectors; the sum of consumption, investment, government spending, and net exports.

aggregate supply (AS)

The relationship between the price level and the total quantity of goods and services supplied by the producers in the economy.

allocative efficiency

A condition in which a business produces the quantity of goods and services consumers value, so that price is equal to marginal cost.

animal spirits

A term coined by Keynes to describe the somewhat arbitrary future expectations of business owners.

arbitrage

Using a situation in which the same good has two different prices in different locations to earn a profit. In arbitrage, the good is bought at a low price and then resold at a higher price.

asset

An object that a business, household, or government owns, such as a building, equipment, or a loan made to others.

autonomous

An activity that occurs independently, regardless of any outside influences.

autonomous consumption

The spending that a household does, regardless of their income level.

average propensity to consume (APC)

The average amount of a dollar of disposable income spent on consumption.

B

balance of payments
The balance on the current account plus the balance on the capital account. The balance of payments equals zero.

balance on the capital account
The sum of all capital inflows minus the sum of all capital outflows.

balance on the current account
Current account exports minus current account imports.

balance sheet
A system of keeping track of a business's assets and liabilities over time.

balanced budget
A situation in which the government's spending is equal to its tax revenues.

balanced budget multiplier
The increase (or decrease) in real GDP when government spending and taxes are both increased (or reduced) by one dollar. The balanced budget multiplier always equals one.

Bank Deregulation Act of 1980
A law enacted by Congress that introduced several changes into the banking sector, such as the requirement that all banks follow the required reserve ratio that the Fed mandates.

bank run
A situation in which a bank's depositors want to remove all their deposits at the same time. Since a fractional reserve bank does not keep all of its depositors' funds, it cannot deal with this situation and is forced out of business.

bartering
Trading goods and services for other goods and services.

base year
The year in which the composition of the market basket is set for the consumer price index.

bond
A contract issued by a borrower that allows the holder to receive interest payments as well as the repayment of the savings the borrower originally received.

bond resale market
A market in which people can buy and sell bonds that were previously issued.

Bretton Woods Agreement
An agreement made between the major industrial nations at the close of World War II that fixed exchange rates and pegged them to the U.S. dollar. It also created the International Monetary Fund (IMF) to help maintain the exchange rate system.

Brumberg, Richard
(1930–1955) An economist who helped develop the life-cycle theory of consumption concurrently with Friedman's development of the permanent income theory of consumption.

budget deficit
A situation in which the government's spending is greater than its tax revenues.

budget surplus
A situation in which the government's spending is less than its tax revenues.

business cycle
A pattern over time in which increases in real GDP are followed by decreases in real GDP, and decreases are followed by increases.

business sector
A part of a nation's economy composed of the people who rent or buy factors of production and use them to create goods and services.

C

capacity utilization
A measure of the amount of capital possessed by businesses that is being used as compared to the total amount available for use.

capital
Equipment, buildings, and human abilities that are used in producing goods and services.

capital account
A listing of the value of real assets and financial assets that are exchanged between a nation and the rest of the world.

capital account deficit
When total capital outflows are larger than total capital inflows, the balance on the capital account is negative. This means the nation is purchasing more foreign assets than the rest of the world is purchasing domestic assets.

capital account surplus
When total capital inflows are larger than total capital outflows, the balance on the capital account is positive. This means the rest of the world is purchasing more of a nation's assets than the nation is purchasing the assets of the rest of the world.

capital goods
Produced goods that are used to make other goods and services (such as machinery and buildings), and that aren't used up when making those other goods and services.

capital inflow
A sale of a real or a financial asset by a nation to the rest of the world.

capital outflow
A purchase of a real or a financial asset by a nation from the rest of the world.

capitalist economy
See *pure market economy*.

central bank
An organization that controls a nation's money supply.

certificate of deposit (CD)
A financial instrument, similar to a bond, issued by a bank and guaranteed by the FDIC.

ceteris paribus
A Latin phrase meaning that all other variables are held constant. Only one independent variable is allowed to change, and resulting changes in the dependent variable are then studied.

chaining
A method of calculating real GDP by using the average growth rates of output between successive years.

change in aggregate demand
A change in consumption, investment, government spending, or net exports (but not caused by a change in the price level), that causes the AD curve to shift.

change in aggregate quantity demanded
A change in the price level that causes the economy to move to a new point on the AD curve.

change in aggregate supply
A change in production costs, not caused by a change in the price level, that causes the AS curve to shift.

change in the value of aggregate quantity supplied
A change in the price level that causes the economy to move to a new point on the AS curve.

circular flow of economic activity

The combined economic activity in the factor, product, and financial markets; an examination of the flow of income, expenditures, and goods and services between the sectors of the economy.

classical view of economics

A view that holds that flexible wages and prices will automatically eliminate any recessions and return the entire economy to equilibrium, where output is at full employment.

command economy

An economic system that uses central government planners to determine the production and distribution of goods and services.

commodity money

Money that has uses in addition to being a medium of exchange, a unit of account, and a store of value. In other words, money that has intrinsic value.

comparative advantage

The ability to produce a good or service at a lower opportunity cost than other producers.

consumer price index (CPI)

A price index created by using a market basket. The CPI is intended to show the cost of the purchases of an "average" household. The CPI measures the price level.

consumption (C)

Expenditures by the household sector on goods and services for a period of one year.

contraction

The period of time over which real GDP goes from a peak to a trough.

contractionary fiscal policy

Fiscal policy with the goal of decreasing real GDP. Used to deal with inflation, it might include increases in taxes and decreases in government spending.

contractionary monetary policy

Monetary policy, usually used to deal with inflation, that has the goal of decreasing the money supply.

cost–benefit analysis

A process of weighing the costs and benefits of a decision in order to make a choice.

cost–push inflation

Inflation caused by general decreases in businesses' supply of goods and services.

coupon payment

Periodic interest payments made by bond issuers to bond holders.

credit card

A card that can be used to purchase goods and services electronically. The credit card company reimburses the vendor and issues a loan to the purchaser.

credit union

A type of financial intermediary that accepts deposits from and makes loans to only certain types of workers.

crowding out effect

The government borrows money to finance a budget deficit, which increases the demand for loanable funds, which increases the interest rate, which decreases the amount of investment that firms pursue.

currency in circulation

The paper money and coins used to pay for daily expenditures in the economy.

current account

A listing of the value of goods and services imported and exported into and out of a nation.

current account deficit

A situation in which current account imports are larger then current account exports. The balance on the current account is negative.

current account exports

The total value of all goods and services exported to other nations plus the income earned from domestically owned assets in other nations.

current account imports

The total value of all goods and services imported from other nations plus the income paid to foreigners who own domestic assets.

current account surplus

A situation in which current account exports are larger then current account imports. The balance on the current account is positive.

cyclical

A variable that increases (or decreases) when real GDP increases (or decreases).

cyclical unemployment

Unemployment caused by fluctuations in production associated with the business cycle.

D

debit card

A card that can be used to purchase goods and services electronically: The bank reimburses the vendor that accepts the debit card as payment and then deducts the purchase from a checking account.

debt

Money a borrower owes to a lender.

deflation

An decrease in price level over time, in which many or all prices decrease.

demand

The relationship between the price of a good or service and the quantity people are willing and able to buy.

demand curve

A graphical representation of demand.

demand deposits

Checking account deposits; traditionally, these deposits do not earn interest.

demand for currency

The group of people who want to purchase a currency being traded in a foreign currency market, e.g., in the market for Mexican pesos, Americans who want to trade U.S. dollars for pesos constitute the demand for pesos.

demand shock

See *change in aggregate demand*.

demand–pull inflation

Inflation caused by general increases in consumers' demand for goods and services.

dependent variable

The variable whose value is determined by the other variable in a functional relationship

depreciation

The value of the capital that wears out over the course of a year.

direct relationship

A type of functional relationship in which an increase in the independent variable causes an increase in the dependent variable, and vice versa.

discount rate

The interest rate the Fed charges to banks for discount window loans.

discount window loan

An overnight loan issued by the Fed to allow a bank to meet its reserve requirement at the end of the day.

discouraged worker

A person who has given up looking for a job after trying to get one. A discouraged worker is not counted as a member of the labor force.

disequilibrium

A condition in which the quantity demanded is not equal to the quantity supplied at the current market price.

disinflation

A situation in which prices are increasing at a slower rate.

disintermediation

A situation that occurs when depositors withdraw their money from financial intermediaries.

disposable income

The income that households have left after they pay taxes.

double counting

An inclusion of the value of an intermediate good or service in the calculation of GDP.

durable goods

A good used up at a slow rate when it is consumed.

E

economic growth

An increase in total output over time.

economic system

A collection of institutions that are used to determine the production and distribution of goods and services.

economics

A social science concerned with the study of human behavior constrained by scarcity.

effect of fiscal policy in an open economy

Expansionary (or contractionary) fiscal policy that increases the budget deficit (or surplus) drives up (or down) interest rates and the price of the U.S. dollar. This causes the trade deficit to grow (or shrink), and creates net capital inflows (or outflows) into (or out of) the economy.

effect of monetary policy in an open economy

Expansionary (or contractionary) monetary policy drives down (or up) the interest rate and the price of the U.S. dollar. This causes the trade deficit to shrink (or grow), and creates net capital outflows (or inflows) out of (or into) the economy.

efficiency

A condition in which a reallocation of resources among producers will not lead to an increase in their combined output. In other words, no resources are being wasted.

efficient

A combination of goods that is on the productions possibilities frontier. With the given resources, the economy can only make more of one good by making less of another.

elastic

A condition in which the price elasticity of demand (or supply) is greater than one. The percent change in quantity demanded (or supplied) is greater than the percent change in price, so demanders (or suppliers) are sensitive to price changes.

embargo

A law that prohibits a nation's members from trading certain goods with members of another nation.

Employment Act of 1946
See *Full Employment Act*.

entitlement
See *transfer payments*.

entrepreneurship
The ability to come up with new ways to combine the factors of production to create new products or produce old products more efficiently.

equation of exchange
The quantity of money (M) times money's velocity (V) equals nominal GDP, which equals the price level (P) times the real GDP (Q). M x V = P x Q.

equilibrium
See *market equilibrium*

equilibrium interest rate
The interest rate at which the quantity of money supplied equals the quantity of money demanded. The money supply curve and money demand curve intersect at the equilibrium interest rate.

equilibrium price
See *market price*.

equilibrium quantity
The quantity that is demanded (or supplied) at the equilibrium price, where the quantity demanded equals the quantity supplied.

excess demand
A condition in which the quantity demanded is greater than the quantity supplied at the current market price. The current market price is below the market equilibrium price.

excess reserves
The total deposits at a bank minus its required reserves.

excess supply
A condition in which the quantity demanded is less than the quantity supplied at the current market price. The current market price is above the equilibrium price.

exchange rate
The price of one unit of currency, in terms of another country's currency.

excise tax
A tax placed on expenditures for a particular good or service.

expansion
The period of time over which real GDP goes from a trough to a peak.

expansionary fiscal policy
Fiscal policy with the goal of increasing real GDP. Used to help a recession economy, it includes increases in government spending and decreases in taxes.

expansionary monetary policy
Monetary policy with the goal of increasing the money supply; this policy is usually used to deal with a recession.

expenditure
The amount of money used to buy goods or services within a period of time.

exports (X)
Expenditures by the foreign sector on domestic goods and services for a period of one year.

F

factor market
A market in which resources and semi-finished products are exchanged.

factors of production
Something used in creating a good or a service, including land, labor, capital, and entrepreneurship.

Federal Deposit Insurance Corporation (FDIC)
An insurance program administered by the federal government that guarantees up to $100,000 of an individual's deposits in a bank.

federal funds market
A loanable funds market in which banks borrow and lend funds to other banks.

federal funds rate
The interest rate banks charge each other on overnight loans.

Federal Open Market Committee (FOMC)
A group composed of the Board of Governors, the president of the New York district's Fed bank, and the presidents of four other Fed district banks. This group selects the open market monetary policy the Federal Reserve will implement.

Federal Reserve (the Fed)
The central bank of the United States.

Federal Reserve Act of 1913
A law that established the Federal Reserve and made it responsible for providing money for economic activity and overseeing the health of banks and the economy.

Federal Reserve Board of Governors
A group of seven governors, each of whom is appointed by the president and confirmed by the Senate to one 14-year term. The board helps to manage the Federal Reserve.

Federal Reserve District Bank
A part of the Federal Reserve that implements its policy and keeps track of economic activity for a certain geographic region of the nation.

Federal Savings and Loan Insurance Corporation (FSLIC)
A now defunct insurance program administered by the federal government, similar to the FDIC, except it insured deposits at savings and loan associations; it went bankrupt during the Saving and Loan Crisis of the 1980's.

fiat money
Money that has no use besides being a medium of exchange, a unit of account, and a store of value. In other words, money with no intrinsic value.

final good
A good being sold to the final consumer.

financial instrument
A tool that uses a person's savings to earn interest.

financial market
A market in which financial intermediaries enable borrowers and lenders to trade savings and interest income.

fiscal policy
Altering government spending or taxation with the goal of promoting economic health. This policy is pursued by the U.S. Congress and the president.

flow variable
A variable whose value is determined over a period of time.

foreign official assets
Foreign currency, gold, and foreign government bonds that are owned by a nation's central bank.

foreign sector
See *rest of the world sector*.

fractional reserve banking
A banking system in which banks keep a small share (a fraction) of their depositors' funds on hand (in reserve), and loan out the rest. Banks do not keep all of their depositors' funds.

free enterprise
An economic system in which buyers and sellers freely decide what to trade and with whom to trade.

free good
A good that people want that isn't scarce, and that people can obtain at no cost.

free trade
A situation in which the government does not use quotas and tariffs to inhibit international trade.

frictional unemployment
Unemployment caused by people moving between jobs.

Friedman, Milton
(1912–) An American economist who advocates a laissez faire approach to fiscal policy and who developed the permanent income theory of consumption.

full capacity
The amount of real GDP that can be produced when all of a nation's resources are devoted to production.

full employment
The level of employment at which cyclical unemployment does not exist.

Full Employment Act (1946)
A law that requires Congress to use fiscal policy to achieve and maintain full employment.

Full-Employment and Balanced Growth Act of 1978
A law that reiterated the intentions of the Employment Act of 1946.

G

GDP gap
The difference between the actual real GDP and the potential real GDP.

gold standard
A type of fiat currency in which the government agrees to buy and sell gold for the currency it issues.

good
A object that satisfies a want.

government budget
A listing of the government's spending and income for a period of one year.

government expenditures on goods and services (G)
Expenditures by the government sector on goods and services for a period of one year.

government sector
A part of a nation's economy composed of the local, state, and federal governments.

government spending
All types of government spending, including purchases of goods and services and transfer payments.

government taxation
The main source of government income.

Great Depression
A severe recession beginning in 1929 and lasting until World War II during which real GDP drastically fell and unemployment was widespread.

Gresham's law
Bad money drives good money out of circulation, the type of commodity money that has the lowest intrinsic value will become the dominant type of money, and the money with the highest intrinsic value will be hoarded rather than used as money.

gross domestic product (GDP)
The total value of all final goods and services produced within a nation's borders in one year. Also called *nominal GDP*.

gross national product (GNP)
The total value of all final goods and services produced by all the members of a nation in one year.

H

household sector
One part of a nation's economy, composed of those who own factors of production. This group rents/sells the factors to the business sector, and buys the goods and services produced by the business sector.

human capital
Intangible types of capital possessed by people, such as knowledge and skill.

I

identity
A relationship that is true by definition.

imports (M)
Expenditures by the household, business, and government sectors on goods and services made by the foreign sector for a period of one year.

income
Money earned by the owners of the factors of production.

income distribution
A description of the way earnings are spread throughout the economy.

income effect
See *real balances effect*.

independent variable
The variable that determines the value of the other variable in a functional relationship.

index of leading indicators
A number that represents a collection of certain economic variables. The index is meant to predict future changes in real GDP.

inefficient
A combination of goods that is inside the productions possibilities frontier. In other words, using the given resources, it would be possible to produce more of one good or service without decreasing the number of other goods produced.

inelastic
A condition in which the price elasticity of demand (or supply) is less than one. The percent change in quantity demanded (or supplied) is less than the percent change in price, so demanders (or suppliers) are insensitive to changes in price.

inflation
A general increase in prices over time, during which many prices in the economy rise.

inflation rate
The percent change in the price level from one year to the next.

injections
An expenditure by the business, government, or foreign sectors on domestic goods or services, including investment, government purchases, and exports.

input
See *factors of production*.

interest
The payment received by capital owners in a factor market. Also, a payment a borrower makes to a lender in exchange for the use of the lender's funds.

KAPLAN

interest rate

The interest payments made on a loan, expressed as a percentage of the amount of the loan.

interest rate effect

An increase (or decrease) in the price level will increase (or decrease) the demand for loanable funds, and thus, the interest rate. In turn, the amount of investment pursued falls (or rises), which decreases (or increases) the aggregate quantity demanded.

intermediate good

A good used up in making and selling another good or service. It is produced by one firm and sold to another firm.

inverse relationship

A type of functional relationship in which an increase (or decrease) in the independent variable causes a decrease (or increase) in the dependent variable.

investment (I)

Expenditures by the business sector on capital goods for a period of one year.

investment demand

An inverse relationship that shows the amount of capital goods businesses are willing and able to purchase at various interest rates.

investment demand curve

A graphical representation of investment demand.

invisible hand

Used by Adam Smith to describe the natural forces in a market economy that harness self-interest, achieving the greatest benefit for the economy. In other words, when people are allowed to seek their own rewards, the common interest naturally takes care of itself.

K

Keynes, John Maynard (1883–1946)

An influential English economist who wrote *The General Theory of Employment, Interest, and Money*, which explained how economic factors might not automatically eliminate recessions.

Keynesian segment of the AS curve

The horizontal section of the aggregate supply curve.

Keynesian theory

A theory that demand determines supply, and prices and wages are not adequately flexible to ensure that the economy will return to equilibrium.

L

labor

Human physical and mental effort that is used in producing goods and services.

labor force

The members of a nation who are actively looking for work, and are not retired, under age 16, suffering from a disability that prevents their being employed, in jail, or in the military.

laissez-faire

A French term meaning "let them be." A government that follows a laissez-faire policy will do little or nothing to regulate the economy.

land

Natural resources that are used in producing goods and services.

large time deposits

A financial instrument that is similar to a savings account since it earns interest. The account is more than $100,000, the funds are deposited for fewer than 90 days but for a specified length of time, and there's a penalty for early withdraw of funds.

law of demand

As the price of a good or service rises, the quantity consumers are willing and able to buy decreases, and as the price drops, the quantity demanded increases, *ceteris paribus*.

law of increasing opportunity costs

As more resources are devoted toward the production of one good, the sacrifice of producing one more unit of the good—or the opportunity cost measured in terms of the production of another good forgone—becomes higher.

law of one price

The idea that, after accounting for transportation costs and converting between currencies, a good in one place should have the same price as the same good in a different place.

law of supply

As the price of a good or service rises, the quantity producers are willing and able to sell increases, and as the price drops, the quantity supplied decreases, *ceteris paribus*.

leakages

Uses of household income on things other than consumption, savings, imports, or taxes.

lender of last resort

One duty of the Federal Reserve, which is to lend funds to banks that cannot obtain the funds from anywhere else.

liability

An object that a business, household, or government owes, such as a loan received from others.

life insurance company

A company that takes small amounts of money from a lot of policy holders, invests the money, and then pays large amounts to the beneficiaries of the small number of policy holders who die.

life-cycle theory of consumption

See *permanent income theory of consumption*.

liquidity

The ease with which an asset can be converted into its full cash value.

loanable funds market

A market in which households trade their savings with businesses in exchange for interest payments.

long run

A time horizon over which the prices of all factors of production can change.

long-run aggregate supply

The relationship between the price level and the aggregate quantity supplied in the long run, when all resource use can be altered.

long-run Phillips curve

Based on the natural rate hypothesis, a vertical line at the natural rate of unemployment, on a graph comparing inflation and unemployment rates.

M

M1

A measure of the most liquid parts of the money stock. M1 is the sum of the currency in circulation, the value of demand deposits, and the value of traveler's checks.

M2

A measure of the money stock. M2 equals M1 plus less liquid forms of money, which include savings deposits, small time deposits, and money market mutual funds.

M3

A measure of the money stock. M3 equals M2 plus near monies.

macroeconomics
The study of the collective behavior of a society of individuals constrained by scarcity.

marginal
The addition of one more unit.

marginal analysis
A type of decision making that compares the additional benefits of a decision to the additional costs.

marginal propensity to consume (MPC)
The portion of one additional dollar of disposable income spent on consumption.

marginal propensity to save (MPS)
The portion of one additional dollar of disposable income that is saved; $MPS = 1 - MPC$.

market
A place where buyers and sellers exchange goods or services for a price on which they agree. The exchange may be concentrated in one location or spread over many places.

market basket
A list of the typical goods and services an urban household buys in one year, used in the calculation of the CPI.

market equilibrium
The price and quantity where the demand and supply curves intersect. At this price, the quantity demanded equals the quantity supplied.

market price
The price where the quantity demanded equals the quantity supplied. The price where the demand and supply curves intersect.

market system
An economic system that uses markets and prices to determine the production and distribution of goods and services.

maturity date
The time at which a bond issuer pays a bond holder the money that was initially borrowed with the bond.

Medicare
A system of transfer payments the federal government makes to the elderly in order to provide health care.

medium of exchange
An object that people use to exchange goods and services indirectly.

menu costs
Costs that businesses incur to update their pricing information when there's a price increase.

merchandise trade balance
The total value of all newly produced goods exported to other nations, minus the total value of all newly produced goods imported into a nation.

microeconomics
The study of individual human behavior constrained by scarcity.

minimum wage law
A law that prevents wages from falling below a predetermined level.

mixed economy
An economic system that combines elements of two or all three types of economic systems.

Modigliani, Franco (1918–)
An economist who helped to develop the life-cycle theory of consumption at the same time that Friedman developed the permanent income theory of consumption.

monetarism
The belief that the Fed's monetary policy should focus on growing the money supply at a constant rate.

monetary policy
Altering the quantity of money in the economy with the goal of promoting economic health. This policy is pursued by the Federal Reserve.

money
An object that people use as a medium of exchange, a unit of account, and a store of value.

money demand
An inverse relationship that shows the amount of money households want to hold at various interest rates; at higher interest rates, people want to hold less money, and at lower interest rates people want to hold more money, *ceteris paribus*.

money demand curve
A graphical representation of money demand.

money market mutual fund
A mutual fund that invests in relatively safe investments, such as short-term bonds.

money multiplier
The increase (or decrease) in the money supply when the Fed increases (or decreases) excess reserves by one dollar; the reciprocal of the required reserve ratio.

money stock
The amount of money in an economy at a point in time. Also called *money supply*.

money supply curve
A graphical representation of money supply. Since the Fed determines the money supply, the money supply curve is a vertical line.

mortgage
A long-term loan used to purchase real estate.

mortgage rate
The interest rate financial intermediaries charge on home loans.

multiplier effect
A change in taxes or spending lead to an even larger change in real GDP.

mutual fund
A financial instrument that invests a group of people's savings into other financial instruments.

N

national debt
The total amount of money the federal government currently owes to lenders.

national income accounting
A system of keeping track of the flows of income in a nation for a period of one year.

natural rate hypothesis
Certain real variables have natural rates of growth that they follow in the long run. Many times, this hypothesis refers to the assumption that there's a natural rate of unemployment to which the economy will always return, in the long run.

natural rate of unemployment
See *full employment*.

near monies
A group of the least liquid types of money, such as large time deposits.

negative externality
A cost imposed on a third party that the decision-maker didn't take into account. Many types of pollution are negative externalities.

net benefits
The benefits that result from a choice minus the costs that accompany the choice.

net domestic product (NDP)
GDP minus depreciation.

net exports (NX)
Exports minus imports.

net exports effect
An increase (or decrease) in the price level makes domestic goods and services relatively more (less) expensive than foreign ones. Thus, imports grow (shrink) and exports shrink (grow), which leads to a decrease (increase) in the aggregate quantity demanded.

net worth
Assets minus liabilities.

New York Stock Exchange
A large market in which people can buy and sell shares of stock of certain corporations.

nominal interest rate
The interest rate that includes a component representing inflation.

nominal variable
A variable that includes a component showing inflation.

nondurable goods
A good used up at a fast rate when it is consumed.

normative economics
A type of economic analysis that uses value judgements to recommend actions and policies that people should take.

North American Free Trade Agreement (NAFTA)
An agreement instituted in 1993 that removed most of the trade barriers between Canada, the United States, and Mexico.

O

official assets
See *foreign official assets*.

OPEC oil crisis
A supply shock that occurred in the early 1970s when the Organization of Petroleum Exporting Countries (OPEC) drastically reduced the supply of oil, which led to a drastic increase in oil prices and production costs.

open economy
An economy whose members can import and export goods and services.

open market operations
The sale and purchase of Treasury bonds by the Fed, with the intent of changing the money supply and the interest rates.

opportunity cost
The value of the next best alternative option that was not chosen.

over-heated economy
A condition in which the economy is producing at a level above the full employment level. Inflation occurs in an over-heated economy.

P

peak
A point in time at which real GDP is at a relative maximum.

pension fund
A financial organization that invests the savings of a large number of workers and then uses the funds to provide the workers with a source of income when they retire.

permanent income theory of consumption
The idea that people base their consumption decisions on the income they expect to earn over their lifetime. This is in contrast to the Keynesian approach of basing consumption on current income.

personal income tax
A tax placed on a household's income.

Phillips curve
The graphical representation of a hypothesized, inverse relationship between the unemployment rate and the rate of inflation.

physical capital
Tangible types of capital, such as machinery and buildings.

positive economics
Economic analysis that describes economic behavior and the functioning of the economy without making judgements about how people should behave.

positive rate of time preference
An expression of the fact that people prefer to receive money today, rather than waiting until tomorrow to receive it.

potential RGDP
The level of real GDP that occurs at full employment.

precautionary motive
The desire to hold money, instead of investing it in a financial instrument, to pay for future unexpected expenditures.

price
The terms of trade established in a market when buyers trade money to sellers in exchange for goods and services.

price ceiling
A regulation that prevents the market price from rising above a stated level.

price elasticity of demand
A measure of how responsive consumers are to price changes, which is the percent change in quantity demanded divided by the percent change in price.

price elasticity of supply
A measure of how sensitive firms are to price changes, which is the percent change in quantity supplied divided by the percent change in price.

price floor
A regulation that prevents the market price from falling below a stated level.

price index
A number used to measure general price trends in an economy. This number is based on the prices of a selection of goods and services.

prime rate
The interest rate banks charge their very best customers.

producer price index (PPI)
A price index created by using the prices of production goods.

product market
A market in which finished goods and services are exchanged.

production possibilities frontier (PPF)
A graphical description of the economy that shows the maximum amounts of two or more goods that can be produced given the inputs available. The PPF shows a range of different combinations of efficient production.

productive efficiency
A condition in which given resources are used to produce the most possible output. The output combination is on the PPF.

productivity
The amount of output that a given unit of input can produce.

profit
The total revenue earned from sales of products minus the total cost of the resources used.

progressive tax
A tax structured so that as a household's income rises, the percentage of its income it pays in taxes will also rise.

property tax
A tax placed on ownership of real property, such as land owned by a household.

protectionism
The idea that international trade should be restricted to protect a nation's economic health.

purchasing power
The goods and services an amount of money can purchase.

purchasing power parity (PPP)
The idea that one unit of a nation's currency should have the same purchasing power in another nation when it is converted into that nation's currency.

pure market economy
An economic system in which resources are privately owned and economic activity is unregulated by the government.

Q

quantity demanded
The amount of a good or service consumers are willing and able to buy at a specific price.

quantity supplied
The amount of a good or service that firms are willing and able to offer for sale at a specific price.

quantity theory of money
A theory holding that a change in the money supply leads to a change in the price level, but not to a change in real GDP.

quota
A limit on the amount of goods that can be imported imposed by the government.

R

rational
Logical, based on thoughtful analysis. It refers to a decision-making process that compares the benefits and costs of an action.

rational expectations theory
The idea that people make their decisions based on all the information they can gather, including events from the recent past, news media reports, and their understanding of how the economy works.

real assets
Property and capital goods that may be used as factors of production.

real balances effect
An increase (or decrease) in the price level decreases (or increases) the purchasing power of financial instruments, which in turn decreases (or increases) the aggregate quantity demanded.

real GDP per capita
The value of total output in an economy in one year, calculated using constant dollars divided by the number of people in the economy.

real gross domestic product (RGDP)

A calculation of GDP using chaining, so that changes in real GDP reflect only changes in production.

real interest rate

The interest rate that does not include an inflation component. The real interest rate equals the nominal interest rate minus the rate of inflation.

real variable

A variable that does not include a component showing inflation.

recession

A contraction of the economy characterized by declines in the total output of the economy for six or more consecutive months. More technically, it is a decrease in total output over two consecutive quarters.

rent

The payment received by land owners in a factor market.

rent control law

A law that prevents apartment rental rates from rising above a predetermined level.

repurchase agreement

A type of loan that a bank receives from its customers.

required reserve ratio

The ratio of (a) the deposits a bank does not loan to others to (b) the total deposits at the bank. This ratio is determined by the government and must be met by all banks.

research and development (R&D)

Investment spending by firms on finding and implementing new ideas and new technologies.

resource

See *factors of production*.

rest of the world sector

A group of people who participate in a nation's economy, but who aren't a part of that nation.

Ricardo, David (1772–1823)

An English economist who advocated trade based on comparative advantage and specialization.

S

sales tax

A tax placed on expenditures for many types of goods and services.

savings account

Money a household keeps in a bank to earn interest payments, to keep the money safe, and to allow easy access to their funds.

savings and loan association

A type of financial intermediary that accepts long-term deposits and specializes in making long-term loans for real estate purchases.

savings and loan crisis

A collapse of many saving and loan associations in the late 1980s caused by improper deregulation and risky investments. The federal government was forced to spend a lot of money to correct the situation.

Say's Law

Supply creates its own demand. Producing goods and services creates income, and that income is spent on goods and services.

scarcity

A situation in which there aren't enough resources to satisfy everyone's wants.

seasonal unemployment
Unemployment caused by fluctuations in production due to changes in the time of year.

self-interest
Regard for what matters to oneself. It refers to the decision-making process in which people choose the option that maximizes their own net benefits.

service
An activity that satisfies a want.

short run
A time horizon over which the prices of some factors of production are fixed.

short-run aggregate supply
The relationship between the price level and the aggregate quantity supplied in the short run, when it is possible for some resource use to be changed.

shortage
A situation in which demand exceeds supply at a price ceiling enforced by the government.

small time deposits
A financial instrument similar to a savings account since it carns interest. The account is less than $100,000, the funds are deposited for less than 90 days but for a specified length of time, and there's a penalty for early withdraw of funds.

Smith, Adam (1723–1790)
An early, influential, Scottish economist who wrote *The Wealth of Nations*, which explained the ability of markets to coordinate economic activity.

Social Security
A system of transfer payments the federal government makes to the elderly and others in order to provide them with disposable income.

specialization
Concentrating in the production of one or a few goods and services, usually one in which the producer has a comparative advantage.

spending multiplier
The increase (or decrease) in real GDP when autonomous consumption, investment, government spending, or net exports are raised (or reduced) by one dollar.

stagflation
A period of time in which there is low or negative real GDP growth, and high rates of inflation.

standard of living
A loose analysis of how "well off" the members of an economy are. One way of measuring this is by measuring the amount of goods and services an individual can purchase with a given level of income.

sticky price
A price that does not automatically adjust to a change in either supply or demand.

sticky wage
A wage that does not automatically adjust to a change in either supply or demand.

stock
A share of ownership in a company.

stock variable
A variable whose value is determined at a point in time.

store of value
An object that can be used to hold onto purchasing power.

structural unemployment

Unemployment caused by factors affecting the structure of the economy, such as the types of goods and services produced, the types of education workers have, government subsidies, and laws that regulate economic activities.

substitute

A good or service that will satisfy the want of another good or service.

substitution bias

A condition that leads to the CPI overstating the price level. Price increases cause consumers to substitute lower priced items for higher priced ones. However, the fixed market basket results in the CPI showing an inaccurate increase in spending.

sunk cost

A cost that is not part of a decision's opportunity cost. It is the cost of a choice made in the past.

supply

The relationship between the price of a good or service and the quantity firms are willing and able to offer for sale.

supply curve

A graphical representation of supply.

supply of currency

The group of people who want to sell a currency being traded in a foreign currency market. In the market for Mexican pesos, for instance, Mexicans who want to trade pesos to Americans in exchange for U.S. dollars constitute the supply of pesos.

supply shock

See *change in aggregate demand.*

supply-side economics

The idea that the government should encourage economic growth by using fiscal policies to alter aggregate supply. This can be achieved by reducing taxes, decreasing cumbersome regulations, etc.

surplus

A situation in which supply exceeds demand at a price floor enforced by the government.

T

T-bill

A bond issued by the U.S. Treasury Department that pays interest for less than one year.

T-bond

A bond issued by the U.S. Treasury Department.

T-note

A bond issued by the U.S. Treasury Department that pays interest for 1–10 years.

tariff

A tax placed on imports.

tax bracket

A range of incomes on which income is taxed at the same rate.

tax multiplier

The increase (or decrease) in real GDP when taxes are reduced (or raised) by one dollar.

thrift

A type of financial intermediary that uses depositors' funds to make loans, such as credit unions, and savings and loans.

total consumption

The sum of autonomous household spending and household spending that depends on income.

total cost
The total amount of money paid for resources used in production.

total output
The total production of goods and services, usually measured by adding up the prices of all the goods and services produced in an economy in one year.

total revenue
The total amount of money earned by the sale of products.

trade balance
A term the media uses to refer to the merchandise trade balance.

trade barrier
A device used to inhibit international trade, such as quotas, tariffs, and embargoes. Also called *trade restriction*.

traditional economy
An economic system that uses the customs and religious practices of its ancestors to determine the production and distribution of goods and services.

transaction motive
The desire to hold money, instead of investing it in a financial instrument, because money enables a household to purchase goods and services.

transfer payments
Money and services given by the government to households or businesses. They are not given in exchange for a good or service.

transitional economy
An economic system that is transforming from one economic system to another.

traveler's checks
A check issued by a financial intermediary that households can use as they would use a regular check.

Treasury securities
Bonds issued by the U.S. Treasury Department.

trickle-down economics
See *supply-side economics*.

trough
A point in time at which real GDP is at a relative minimum.

twin deficits effect
A situation in which a government budget deficit leads to a current account deficit.

U.S. Treasury Department
A part of the executive branch of the federal government. This department acts like a bank for the federal government by collecting its tax revenues, handling its payments, and obtaining loans for it.

U

unattainable
A combination of goods that is outside the PPF. It is impossible to produce this combination of goods with the given resources.

unemployment rate
The percentage of the workforce currently unemployed and actively looking for employment.

unit of account
An object that can be used to measure the value of a good or service.

unregulated market
A market in which the government does not intervene in buyers' and sellers' decisions.

V

velocity of money
The number of times, on average, that a dollar is used to purchase final goods and services over a period of one year.

Volcker, Paul
The chairman of the Fed during the late 1970s and early 1980s who presided over a contractionary monetary policy to combat inflation.

W

wage.
The payment received by labor providers in a factor market.

want
A desire that can be fulfilled by a good or a service.

The Wealth of Nations
A book, written by Adam Smith in 1776, which explains the functioning of markets and put forth the claim that the market economy is the best way to structure an economy.

workforce
See *labor force.*

Glossary of Microeconomic Terms

16th Amendment
The amendment to the U.S. Constitution that legalized income taxes, ratified in 1913.

A

"ability to pay" principle of taxation
The idea that those who are more able to pay taxes should be taxed more heavily.

absolute advantage
Ability to produce a good or service using fewer resources than other producers.

absolute value
The numerical value of a number without reference to whether it is positive or negative.

accounting profit
Total revenue minus explicit costs.

aggregate income
The total amount of income earned by all people in a society.

algebraic model
Simplification that shows the relationship between two or more variables with an equation.

allocative efficiency
The output level at which price equals marginal cost—producing every unit that consumers value at least as much as the unit's marginal cost.

alternative good
A good that uses some of the same production resources as another good.

annuity
An insurance contract that makes specified payments over time, often after retirement.

antitrust legislation
Government laws designed to restrict the anticompetitive activities of firms with market power.

arbitrage
Reselling a good or service to make a profit. The reseller is able to do this because the firm sells the same product to different people at different prices.

average cost pricing
Regulatory method for monopolies that sets price equal to average total cost.

average fixed cost
Fixed cost divided by the quantity of output.

average product
Total production divided by the quantity of a particular input.

average revenue
Total revenue divided by output.

average total cost
Total cost divided by the quantity of output.

average variable cost
Variable cost divided by the quantity of output.

B

bar chart
A graph that shows values of a variable (or variables) with bars that run up or across a graph.

barriers to entry
Variables that prevent firms from entering an industry.

barter
Exchanging goods and services directly for other goods and services.

behavior assumption
An assumption about how people will act. Economists assume that people act to pursue their own self interest.

"benefit" principle of taxation
The idea that those who benefit more from government services should be taxed more heavily.

benefits
In labor contracts, benefits refer to nonmoney employee compensation, such as health insurance, bus passes, and so on.

bilateral monopoly
A single buyer bargains with a single seller, such as when a monopsonist firm bargains with a union.

binding arbitration
A dispute resolution method in which both parties in a dispute agree to accept a mediator's resolution of the disputed issues.

break-even point
Output level at which total revenue equals total cost

C

capital
Factor of production that includes factories, machinery, tools, computers, buildings, and human capital, such as managerial skill.

capital income
Interest and profits households receive in the loanable funds market.

capital market
See *loanable funds market.*

capitalism
Economic system characterized by private ownership of property and unregulated markets. See *market system.*

cartel
A collection of firms that make production, pricing, and other decisions jointly.

Celler–Kefauver Act
A 1950 amendment to the Sherman Act prohibiting one firm from merging with another in same industry, by buying the capital of the second firm, if the overall effect of the merger significantly reduces competition.

ceteris paribus
Latin phrase meaning "all other things held constant." A key for successful experimenting is to control all variables, making sure only the ones you're observing change. This controlling of all other variables is called *ceteris paribus.*

change in demand
A shift of the demand curve caused by changing something other than the price (one of the determinants of demand).

change in quantity demanded
Movement along the demand curve caused by a change in price.

change in quantity supplied
Movement along the supply curve caused by a change in price.

change in supply
A shift of the supply curve caused by a change in something other than price (one of the determinants of supply).

circular flow of economic activity
A diagram that shows the flow of economic activity in a society as goods, resources, and dollar payments are circulated from households to firms and from firms to households.

Clayton Act of 1914
A major piece of antitrust legislation that designates specific activities as illegal when they restrict competition.

Coase theorem
If property rights are well defined, and the costs of negotiation are small or zero, people can bargain with each other to reach efficient resource allocation and efficient solutions to externalities (in other words, avoiding the problem at the lowest cost).

collective bargaining
Negotiations between management and labor over wages, benefits, and working conditions.

collusion
When firms make joint production or pricing decisions.

command economy
An economic system characterized by government ownership of property and in which resources are allocated by specific instructions from the government.

common pool problem
The unrestricted use of a resource leads to overuse, and the net marginal value of an additional use of the resource drops to zero. Also known as *common property problem*.

comparative advantage
Ability to produce a good while sacrificing less production of another good than other producers.

competing interest legislation
Legislation that provides benefits to a relatively small group of people and imposes costs on another relatively small group of people.

complement good
A good that tends to be consumed with another good. If the price of one good goes up, demand for its complement good decreases (and vice versa).

concentration ratio
The share of the total production in an industry produced by the four largest firms in the industry.

conglomerate
A large corporation made up of unrelated firms.

consent decree
Approval by a judge of an agreement between disputing parties.

constant elasticity of demand
Elasticity of demand that's the same at all prices.

constant returns to scale
Average cost is the same over the whole range of production.

constant cost industry

An industry in which increases in production do not cause an increase or a decrease in the firms' average total cost.

consumers

The people in an economy who buy and use the goods and services firms produce.

consumer equilibrium

When a consumer's budget is completely spent, and he gains an equal amount of marginal utility from the last dollar spent on every good.

consumer surplus

The difference between what a consumer pays for a good and what she would have been willing to pay for that good.

consumption tax

See *sales tax*.

contestable market

A market in which the threat of entry by a rival firm keeps a monopolist from earning monopoly profits.

copyright

An exclusive right granted by the government to copy, publish, and sell items such as books, art, and film.

corporation

A firm that is a legal entity, in which the stockholders are not held financially liable for the actions or debts of the firm.

cost envelope

The long-run average-total-cost curve, which includes the minimum point of every short run average-total-cost curve.

cost–benefit analysis

The analysis of alternatives that considers the costs and benefits of each alternative. This is usually done in search of the alternative with the highest net benefit.

cost–plus pricing

Adding a percentage mark-up to the average variable cost; one of the major models of behaviors of oligopolies.

craft union

An early form of labor organization whose members all possessed a similar skill or worked in a similar craft.

cross-price elasticity of demand

The percentage change in demand for one good at a given price that results from the percentage change in price of another good.

cross-subsidization

Using the profits generated in one part of its operations to support the losses generated by another part of its operations.

cyclical majority

A condition in which no choice dominates all others, and votes on an issue depend on the order in which the series of issues are considered.

D

deadweight loss

When firm operates with allocative inefficiency, the gains from trade are not maximized; the excess value above marginal cost that consumers place on the production of the units that are not produced by a price searcher, but that consumers value more than the marginal cost of production. Also called *welfare loss*.

decreasing-cost industry
An industry in which increases in production cause a decrease in the firms' average total cost.

delta (Δ)
A Greek letter used in economics (and other sciences) to mean "change."

demand
The different amounts of a good that consumers are willing and able to buy at different prices.

demand curve
A graph that shows quantity demanded for a good at each of a range of prices.

demand for loanable funds
Firms borrow money in the loanable funds market to purchase capital goods; in doing so, firms are the demanders of loanable funds.

demand schedule
A table that shows quantity demanded for a good at each of a range of prices.

dependent variable
A variable that changes in response to changes in the independent variable.

deregulation
Removing government restrictions on the actions of suppliers.

derived factor demand
The demand for a factor of production: land, labor, or capital. The factor demand depends on the demand for the good or service produced using that factor.

determinant of elasticity of resource demand
Something that influences the responsiveness of resource demanders to a change in resource price.

determinants of demand
Things that cause a change in demand-a shift of the entire demand curve (not movement along the demand curve). The determinants of demand include tastes, income, population, substitute and complement goods, and expectations of consumers.

determinants of price elasticity of demand
The things that make consumers more or less sensitive to a change in a good's price. As such, they determine a good's price elasticity of demand. They are as follows: the availability of substitutes, the time necessary to find substitutes, and the portion of a consumer's budget spent on the good.

determinants of supply
The things that make consumers more or less sensitive to a change in a good's price. They determine a good's price elasticity of demand and include these items: the price of inputs, the price of alternative goods, the expectations of producers, the level of technology, and government policies.

differentiation
A firm's ability to establish its product as unique or different from its rivals' products.

diminishing marginal returns
See *law of diminishing marginal returns.*

direct relationship
When a change in one variable causes another variable to change in the same direction.

discount rate
The interest rate that the Federal Reserve (the Fed) charges banks when they take overnight loans (from the Fed) to meet their required reserves.

discounting

Reducing the value of something. For example, people discount the value of money received in the future as compared to money received in the present, so that having $100 today is valued more than having $100 next year (even in real dollars).

diseconomies of scale

Increased production brings about a higher average cost of production.

disequilibrium

A (usually) temporary imbalance between quantity supplied and quantity demanded in a market, which occurs when price is above or below the market-clearing price.

disequilibrium price

Price of a good when the market for that good is in disequilibrium.

dividend

The per share portion of profits distributed to the owners of a corporation.

division of labor

Breaking up the production of a good or service into subdivisions.

double taxation

Income is taxed twice because corporations pay corporate income taxes on income before dividends are paid, and shareholders pay personal income tax on the dividends they receive.

E

earnings

Wages, salaries, or more frequently, the total compensation paid for a job.

economic profit

Total revenue minus explicit and implicit costs.

economic regulation

The category of government regulations concerned with the workings of the economy.

economic rent

Income earned in excess of the resource owner's opportunity cost.

economic system

The laws and institutions through which a society allocates resources to produce goods and services.

economics

The study of the behavior of people in the face of scarcity.

economies of scale

Higher production results in a lower average costs of production.

efficiency

In the context of production, efficiency means producing the maximum amount of goods or services possible, given the resources available.

elastic demand

When consumers are sensitive to a change in price, so that the percentage change in quantity demanded is greater than the percentage change in price.

elastic supply

When suppliers are sensitive to a change in price, so that the percentage change in quantity supplied is greater than the percentage change in price.

elasticity

A measure of how much quantity demanded or quantity supplied changes when the price of a good changes, when the price of a related good changes, or when income changes.

entrepreneurship
The talent certain people have for organizing resources to produce goods or services, find new business opportunities, and create new ways of doing things. Some economists consider entrepreneurship one of the factors of production.

equation
A mathematical formula relating the relationship between two or more variables.

equilibrium
When quantity supplied in a market matches quantity demanded, which occurs when the price is at the market-clearing price.

equilibrium price
The price at which quantity supplied equals quantity demanded.

equilibrium quantity
Quantity at which quantity supplied equals quantity demanded.

equilibrium rate of interest
An interest rate in which the quantity of loanable funds supplied is exactly equal to the quantity of loanable funds demanded.

excess capacity
Producing below the level where average total cost is at a minimum. The firm has the ability to increase production while decreasing the average total cost of production.

excess demand
The amount that quantity demanded exceeds supply at a given price, below the equilibrium price.

excess supply
The amount that quantity supplied exceeds quantity demanded at a given price above the equilibrium price.

exclusive dealing
The practice in which a supplier agrees to limit its interactions with other firms in exchange for the right to sell a particular good or the right to sell at a particular price or in a particular area. This practice, along with others, was outlawed by the Clayton Act.

exhaustible resource
A natural resource that doesn't renew itself, such as iron or oil.

explicit cost
The cost a firm pays in money for the resources it uses.

externality
A benefit or cost to an unrelated party imposed by another decisionmaker's actions. Externalities often occur in a transaction between two parties, with the third party paying the cost.

F

factor market
The market in which the factors of production and semi-finished goods are exchanged.

factors of production
The inputs or resources—land, labor, capital, (and for some economists, entrepreneurship)—used to make goods and services.

fair return
See Also average cost pricing.

fallacy of composition
The incorrect belief that what's good or true for an individual is good or true for the group.

fallacy that association is causation
The incorrect belief that because two things happen at about the same time, one caused the other.

faulty *ceteris paribus*
The incorrect assumption that variables are constant when they aren't.

Federal Trade Commission Act of 1914
The act that established the Federal Trade Commission to investigate unfair competitive acts of business firms.

financial intermediary
A business firm such as a bank or investment company that brings together the borrowers (businesses) and lenders (households) in the loanable funds market.

firm
A business formed by an entrepreneur to organize and combine factors of production in order to make a good or service, usually in the hope of making a profit.

fiscal policy
The use of government spending and taxes to meet macroeconomic goals, such as controlling inflation or unemployment or promoting growth.

fixed cost
The costs a firm must pay in the short run regardless of how much the firm produces; the costs of the factors that cannot be changed in the short run.

fixed factor
A factor or input in production that cannot be changed in the short-run.

fixed-production technology
The relationship between production and the creation of an externality is fixed, so that the only way to decrease (or increase) the externality is to reduce (or increase) the production.

free enterprise
A market economy free from government regulation.

full employment
The percentage of the work force that is employed when the economy grows at its long-run sustainable growth rate. In the United States, this corresponds to approximately 95 percent employment.

G

game theory
One of the main tools for analyzing oligopoly behavior, providing a way to predict the behavior of oligopolists who base their decisions on expectations about their rivals' decisions.

golden rule of profit maximization
To maximize the profits of a firm, the firm owners should produce where marginal revenue equals marginal cost.

Gompers, Samuel
The founder of the union called the American Federation of Labor.

good
An item, usually something tangible, that satisfies a want.

government corporation
A government-owned firm.

graduate tax
See *progressive taxation.*

graph
Data expressed in a visual manner, usually on a grid that measures numerical data.

graphical model
A simplification of the relationship between two or more variables, shown on a graph.

Great Depression
The period between World Wars I and II when many world economies suffered severe recessions. In the United States, from 1929 to 1933, the unemployment rate rose from 3 percent to 25 percent, and national income fell by half.

growth
Increases in quantity and quality of goods and services produced by an economy. Alternatively, an increase in the standard of living of a country.

H

Hart-Scott-Rodino Anti-Trust Procedural Improvement Act
The 1980 law that extended anti-trust legislation by allowing the government to investigate sole proprietorships and partnerships for anti-competitive business practices. The law also required all proposed mergers and acquisitions be reported to the Justice Department for review.

Herfindahl index
An index that measures the concentration of an industry.

homogeneous product
A product without significant differences among different manufacturers.

horizontal axis
See also *x-axis*.

horizontal merger
A merger between firms producing the same type of good or service.

household
The part of a society that supplies labor and other resources in the factor market and purchases goods and services in the product market.

human capital
Productive ability of the labor force acquired through education and training.

I

imperfect competition
A competitive situation in which firms in a market have some ability to set price. (This is the case in all market structures except perfect competition).

implicit cost
The costs a firm incurs for using resources they don't pay for.

income distribution
How income is distributed among the people in a society.

income effect
When the price of a good drops, increasing consumers' real income (or purchasing power) and enabling them to buy more of that good.

income elasticity of demand
A measure of how much the quantity demanded for a particular good at a particular price changes when income changes. It's the percentage change in demand divided by the percentage change in income.

income inelastic demand
When consumers are not sensitive to a change in income, so the percentage change in demand is less than the percentage change in income.

income tax
A tax on income (income is the tax base).

increasing marginal returns
Marginal cost decreases as output increases.

increasing-cost industry
An industry in which cost curves increase as total output increases; these industries experience diseconomies of scale.

independent variable
A variable that causes a dependent variable to change.

indeterminate change
When it's not possible to tell if equilibrium quantity or equilibrium price will increase or decrease. This happens in some cases when both supply and demand change.

indirect relationship
When a change in one variable causes another variable to change in the opposite direction.

industry
A collection of firms making similar or identical products that can be defined broadly, such as baked goods, or more narrowly, such as croissants.

inefficiency
In the context of production, inefficiency means producing less than the maximum amount of goods or services possible, given the resources available.

inelastic demand
When consumers are insensitive to a change in price, so the percentage change in quantity demanded is less than the percentage change in price.

inelastic supply
When suppliers are insensitive to a change in price, so the percentage change in quantity supplied is less than the percentage change in price.

inferior good
A good for which demand decreases when consumer income increases, and demand increases when consumer income decreases.

inflation
A general rise in the price level, meaning that many—but not necessarily all—prices and wages rise approximately the same percent.

injunction
A court order that stops someone from doing something, or makes someone do something.

innovation
A new idea for combining the factors of production to make a good or service.

inputs
Resources, or factors of production, used to make goods and services, categorized as land, labor, and capital (and for some economists, entrepreneurial ability).

intercept
Point where a line or curve touches an axis.

interest
The payment resource owners receive in the factor market in exchange for capital.

interest rate
Payment for the use of money today; the payment is a percentage of the total amount borrowed.

interlocking directorates
The practice in which members of the board of directors of one company serve on the board of directors of another firm in the same industry. This practice, along with others, was outlawed by the Clayton Act.

invisible hand
Economist Adam Smith's idea that an unregulated economy would direct the society's resources to their most efficient use, as if the people in the society were guided by an "invisible hand.".

K

kinked demand curve
A model that explains the behavior of an oligopolist in an industry where the firm expects its rivals to match its price decreases but not its price increases; one of the major models of oligopoly behavior.

Knights of Labor
One of the early labor organizations in the United States.

L

labor
All human effort used to produce goods or services. Includes both physical and mental effort. Labor is one of the factors of production.

labor union
An organization of workers who join together to improve their working conditions through collective bargaining.

laissez-faire
Policy of allowing market systems to operate without government involvement.

land
All the natural resources that come from the earth. Land is one of the factors of production.

law
A theory that has been repeatedly tested and shown to be true. A law is not indisputable; it could conceivably be proven untrue.

law of comparative advantage
The law that says a person or nation benefits when producing those goods and services in which they have a comparative advantage and trading those goods and services for other goods and services.

law of demand
The law that says the amount people are willing and able to purchase increases when prices decrease, and the amount people are willing and able to purchase decreases when prices increase, ceteris paribus.

law of diminishing marginal returns
The law that says as more and more units of a variable resource are added to the production process (as long as there's a fixed resource), the marginal product of that variable input eventually declines.

law of diminishing marginal utility
The law that says as more and more units of a good are consumed, the additional satisfaction from consuming each additional unit becomes smaller and smaller.

law of increasing opportunity costs
The law that says as more and more of a good is produced, the opportunity cost of producing each additional unit of the good increases.

law of supply
The law that says when prices increase, suppliers are willing and able to supply more, and when prices decrease, suppliers are willing and able to supply less, *ceteris paribus*.

least-cost combination of factors
The combination of factors for which the marginal physical product per dollar spent on the last of each factor is the same for each factor used.

limited partnership
A partnership that allows the owners, or partners some protection from personal liability for the firm's debts or actions.

line graph
A graph that shows values of two related variables on one line.

linear demand curve
A demand curve that's a straight line.

loanable funds market
A market where suppliers (households) and demanders (businesses) of loanable funds exchange money and loan contracts.

logrolling
Trading votes or promising to support future proposals in exchange for support of a current proposal.

long run
The period in which all a firm's factors of production can be altered.

long-run average total cost
Average total cost in the long run, when all factors can be changed. This includes the minimum point of every short-run average cost curve.

long-run average cost curve
The curve that represents the average cost (or average total cost) for a firm, for the period in which all factors of production can be changed.

long-run supply curve
The supply curve for a firm or industry for the period in which all factors of production can be changed. The long-run supply curve is tangent to all the short-run supply curves for a firm or industry.

Lorenz curve
A curve showing how income is distributed in an economy. It relates the population to the proportion of the total income it receives. The straighter the Lorenz curve is, the more equally income is divided. The more curved it is, the less equally income is divided.

M

macroeconomics
The study of the economic behavior of large groups of people, such as a state or nation.

marginal analysis
The study of the effects of an incremental change— one more or one less.

marginal cost
The additional cost incurred to produce one more unit of output.

marginal cost curve
The marginal cost of each unit of output.

marginal physical product
The increase in total output with the addition of one more unit of input.

marginal product
The additional production from adding one more unit of an input.

marginal productivity theory
Determines the quantity of an input a producer will employ, based on marginal physical product, marginal revenue product, and marginal resource cost.

marginal rate of return on an investment
The rate of return on an additional dollar of investment.

marginal resource cost
The additional cost incurred by a firm with the addition of one more unit of input.

marginal revenue
Additional revenue gained from the production of one more unit of a good.

marginal revenue product
The increase in total revenue with the addition of one more unit of input.

marginal social benefits
The added benefit of doing a little more of some action (both to the person doing the action and to any others). Also, the sum of the marginal private benefits and the marginal external benefits of production or consumption.

marginal social costs
The added costs of doing a little more of some action, including both the cost to the person doing the action and any external cost to others. Also, the sum of the marginal private costs and the marginal external costs of production or consumption.

marginal utility
The additional satisfaction (utility) that comes with consuming one more unit of a good.

marginal valuation
Value of the utility that comes with consuming one more unit of a good, as expressed in dollars.

market concentration
A measure of how much market power the firms in an industry have.

market economy
An economic system characterized by private ownership of property and unregulated exchange of goods and services in markets.

market equilibrium point
The price at which the quantity demanded equals the quantity supplied.

market failure
The result when unregulated markets produce socially undesirable outcomes. Causes of market failure include externalities, public goods, incomplete information, and natural monopolies.

market power
Firms' ability to set their own prices above marginal cost.

market structure
One of four models of the way firms in an industry interact. (The four models are perfect competition, monopolistic competition, oligopoly, and monopoly).

market-clearing price
Price at which the quantity demanded equals the quantity supplied. See Also equilibrium price.

maximum-profit combination of factors
The combination of factors for which the last dollar spent on each resource yields one dollar's worth of marginal revenue product.

means-tested program
A government program that benefits individuals based on their wealth or income. Generally, those with higher wealth or income will receive fewer benefits under a means-tested program.

median income
The level of income at which half the population earns less income and half earns more.

median voter model
A model of voting in which the policy or program desired by the median voter will beat any other policy in an election. The median voter is a voter whose preferences are in the middle of all voters' preferences.

mediation
An impartial third party acts as a mediator, listening to both parties in a dispute and trying to help them find a resolution.

medium of exchange
Something that people generally accept in exchange for a good or service, such as money.

merger
Two or more firms joining together to become one firm.

microeconomics
The study of the economic behavior of individuals.

midpoint formula for price elasticity of demand
Percentage change in quantity demanded divided by the percentage change in price, using the average of the two different quantities demanded and the two different prices to determine the percentage change.

midpoint formula for price elasticity of supply
Percentage change in quantity supplied divided by the percentage change in price, using the average of the two different quantities supplied and the two different prices to determine the percentage change.

minimum efficient scale
Output level where long-run average-total-cost curve quits declining and flattens.

mistake of ignoring secondary effects
The mistake of not noting changes in other variables when the variable being studied changes.

mistake of ignoring unaccounted variables
Overlooking changing variables that may be responsible for the change of other variables.

mixed economy
An economic system that includes elements from more than one of the main categories of economic systems (command, market, and traditional).

monetary policy
The use of the money supply and interest rates to meet macroeconomic goals.

money
Anything that is widely accepted as a medium of exchange for goods and services.

monopolistic competition
A market structure characterized by many producers of a product that can be slightly differentiated, allowing a small amount of price-setting ability.

monopoly
The market structure in which there is one seller of a good that has no close substitutes.

monopsonistic labor market
A labor market with only one demander for labor.

monopsony
A market with only one buyer.

N

National Labor Relations Act
The act that guarantees American workers the right to join unions and requires management to participate in collective bargaining if the majority of the workers desire it. Also called the *Wagner Act*.

natural monopoly
When one firm can provide a good or service at a lower cost than two or more firms, because it has decreasing average total costs over the whole range of production.

negative elasticity
Elasticity of demand is usually measured as an absolute value. However, since price and quantity demanded move in opposite directions, the percentage change in quantity demanded divided by the percentage change in price is negative. If income elasticity of demand is negative, the good is an inferior good. If cross-price elasticity of demand is negative, the good is a complement.

negative externality
A cost to an unrelated party caused by a decision-maker's actions. Negative externalities often occur as a result of a transaction between two parties (with a third party paying the cost).

negative slope
A line in which a positive change on the horizontal axis is associated with a negative change on the vertical axis, and a negative change on the horizontal axis is associated with a positive change on the vertical axis.

negative-sum game
A situation in which the total benefits and total costs add up to less than zero (a net cost), although an individual in the situation can come out ahead, or benefit. This is often used to describe the costs and benefits of political action.

net benefits
Total benefits minus total costs.

nominal rate of interest
The interest rate expressed in nominal dollars, which are dollars that do not have constant purchasing power; it's the real interest rate plus the rate of (anticipated) inflation.

nonexclusionary
The term describing a good that is difficult or impossible to prevent a person from consuming or enjoying.

nonprice competition
When rivals compete with each other through means other than price, such as quality, product differentiation, service, or advertising.

nonrenewable resource
A factor of production that can't be replaced as it is used up; some factors, such as oil and diamonds, take so long to renew that they're called nonrenewable.

nonrival
The term describing a good whose quantity available is not reduced by consumption; also, a good that many people can enjoy at the same time without reducing each other's enjoyment.

nonprofit institution
A business that organizes resources for the production of a good or service, but cannot distribute profits to shareholders or individuals.

normal good
A good for which demand increases when incomes rise. Similarly, when incomes drop, demand for this good decreases.

normal profit
Zero economic profit; also, total revenue equals implicit plus explicit costs.

normal rate of return
The return on an investment, expressed as a percentage (rate) of the total investment that equals the percentage earned on the next best alternative investment.

normative analysis
Analysis that includes value judgements and suggests a specific action or actions.

North American Free Trade Agreement (NAFTA)
A trade agreement between Mexico, Canada, and the United States that went into effect in 1994, and eliminated most trade barriers between the three nations.

numerical model
A simplification showing the relationship between two or more variables using numbers in a table.

O

oligopoly
A market structure characterized by a few sellers with a high ratio of market concentration who make pricing and output decisions interdependently.

open-access resources
Resources that may be used by any person at any time.

opportunity cost
The value of the next best alternative sacrificed when an alternative is chosen.

origin
A graph's frame of reference, usually the point (0, 0).

P

partnership
An unincorporated firm owned by two or more people.

patent
An exclusive right granted by the government to inventors to make, use, or sell their inventions. A patent is used to protect an innovative idea or process; the exclusive right usually lasts for 17 years.

payoff matrix
The visual representation of game theory.

per se illegality
Per se means "of and in itself," or intrinsically. Some aspects of anti-trust legislation make actions illegal only when they restrict competition; other actions are illegal in all cases, or per se illegal.

perfect competition
A market structure characterized by many buyers and sellers, homogeneous products, and no barriers to entry.

perfect information
A situation in which all participants in an industry (consumers and producers) know the product, who's selling it, the quality, and the price; also when the information is readily available.

perfectly discriminating monopolist
A monopolist that charges each consumer the most he or she is willing to pay for a good or service.

perfectly elastic demand
When any price increase reduces the quantity demanded to zero. This is represented on a graph as a horizontal straight-line demand curve.

perfectly elastic supply
When any price drop reduces the quantity supplied to zero. This is represented on a graph as a horizontal straight-line supply curve.

perfectly inelastic demand
Price elasticity of demand that equals zero and is characterized by a vertical demand curve. The quantity demanded doesn't change when price changes.

perfectly inelastic supply
Price elasticity of supply characterized by a vertical supply curve. The numerical value of elasticity is zero, and quantity supplied does not change when price changes.

Phillips curve
A curve that shows the short-run negative (or inverse) relationship between unemployment and inflation.

physical capital
Goods, such as buildings, machines, and tools, that are used to produce other goods but are not used up in the production process. A mixing bowl is physical capital, while an egg is not.

pie chart
A chart in which different pieces of something are represented as "wedges" within a circle. When added together, the sum of the wedges equals the whole. The size of each wedge is proportional to its percentage of the whole.

positive analysis
Analysis that tries to be objective and avoid making value judgments.

positive externality
A benefit to an unrelated party caused by a decision-maker's actions. Positive externalities often occur as a result of a transaction between two parties—with a third party reaping the benefit.

positive rate of time preference
People prefer to have purchasing ability today rather than wait for it later; this is a major component of the real interest rate.

positive relationship
See *direct relationship*.

positive slope
A line in which a positive change on the horizontal axis is associated with a positive change on the vertical axis, and a negative change on the horizontal axis is associated with a negative change on the vertical axis.

positive-sum game
A situation in which the total benefits and total costs add up to more than zero (a net benefit), although an individual in the situation can come out behind, or pay a net cost. This is often used to describe the costs and benefits of political action.

poverty
In the United States, poverty is defined as earning less than a specific amount of money, depending on the size of the household.

predatory pricing
Selling at a price below cost to drive rivals out of business, with the intention of raising prices and earning high profits once the rivals are gone.

present value
The value today of something that will be received in the future.

price

The amount of money a buyer must give a seller in exchange for a good or service.

price ceiling

Maximum price for a good or service set by the government. When set below the equilibrium price, it causes a shortage.

price discrimination

Charging different prices to different customers for the same good or service.

price elasticity of demand

A measure of how sensitive consumers are to a change in price. It measures the amount that quantity demanded changes in response to a change in price; measured as the percentage change in quantity demanded divided by the percentage change in price. The formula for price elasticity of demand is % quantity demand divided by % price.

price elasticity of supply

A measure of how sensitive producers are to a change in price. It measures the amount that quantity supplied changes in response to a change in price; measured as the percentage change in quantity supplied divided by the percentage change in price. The formula for price elasticity of supply is % quantity supplied divided by % price.

price floor

A minimum price set by the government When set above the equilibrium price, it causes a surplus.

price leadership

A model that explains the activity in an industry where one firm clearly dominates and the other firms follow the lead of the dominant firm; one of the major models of oligopoly behavior.

price searcher

A firm with some price-setting ability; it can set price above marginal cost.

price taker

A competitive firm that must sell at the market price, having no price-setting power.

prime rate of interest

The interest rate that banks charge their very best customers.

prisoner's dilemma

A standard game theory model: When each party acts independently, the resulting outcome is less desirable than if the parties colluded.

private property rights

The rights of an owner to use, sell, or destroy, the thing owned.

private sector

The part of an economy that includes firms and households but not the government, in contrast to the part of the economy that the government is involved in (the public sector).

producer surplus

The difference between the lowest amount for which a producer is willing and able to supply a good or service and the revenues the producer receives for doing this.

product

A good or service produced by a firm.

product market

The market in which goods and services are exchanged.

production possibilities frontier (PPF)

A curve that shows all the different combinations of two or more goods or services that can be efficiently produced, given the current resource availability and technology.

productive efficiency
Using resources in such a way that in order to produce more of one good or service, the society (or firm) has to produce less of another good or service.

profit
Total revenue minus total costs.

profit maximization
The output level at which the highest possible profit is earned, given a set of conditions.

profitable investment
An investment that provides a positive rate of return. If it's economic profit, then the rate of return is greater than the normal rate of return.

progressive taxation
The system in which income tax rates rise as income rises. That is, people with higher income pay a higher average tax rate.

proportional taxation
The system in which income tax rates are the same regardless of income level.

public good
A good which is both nonrival (many people enjoy/consume it simultaneously) and nonexclusionary (it's difficult or impossible to keep people from enjoying it).

purchasing power
Quantity of goods and services that can be bought with a given amount of money. As prices go up, purchasing power goes down. As prices go down, purchasing power goes up.

Q

quantity demanded
The amount of a good or service people are willing and able to buy at a given price.

quintile
One portion of a data set divided into five equal portions. This division is done for statistical purposes. Economists usually use quintiles to rank a society's income distribution from lowest to highest.

quota
Legal limit on the amount of a good or service that can be imported.

R

random measurement error
Differences in measurements that occur when measuring the same object more than once.

rate structure
The system of tax rates applied to a tax base.

rational ignorance
The decision by people not to become informed about public issues (or even vote) because the cost of information is greater than the benefit of being informed.

real income
The purchasing power of income, determined by taking nominal income and adjusting it for changes in price. As prices increase, real income decreases, and as prices decrease, real income increases, *ceteris paribus*.

real rate of interest
The interest rate expressed in real dollars; that is, dollars that have constant purchasing power. It is the nominal interest rate minus the rate of (anticipated) inflation.

recession
Six or more months during which national output or national production decreases.

regressive taxation
The system in which tax rates fall as income rises: People with higher income pay a lower average tax rate.

relevant resources
Inputs used in the production of a particular good or service.

renewable resource
A resource (factor of production) such as timber, fish, or fresh water, that is renewed over a relatively short period.

rent seeking
Spending money solely in an attempt to increase profits (such as lobbying politicians).

resource
Another term for factor of production, or input.

resource market
See *factor market*.

resource price searcher
A firm that directly affects the price of a resource when it buys the resource.

resource price taker
A firm that has no direct effect on the price of a resource when it buys the resource.

rival
Competitor; another firm in the same industry.

rule of reason
Refers to anti-trust court cases; a firm is typically found guilty of violating anti-trust legislation if it fails to provide evidence that its activity was in the interest of efficiency rather than an attempt to monopolize the industry.

S

sales tax
A tax on goods purchased based on a percentage of the purchase price.

sample selection bias
When a small subsection of a group is used to represent the group as a whole for statistical purposes, but doesn't share the characteristics of the group as a whole.

scarcity
Insufficient availability to meet the needs of what is desired.

scientific method
A four-step process used by all scientists (including economists, who are social scientists). 1) Identify and define the key variables; 2) specify assumptions; 3) develop a hypothesis; and 4) test the hypothesis.

secondary effects
The effects other than the expected primary effects caused by the change of a variable. Secondary effects tend to occur later and with less intensity than primary effects.

self interest
An individual's wants and desires, which may include the well being of others.

service
Something, usually intangible, that satisfies a want.

Sherman Act of 1890
The first major piece of antitrust legislation, which made it illegal to monopolize or attempt to monopolize an industry.

shift of demand curve
Movement of the entire demand curve, either left or right. A shift of the demand curve is a change in demand. It's caused by a change in one of the determinants of demand (not a change in price).

short run

The period during which at least one factor of production is fixed (or can't be changed).

short-run firm supply curve

The supply curve for a firm for a period in which at least one factor of production cannot be changed.

short-run industry supply curve

The supply curve for an industry in a period during which at least one factor of production can't be varied.

shortage

When price is held below equilibrium price, usually by government intervention in the form of a price ceiling, causing the quantity demanded to be greater than the quantity supplied.

slope

Ratio of change in the variable on the vertical axis to the change in the variable on the horizontal axis. Also described as the "rise" over the "run.".

Smith, Adam

Eighteenth century English economist who wrote *Wealth of Nations* in 1776, advocated free enterprise, and spoke of the "invisible hand.".

social regulation

The category of government regulations concerned with social welfare.

special-interest legislation

Laws and regulations that benefit a small number of people, often at some cost to a large number of people.

specialization

When an individual spends time on a particular task or tasks, rather than producing all the goods and services they consume.

standard of living

The measure of how well-off the people of a society are. Standard of living is often measured as total output, or production, per person.

stock

The total value of a corporation, which is divided into shares. The owners of the corporation receive stock shares in exchange for their purchase of ownership.

straight-line relationship

When the change of a line's position on one axis is associated with an equal change of the line's position on the other axis.

strike

Workers uniting and refusing to work, in hopes of influencing their employers' stand on contract negotiations.

subsidy

Government payment to producer of a good or service.

substitute good

A good that can be substituted for another good. People tend to consume one or the other.

substitution effect

When the price of a good drops, the good is relatively cheaper than its substitutes, so people buy more

sunk cost

A cost that must be paid regardless of any current decision. Because a sunk cost has to be paid no matter what, it's irrelevant to any current decision.

supply curve

A graph that shows the willingness and ability of producers to produce and offer for sale different quantities of a good or service at different prices.

supply of loanable funds
The money provided in the loanable funds market by households.

supply schedule
A table that shows the willingness and ability of producers to produce and offer for sale different quantities of a good or service at different prices.

surplus
When the market is held above equilibrium price, usually by government intervention in the form of a price floor, the quantity supplied is greater than the quantity demanded, and there is a surplus.

T

tacit collusion
Collusion that occurs even though the parties don't communicate with each other directly or through a third party.

tangent
A line or curve that touches a curve at only one point, but does not intersect the curve.

tax
Legally required payments by households or firms to the government.

tax base
A thing taxed, or the total property value or total amount of economic activity on which a tax is placed.

tax equity
Fairness in taxation. "Fair" depends on the context and on who is making the judgment.

tax incidence
How the total amount of tax paid is divided among different groups within a society. These groups may be buyers and sellers, people with different income levels, or people from different geographical areas.

term structure of interest rates
The relationship between duration of a loan and interest charged.

total cost
All the costs the firm incurs to produce a given quantity of output.

total cost curve
Shows the relationship between the quantity of output and the total cost of that quantity of output for all output.

total product
The quantity of output produced with a given quantity of inputs.

total revenue
Price times the quantity sold.

total utility
The total satisfaction a person receives from consuming a particular quantity of a good or service.

traditional economy
An economic system that's based on the ways of ancestors.

transaction costs
Costs incurred by buyers and sellers due to the time and effort needed to look for, negotiate, and finish an exchange of goods or services.

transitional economy
An economic system that's moving from one of the main categories of economic systems to another.

trust
A group of firms or corporations that have an agreement binding them together. At the end of the 19th century, the existence of large trusts significantly reduced market competition, prompting the need for the Sherman Act of 1890.

tying contracts
The practice in which the seller of one product also requires the buyer to buy another product. This practice, along with others, was outlawed by the Clayton Act.

U

underground economy
The goods and services produced and sold that, though not necessarily illegal, are not reported to the government, often to avoid regulation or taxation.

unit elastic demand
When the percentage change in quantity demanded equals the percentage change in price.

unit elastic supply
When the percentage change in quantity supplied equals the percentage change in price.

unregulated economy
An economy without government intervention in its markets.

unregulated market
See *market system*.

util
An arbitrary unit used for measuring the satisfaction, or utility, a person gets from consuming a good or service. A util for one person is not the same as a util for another person.

utility
A measure of the satisfaction a person gains from consuming a good or service.

V

variable
Something that changes.

variable cost
The costs of producing a given quantity of output associated only with the inputs that can be changed in the short run.

variable factor
A factor of production, or input, that can be changed in the short run.

variable technology
A technology with an associated externality that can be reduced by altering the production process instead of altering the output.

vertical intercept
Position on y-axis at which a line intersects the y-axis.

vertical merger
A merger between firms that are part of the same production process but that produce at different points in the process.

W

wage
Payment that resource owners receive in exchange for their labor in the factor market.

Wealth of Nations
An influential book written by economist Adam Smith and published in 1776. Smith said that the market system was the best economic system, and that it worked best when markets were allowed to function with no (or little) government regulation. Smith explains his notion of the "invisible hand" in this book.

wealth tax
A tax on the total value of individuals assets, regardless of their income.

welfare
Government payments to people who are, in some way, economically disadvantaged.

X

x-axis
Horizontal axis of a graph.

Y

y-axis
Vertical axis of a graph.

yellow dog contract
A now-illegal labor contract in the U.S., in which prospective new employees promised their employers that, if hired, they wouldn't join a union.

Z

zero-sum game
A situation in which the total benefits and total costs add up to zero.

How Did We Do? Grade Us.

Thank you for choosing a Kaplan book. Your comments and suggestions are very useful to us. Please answer the following questions to assist us in our continued development of high-quality resources to meet your needs.

The title of the Kaplan book I read was: _____

My name is: _____

My address is: _____

_____

My e-mail address is: _____

What overall grade would you give this book? Ⓐ Ⓑ Ⓒ Ⓓ Ⓕ

How relevant was the information to your goals? Ⓐ Ⓑ Ⓒ Ⓓ Ⓕ

How comprehensive was the information in this book? Ⓐ Ⓑ Ⓒ Ⓓ Ⓕ

How accurate was the information in this book? Ⓐ Ⓑ Ⓒ Ⓓ Ⓕ

How easy was the book to use? Ⓐ Ⓑ Ⓒ Ⓓ Ⓕ

How appealing was the book's design? Ⓐ Ⓑ Ⓒ Ⓓ Ⓕ

What were the book's strong points? _____ .

How could this book be improved? _____

Is there anything that we left out that you wanted to know more about?

Would you recommend this book to others? ☐ YES   ☐ NO

Other comments: _____

_____

_____

Do we have permission to quote you? ☐ YES   ☐ NO

Thank you for your help.
Please tear out this page and mail it to:

Managing Editor
Kaplan Publications
1440 Broadway, 8th Floor
New York, New York, 10018

KAPLAN®

Thanks!